RADICAL DREAMING

RADICAL DREAMING
Use Your Dreams to Change Your Life

JOHN D. GOLDHAMMER, PH.D.

CITADEL PRESS
Kensington publishing Corp.
www.kensingtonbooks.com

Author's Note: Names and certain identifying details have been changed when necessary to protect confidentiality and privacy. Some dreams have been condensed for clarity.

CITADEL PRESS BOOKS are published by

Kensington Publishing Corp.
850 Third Avenue
New York, NY 10022

All Kensington titles, imprints, and distributed lines are available at special quantity discounts for bulk purchases for sales promotions, premiums, fund-raising, educational, or institutional use. Special book excerpts or customized printings can also be created to fit specific needs. For details, write or phone the office of the Kensington special sales manager: Kensington Publishing Corp., 850 Third Avenue, New York, NY 10022, attn: Special Sales Department, phone 1-800-221-2647.

CITADEL PRESS and the Citadel logo are Reg. U.S. Pat. & TM Off.

First printing: July 2003

10 9 8 7 6 5 4 3 2 1

Printed in the United States of America

Designed by Leonard Telesca

Library of Congress Control Number: 2002116153

ISBN 0-8065-2495-2

*This book is dedicated to the memory of
my father,
David Eugene Goldhammer,
who told me there was no such word as "can't."*

Contents

Acknowledgments

This book would not have been possible without the remarkable dreams and experiences of countless friends, clients, and dream group and workshop participants with whom I have had the honor and privilege to work over many years. My heartfelt thanks and gratitude to each person.

Special thanks go to my courageous editor, Ann LaFarge, whom I overwhelmed with about forty thousand extra words. Finally, I want to thank my wife, Terri (Nazarita), for her support, her patience, and her excellent editing help.

Prologue: Modern Dreamwork—the Missing Piece

Naturally nature has so disposed me. —Leonardo da Vinci

What the crowd requires is mediocrity of the highest order.
—Auguste Préault

Prior to my thirty-fourth year, the occasional dreams I remembered appeared to be either unintelligible nonsense or endless dramas about frustrating work scenarios. I would wake up panicked, relieved it was just a dream. But one December night everything changed. I dreamt that I was looking through a large door to see what was in a mysterious room. I saw a huge single eye looking back at me intently. Someone had opened the floodgates and a torrent of dreams spilled over the banks of my well-planned and quite ordinary life. Some dreams were life-transforming, others catastrophic, euphoric, nightmarish. Some were shocking. Bottom line: I was hooked, fascinated, drawn into the house of dreams, a world that demanded exploration and attention. That winter night I began a remarkable journey that forever changed my life, an adventure that continues to this day.

As I began to explore the vast landscape of dreaming, I realized that dreams were far more than psychological curiosities, circus side shows we visit every so often for entertainment. I discovered that dreams have shaped and influenced the stream of history for thousands of years.

Dreams have inspired poets, scientists, heads of state, emperors, people from every walk of life. Dreams have saved countless lives from lethal illness, providing individuals with uncanny medical knowledge and healing remedies, often at the eleventh hour. Dreams have ignited wars and created peace. Innumerable lives have been forever changed, transformed by a single dream. But, for the most part, our modern world does not take dreaming seriously. Instead most popular attitudes about dreams turn them into crib toys or video games, or dismiss them as nonsense.

A Bedeviled Genius

I'd like to tell you about a dream that happened over two centuries ago. Dream researcher and author Stuart Holroyd describes the experience of Giuseppi Tartini, a talented, 18th century musician. Tartini dreamt that he made a compact with the Devil, who agreed to be his servant. In his dream, he gave his violin to the Devil to see what kind of musician he was, and the Devil played an exquisite solo that far surpassed anything Tartini had ever heard. The Devil's music so delighted and amazed him that he woke up and immediately tried to reproduce what he had heard in his dream. His best efforts produced a composition he called "The Devil's Trill," which the public regarded as his finest work. But Tartini felt it was so inferior to the Devil's music in his dream that he said he would have broken his violin and abandoned music if he could have found any other way to support himself.[1]

In Tartini's time, the Devil personified the spirit of evil, a demon, the ruler of Hell, and the chief adversary of God. So what or who is this "Devil" and how can *he* create such beautiful music? This important question evokes an answer that threatens to topple some massive ideological structures. Might Tartini's dream be saying that it is his *devilish*, nonconformist rebellion against the accepted musical authorities—the musical gods of his age—that carries the treasure of his unique genius, his authentic, original music? In fact, his dream suggests that his true creative nature *depends* upon characteristics the establishment has rejected and cast out.

Hence *the missing piece in modern dreamwork*: the vital necessity that we understand those dream images and symbols, like Tartini's "Devil," that represent either conformity to outside influences and authority that would smother our essential nature, or, on the other hand, our own hidden genius and creativity that want *into* our life; those priceless qualities that define who we really are and empower each of us to live an authentic life, to become a true *original*, a masterpiece. Or, a dream wants to draw us *out*, save us, pull us outside the narrow passageways and cloned subdivisions that have been *put upon* the land; our dreams want to collapse the gray, concrete garages where we mechanically park our lives each day.

Our dreams relentlessly identify those essential, extraordinary qualities that make us unique and authentic individuals. At the same time, dreams are ruthless and often shocking in exposing influences from others—from society, from family, from groups, from ideologies—that threaten our ability to live our own lives. Any technique of dream interpretation that ignores this powerful dream dynamic is like a child playing in the shallow end of the pool—safe and secure but missing something *tremendous*, a priceless tool for helping us to avoid living a puppetlike life of dull conformity, a life without passion and creativity, a life of depressed potential.

An *Authentic Life* is the expression of our essential nature, the original blueprint, the soul struggling, playing, creating, and recreating life. It is breaking the mold, living outside the boxes of life that want to define, contain, and imprison us. It's the distinct, eccentric, unconventional *you*, your unique sense of who you are in the core of your being.

What We "Put On" Ourselves

I've been wearing glasses since I was about eight years old—a bad case of nearsightedness for which I blame my mother. My parents taught me to read long before I started school, opening the door to a fascinating world of adventure and mystery for me. It wasn't long before I developed a real addiction to reading. I became a five-year-old book worm. I remember secretly climbing the bookshelves in my parents' bedroom to reach the forbidden books on the top shelves—the books I was "too young to read," books like *A Thousand and One Nights.*

I had my special stash of books hidden under my bed. Each night after bedtime my mom would turn the lights out, tuck me in, and close the bedroom door. I would then turn on my lamp and read for hours. Of course I got caught occasionally. Mom would burst through the door, admonishing, "It's way past your bedtime! Turn that light out! You're going to ruin your eyes with all that reading." To this day, I'm convinced my mom psyched me into needing glasses—the power of suggestion.

You're no doubt wondering what all this has to do with dreaming. Well, a curious thing has been happening lately. After all these years, my eyes have been getting gradually stronger. Now I see pretty well without glasses and I don't always need them. My daily routine includes an early morning walk in our neighborhood just outside Portland, Oregon, a quiet little village tucked into a forest with lots of narrow, winding roads that are perfect for walking. On one overcast, windy morning I finally decided to stop wearing my glasses, and as I walked down the hill and toward the street I noticed the colors were more vibrant, and without my eyeglasses on, I felt about a foot taller. I realized that my glasses helped me to see better but they also distorted my perception of the world.

So I'm walking along and I'm thinking how we all see the world through glasses of some sort: We *put on* our religious lenses that see life through a particular religious viewpoint; or we *put on* our political glasses and see the world through one political viewpoint; or we *put on* our familial glasses and see life through the expectations of our parents; or we *put on* societal glasses and live our life by adapting to social pressure to conform to popular ideas. Or we interpret our dreams through the thick dark lenses of some theory.

Our dreams carry the awesome potential to help us see clearly *who we really are*, our natural, inborn potential and unique character, without anything "put on" us.

How This Book Came into Being

A few weeks before I began working on this book, I dreamt that I was looking down on the countryside from high up in the atmosphere at night. I was on my way to some high object, looking for a place to strike—I suddenly realized in the dream that *I was a lightning bolt* and I saw everything from inside the lightning, from the lightning's perspective; I was the *eye* of the lightning. In that same instant I connected to a tall pole on the ground, and then I felt myself spreading out like an electric mandala rippling with brilliant, translucent colors: blues, light magentas, and violets. I felt dangerous, powerful, natural, completely real—elemental. I experienced what it was like to be pure energy, but energy *with consciousness*.

For me, this dream has several layers of meaning. It foretold my actual experience when the idea and realization of *Radical Dreaming* struck me—electrifying, astonishing, beautiful, energizing, and also frightening. Would I be able to articulate what I had gleaned from two-and-a-half decades of dream research and study? What would be the reaction to ideas that don't fit the established, contemporary dream interpretation techniques?

The lightning dream also helped me better understand myself and my love of ideas, words, and images that "shock." And it further convinced me of the awesome power of our *dreams*, their natural autonomy, their unpredictability, how a dream strikes our life from the heavens, rippling through our world, leaving trails of fire and scattering rose petals, changing everything. Suddenly we see ourselves and our environment from a completely new perspective.

This book actually began nearly two-and-a-half decades ago when, seemingly out of nowhere, that torrent of unusual dreams roared into my life. Even though I was unable to interpret the inner, symbolic language* at first, my intuition told me that these dreams were far more than just my brain purging residues from the day. They contained thematic images, symbols, and dramas that moved through my life, leaving strange tracks, exotic fragrances, tearing down old buildings, setting fires. I was captivated. I committed myself to understanding their real meaning. I gradually filled five dream journals with thousands of dreams, all the while voraciously reading everything I could find on dreams, symbols, the imagination, and theories and techniques of dream interpretation.

In the late seventies, I began working with others' dreams and with numerous dream study groups, filling several file cabinets with fascinating examples of individuals' dreams. But the real epiphany for me came *after* I began writing this book. I was well into the first chapter and still in the process of organizing my dream records and research materials, intending to organize the book around types of dreams: relationships, death, sex, warnings, etc., when that lightning bolt in my dream struck! In the process of rereading and selecting dreams from my files, twenty-five years of dreamwork came together. It felt like discovering the long-lost, missing pieces of a beautiful mosaic: Dreams were indeed about our *real* life circumstances, but even more significantly, they were about an *inner revolution*, a *radical* approach to living life. Dreams consistently drag us, usually kicking and screaming, from normality and conformity, into our own life.

I realized that a major category of dreams focused on defining and extracting our *Authentic Self*† from the miasma of collective, outer-

---

*By *symbolic,* I refer to its meaning from the Greek root, *symballein* "to throw together." Thus an unfamiliar face in a dream is symbolic in the sense of a *composite,* a combination of images, a carefully crafted mosaic intended to impart information. An important additional aspect would be looking at the dream as a symbolic whole, like an artist throws together all the elements of a painting on a canvas; Jung ("Definitions," CW 6, par. 817) explained it as "The best possible expression for something unknown."

†I use the term, *Authentic Self,* not in the sense of any personality theory, but rather to describe that constellation of qualities that define our *essential nature*—who we really are, including out fate, our destiny, and our purpose—all the characteristics that combine to make us unique individuals. Instead of a final goal to be attained, the *Authentic Self* is a creative work-in-process, like the seed becoming a unique tree.

world influences and authority that divert us at one time or another from living our own creative life. Moreover, I found that dreams were relentlessly purposive in seeking to move us into living our own Authentic Life, releasing dormant inner potential so that individuals can add unique values and characteristics to society and to our outer world; then we, in Buddha's words, enter into "joyful participation" in the world.

Well, back to the drawing board and a new title: my book had named itself: *Radical Dreaming*—"radical" because our dreams promote *inner revolution*; they mean to overthrow anything that opposes or hinders our essential natures; they seek to give birth to a *radical*, unique, creative life.

About Language

In this book, I use the word *collective* to refer to "the behavior of individuals under the influence of an impulse that is common and collective, in other words, that is the result of social interaction."[2] However, collective influences—good, bad, and everything in between—also infiltrate our psyches like implants, preprogrammed software that propels us into greater and greater conformity and subservience to the demands of the outside world.

Our dreams, a spiritual immune system, relentlessly battle these collective viruses, often with graphic images that rip apart the dull fabric of an *approved* existence, a life frequently dominated by the *group mind* and its often nefarious agendas. Such dreams *intend* to shock and awaken our understanding of the gravity of self-destructive influences and ideologies that place a shroud over the Authentic Self.

Feeling overwhelmed with the excitement of this new approach to dream interpretation, I started rewriting and immediately began having dreams about this book. I also began recalling past dreams that clarified the direction and content of *Radical Dreaming*. After each dream, I would throw up my hands thinking, I don't believe this! Another rewrite! I would have to go back to square one again and revise everything.

For example, the renowned Swiss psychologist Carl Jung had proved to be of immense help to me over the years in understanding dreams, so I was including a lot of Jungian ideas in my book when I dreamt that I was publishing a book with a jacket that looked like a typical book from Jung's *Collected Works*. In the dream I knew my book was an "edited" book. From this dream, I knew I had to write *Radical Dreaming* out of my own experience, not polish someone else's shoes. I was trying to make my experience with dreams *fit* into someone else's theoretical framework. This is not to say that I no longer value Jungian ideas. In fact, I consider Jungian psychology to be one of the most important resources for anyone interested in the connections between dreams, psychology, and spirituality. In any field of human endeavor we necessarily build upon the past and, we hope, add something unique to our store of human experience and knowledge. I simply needed to trust my experience.

Perfumed

I had just finished a major rewrite when I had another dream:

> I was in a small bathroom and I felt very confined. A particular prominent writer and psychologist whom I admire and consider one of my mentors was in the bathroom with me, dressed all in white. He was wearing a potent perfume that was overwhelming. I knew I had to get out of that small room, which I did.

In essence (pun intended), this person's influence was permeating my writing—it smelled of someone else's psychology and methodology. My psyche, *my experience* needed more space; it wanted out of the restrictions of conforming to another's perspective. So, dream by dream, something in me—my dream maker, my soul, my Authentic Self?—would not allow this book to follow someone else's path. I had to set the book free, as much as possible, from preconceived methods and techniques. This has been challenging to say the least, but it has also been deeply gratifying, and it adds further corroboration to the thesis of *Radical Dreaming*. After all, radicals don't follow the status quo, they upset it!

Beyond Authority

One morning, not long after getting "perfumed," I was writing when a puzzling dream I had about eight years ago surfaced out of nowhere:

> I was in Switzerland, explaining to someone that I had to change my name so I would not be persecuted. My new name was

"Paracelsus," and it was going to be the celebration of the 400th anniversary of his death on January 1st.

Paracelsus, a 15th-century doctor and philosopher, was known as "the first modern scientist."* He was a pioneer in microchemistry, modern surgery, homeopathy, and other modern-day accomplishments in medicine. He was born in Einsiedeln, Switzerland, in 1493, and my dream had occurred almost exactly 500 years after his birth. When I did some further research on Paracelsus, I found out that he had changed his name from Philippus Aureolus Theophrastus Bombastus von Hohenheim to *Paracelsus* in order to disassociate himself from "Celsus," who was the preeminent medical authority at the time Paracelsus lived. "Para" means "beyond."

At the time I had this dream, I did not know who Paracelsus was and thus I was stymied as to the dream's essential meaning other than as metaphoric of some aspect of my psyche. And in some gigantic corner of my ego, I entertained the notion of reincarnation—could I have been Paracelsus in a past life?

In short, I now realized that the dream was referring to an aspect of who I am and how I ought to approach my writing and my work with dreams in an original manner, *"beyond"* the establishment, beyond the accepted psychological approaches, as Paracelsus had *radically* departed from the mainstream medical establishment of his day. Certainly I do not intend in any way to depreciate the invaluable contributions many remarkable individuals have made to modern dreamwork, but my dream told me I had to do my best to add something unique out of my own experience.

I understood that this book was my *opus*, my work. For me, it brought my *existence* into clear relief, gave me the "why" of my life, the reason for my being here in this time and place. I felt driven but also deeply content as I recalled another recent dream where I saw an enormous battleship in heavy seas. In the background I heard a symphony that reminded me of the music for the public television documentary "Victory at Sea."

You hold in your hands a *radical* guide for a journey into the night world of dreams that will enrich and change your life. Dreams have painted their images, told their stories, and poured their spirit onto these pages; dreams are the ingredients creating the healing elixir;

---

*Paracelsus, *Paracelsus: Selective Writings*, edited by Jolande Jacobi (Princeton, NJ: Princeton University Press, 1988), p. xxxix.

dreams are the gateways into the Royal City, our passport into the Special World—and your passport into a meaningful life that makes a difference.

And now I invite you to come with me on a journey to explore the miracle of dreaming—that continuously flowing vessel pouring the *water of life*, freeing the tall ship from the sands of the ordinary world.

Radical Dreaming

Introduction

Learn what you are and be such.

—Pindar[1]

The Way of Radical Dreaming

*I went to the woods because I wished to live
deliberately, to front only the essential facts of life,
and see if I could not learn what it had to teach, and
not, when I came to die, discover that I had not lived . . .*

—Henry David Thoreau

Understanding your dreams does not mean you will have to look at them through the smoky glasses of any formal theory. Nor will you have to freeze your dream images in icy psychological labels. Instead, we will look at ways to allow your dreams to interpret themselves. Most traditional dream interpretation techniques drag dreamworld images into the daytime world where the waking ego either depreciates and discards them, or kills their real potential by imprisoning them in professional opinions and expertise.

Dreamwork provides an important intervention between the individual and groups, particularly due to the fact that dreaming provides access to an in-between space in consciousness. In other words, dream imagery reveals collective psychic infection—ailments of the human spirit transmitted from destructive collective agencies—a sort of *pollution by group*.

1

Just as we all learn to read and communicate with each other, to speak and use language, we also need to learn how our dreams communicate. Understanding how to interpret the wisdom and guidance in our dreams enables us to reconnect directly with our own deep inner nature, with the soul, with the Authentic Self, and with our often untapped and unknown creative potential. We then restore a vital *creative tension* in life between the influences of the outside world and our own unique destiny and purpose.

Interpreting dream symbols places us in slippery territory because there are always exceptions to any generality, and because dream images and symbols must be placed within the context and circumstances of the dreamer's life. However, there are broad motifs and images that are red flags, potential indicators that we may be living a collectively driven life. When the powerful currents of societal impulses carry us along, the psyche often produces dream symbology related to the public or mass culture. Thus people have dreamt about: buying a large apartment building, trying to get out of Russia, building an android, wearing a uniform, being inside shopping malls, a man with hooks in his flesh released from bondage. Marie-Louise von Franz found that dreams of officials and civil servants often represent collective adaptation.

Ten Basic Perspectives and Concepts

1. *Intent* and purpose.
2. *Discrimination*: Many images represent *exterior* influences.
3. *Intervention* in the social order.
4. *Protection*: Dreams are protective.
5. *New information*: Dreams do not tell us something we already know.
6. A *natural process*: Dreaming is a part of nature; dreams connect us to our own essential nature and to our *natural* world.
7. *Relevance*: Dreams are relevant to what is happening now or what is about to happen in our lives.
8. *Non-literality*: Dreams are masters of metaphor. For the most part, dreams speak to us in a universal language using symbols and metaphors. They are *seldom* literal.
9. *Synergy*: Dreams strive for a synthesis of opposites, for a unique solution, for a *holding* of tension between opposing forces, for greater integrity and character.
10. *Contradiction*: Dreams expand the ego's often limited percep-

tions of self and others. They also deflate the ego's inflated flights of fancy. Dreams accomplish this through correction, exaggeration, and even intentional *nonsense*.

Dreams, by virtue of their essentially autonomous functioning in the human psyche, often create considerable tension. With a life of their own, they routinely portray dramas that stand in stark contrast to our conscious, waking ego* and personality. They span a mysterious world from terror-producing nightmares to the most profound transformative experiences. We find ourselves doing improbable and unbelievable things, often caught in the worst possible predicaments, escaping dangerous beasts, making love, chopping up tigers, or sublimely flying through space.

1. Intent

Dreams have intent and purpose. They *intend* to free the *Authentic Self*, which then is free to express an *Authentic Life,* which then *will* help create a better world.

Descartes's Dreams

René Descartes (1596–1650), the French mathematician and philosopher, was known for his rationalistic premise, "I think, therefore I am." Exhausted from his intense search for truth, he resolved to focus his awareness within to find his life and his purpose. As he explained in his *Discours de la Méthode*:

> After I had spent some years thus studying in the book of the world and in trying to acquire some experience, I one day made the resolution to study *within myself also*, and to use all the powers of my mind for the choosing of the paths that I ought to follow . . .[2]

---

*I use the term "ego" to put a handle on the cup of our waking persona, to have something to hold on to that refers to our waking *personality structure*. By *ego*, I also mean the individual dynamic of waking awareness, especially as distinct from the world and other individuals. In this sense the ego is a *survivor* by nature, a complex (dreams often use images of different types of structures to represent the waking ego) of influences: genetic, family, societal, experiential, cultural, ideological, political. Similarly, I use the term "dreaming ego" to represent the waking ego's experience in the dream world; the waking consciousness, the waking ego, diving into the dreamscape, becomes the *dreaming ego*—that part of our awareness experiencing the dream, the "me" in a dream.

Not long afterward, in November of 1619, he had a series of unusual, detailed dreams that gave birth to a transformation in his life, turning what had been a keen interest in mathematics and science into a resolve to make that interest his life's work. In one dream, the Angel of Truth appeared and revealed to him that mathematics was the key needed to unlock the secrets of nature. He "was filled with enthusiasm, and discovered the foundations of a marvelous science."[3]

This particular dream opened the door to a lifetime of creative genius in mathematics and science. It also is a rare example of directness and clarity in contrast to the veil of mystery most dreams throw over their real meaning. Descartes ought to have said, "I dreamt, therefore I lived my authentic life"—a life whose impact on the world at the time of the late Renaissance continues to this day.

For Descartes, his "Angel of Truth" apparently knows what it is that he needs to do with his life. His Angel of Truth would have corresponded to the beliefs of the Church at that time and is an example of how dreams *cloak* aspects of the Authentic Self in images that fit a person's dominant religious or philosophic beliefs. We will explore this "cloaking" phenomena in the following chapters because it gives us a major key to deciphering the hidden meaning in our dreams.

Digging Up Stories

Maurice Sendak, the talented writer of children's stories, had a recurring dream that described a beautiful aspect of his Authentic Self: "They're excavating and they find a Brooklyn candy store intact behind ancient brick walls . . . Everything is just as it was when I was a child. All the beautiful toys in their original boxes. There's this overwhelming joy at finding them."[4]

Sendak's dream probably continued until he stopped writing. His dream eloquently depicts his own creative process, his "excavation" of the "candy store" still "intact." If we imagine being a candy store with "beautiful toys in their original boxes," our job would be to make children happy, a job Sendak fulfilled with eminent success. Maurice Sendak kept his child's heart and imagination alive; he had only to dig down through the layers of years to find his "original" stories and the pure gold of his essential nature. His dreams *intended* to inspire and support his writing.

2. Discrimination

Many dream elements, figures, and images represent *exterior* influences, *implanted* attitudes, and popular ideas that are *not* a part of our authentic natures. Just because it's in our dream *does not mean it belongs to us*. The *barbed wire* fence in Robert's dream (chapter 3) that kept him out of Africa becomes the perfect image representing the educational system's demands, restrictions, and pressure to conform—stinging ("barbs") self-judgments that he had internalized.

We will look at numerous ways to identify what belongs to your essential nature and what does not. As this distinction becomes clearer, we begin to feel connected, integrated, self-confident, responsible, and empowered.

Out of Control

Let's look at a dream: "I am in a doctor's waiting room. He hands me a baby with dirty diapers and says, 'Change it.'"[5] The old method of interpreting this dream would be to get associations from the dreamer and then force everything in the dream to be a part of the dreamer. However, what if we simply get rid of any preconceived ideas or theories about the dream and let the dream images interpret themselves? Now the dream takes on some depth; in reality, the "doctor" represents the medical establishment, the approved, licensed authority regarding health issues. And this medical authority figure wants the baby's dirty diapers changed, a *mess* cleaned up. A baby is a *new life* beginning—*natural* and *authentic*. But the doctor will not *tolerate* the fact that it is a natural part of a baby's nature to be out of control in certain areas. The creative process is messy, unpredictable, and it often feels "out of control," particularly to the waking ego's social hypnosis, addiction to survival, adaptation, and conformity.

Perhaps this dream is showing the dreamer that she is allowing lethal outside restrictions to thwart a valuable new beginning for which being out of control at times, making a mess, is *natural*. Moreover the dream is showing the dreamer that her negative self-talk is building a wall of restrictions and intolerance around her "baby." In this sense, a figure like the doctor can best be looked at as a cluster of influences that does not belong to the dreamer and must, like weeds, be pulled from the garden of the Authentic Self.

Dreams and an Ideological Plague

From 1933 to 1939, journalist Charlotte Beradt made records of the dreams of hundreds of Germans, which she smuggled out of the country. In her remarkable book *The Third Reich of Dreams*, she presents those dreams with political content. Beradt's book is an extraordinary illustration of how the dreams of those who lived just prior to and eventually under the Nazis teemed with foreboding imagery about the spreading plague of totalitarianism. Her book also illustrates how dreams graphically portray destructive social and political influences that threaten to trample individual integrity and authenticity.

This unique collection of dreams documents, often with excruciating intensity, how dreams warned people far in advance of an approaching ideological tidal wave. The dreams show how individuals adjusted and adapted to Hitler's regime and how terror can make an accomplice of anyone, even the innocent. Most important, Beradt's book explores the dream images that, like storm warnings, tried to save a citizenry from becoming *accomplices* to mass murder and insanity.[6] It's as though our dreams station guardians at the gates of the soul to prevent barbaric influences from gaining entry.

Dreams pull images out of the mysterious realm called by some the *special world*, the *underworld*, the *dream world*, the Shamanic "lower, middle, or upper world"—similar to what physicist David Bohm terms the "implicate order,"[7] or Rupert Sheldrake's "morphic resonance."[8] All perhaps different ways of looking at what Jung termed the "collective unconscious," which he described as containing ". . . the whole spiritual heritage of mankind's evolution, born anew in the brain structure of every individual."[9] He reasoned, "Our mind has its history, just as our body has its history. We do not need to think that there is anything mystical about it."[10]

Thus, the Roman temple, or that ancient, dusty volume in the Egyptian library, or the medieval village we are walking through, or Buddha sitting in meditation in our dream may be brush strokes from the Self, the *dream maker*, the deft hand of a god, the soul dipping a brush *into* the palette of human experience, *into* the stream of time, and *into* the woods so "lovely, dark and deep." In this sense, our dreams use *nature*—human and the natural world—to create a dialogue, to paint and sculpt our true potential and purpose in life.

3. Intervention

Dreams want the individual life to become a creative *intervention* in the social order; they intend not only to change the dreamer's life; they mean to accelerate the evolution of the human spirit and change the world we live in. Our dreams say that social change begins within each of us.

Beyond Convention

Jasper Johns was working as a window dresser in New York City when he had a dream about painting an American flag. He followed his dream's prompting and went on to play a leading role in mid-20th-century American art, breaking free of the prevailing abstract expressionist movement.[11] Johns's dreams gave him the confidence to step outside convention, to "enter the forest where there was no path," to become a "radical."

President Johnson's Recurring Nightmare

President Lyndon Johnson had a recurring nightmare that began as a child and continued while he was vice-president and then President of the United States. His nightmare worsened after the 1968 Tet offensive in Vietnam. Shortly after a final dream, which bluntly portrayed the impossible predicament he found himself in regarding the Vietnam war, he decided not to seek reelection. His successor quickly ended the war and withdrew U.S. troops.[12]

4. Protection

Dreams warn us about the consequences of our choices, particularly when a decision threatens to compromise any aspect of our authentic life or our real work.

The Sacrifice

While in the midst of her wedding plans, Sue had a startling dream that kept her from making a very bad choice and altered the course of her life:

I'm ascending the Pyramid of the Moon outside Mexico City, which I had actually once visited. I am being escorted up the

steps in my wedding dress. My feet feel like lead. There is a sense
I'm about to be sacrificed. I am filled with dread, panic, and
helplessness. I wake up feeling an incredible sense of relief that
this is only a dream.[13]

Marriage panic? Maybe—maybe not. But she called off the wedding.
Sue's dream impressed upon her a new resolve to live *her* life: "I've got
things to do with my life. And it's not about being a wife, settling down,
and having children.... from that point onward, I was on my own
journey. That's been my driving force." She added, "The dream was so
absolutely *real*, the feeling of impending doom so terrifying, the relief so
huge that I had not been sacrificed.... Something informed me, and I
just followed it in an uninformed way!"[14]

Sue's dream has an ominous image of outside influences in the
Pyramid of the Moon, a place where individuals were sacrificed for the
"good" of society—a pretty transparent message about society's pressure to conform, *outside* pressure to shrink wrap our lives into socially
acceptable roles.

Our dreams also warn us about impending or existing illness, and if
we are alert, they often provide healing solutions, not only for the physical aspects but also the underlying dynamics that are affecting or even,
over time, creating an illness. That is why our dreams often focus on obstacles, boulders blocking our path to living a meaningful, creative life.

People caught in ideological and political movements have dreamt
of: uniformed troops marching in formation, a minister chopping off
people's heads, the slaughter of wild creatures, barbed wire fences, prisons, shopping malls, gurus in pinstripe suits, earthquakes, tidal waves,
sleeping with a politician, being in bed with the boss, a bunch of white
snakes, prostituting themselves, being drugged, aliens breaking into the
house, trees uprooted, a lover dying.

Dumbing It Down

Dave, a good friend and a writer, had just completed his first book
when he had this dream:

I had won a prize—a gleaming, solid gold nugget, round and
oval shaped, about the size of a small egg. I knew it was worth a
fortune. Then I'm seeing if I can sell it in New York, but a man
behind a counter in a jewelry store tells me it's about one ounce
and worth only $425. I'm shocked and notice my nugget has

been pounded down into a thin, fingernail-size piece of gold leaf.
I wake up feeling disturbed.

Dave's dream coincided with feedback from an agent he had approached about representing his book. This agent advised him to
"Dumb it down" if he wanted to make any money with his writing. He
had been seriously considering how to do that when his dream made
him realize he would lose something extremely valuable. The "jeweler"
is someone we normally expect to be an expert, someone who knows,
like an agent. His hard-won treasure was in danger of being beaten
down into a paper thin, insubstantial scrap. His dream saved the *integrity* of his writing.

5. New Information

Dreams do not waste time and energy telling us something we already
know. When a dream appears to be old information, we are certain to
be missing something.

The perception that a dream is going over familiar ground may, paradoxically, mean we are somehow stuck in a literal approach to a dream.
For example at one time or another most of us have had work-related
dreams. Usually these recurring work dreams are so realistic we wake
up trying to sort out the dream situation from real events. Such dreams
seem to hold nothing at all in the way of new information for us. But
what if it is exactly the dream's portrayal of the same *dull routine* "at
work?"—the dullness and the stuckness—that we can't see? What if
these dreams are saying to us that we are stuck, trapped in an ordered,
ordinary life? Perhaps another "ordinary" dream about our endlessly
boring workplace really intends to demolish the *ordinariness* in our
lives, drag us out of some money-lined straitjacket. Suddenly those irri-
tating dreams about work take on a new significance; suddenly there is
some healthy tension between our "ordinary" world and our Authentic
Life.

6. A Natural Process

Dreaming is a part of nature and our dreams connect us to our own essential nature and to our *natural* world.

Dreams select many of their images from our natural world: wild and domesticated creatures, tangled forests, barren deserts, earth, water, rivers, ice, snow, rain, wind, fire, space, stars, floods, storms, eruptions, earthquakes, night and day, moonlight, sunlight, people—a symbolic language connecting us to natural processes that teach us about our life and how life works. Hence people have dreamt of the "Tree Cutter," the sailing ship caught in an ice pack, cutting down an old-growth forest, bees attacking a house, a pine tree uprooted, a garden dying for lack of water, walking on thin ice, trouble getting out of a stream, a bear on fire, being chased by a tiger, a "ravishing bird," a wise Brontosaurus, climbing an icy cliff, getting water for a sick horse.

The Dream That Changed Organic Chemistry

In 1858 the German chemist Kekulé had a remarkable dream that forever changed the face of organic chemistry. He had found his passion and his life's work, chemistry, but he had reached a dead end in his research. This dream opened the door to a startling discovery. Kekulé described his experience: "I turned the chair to the fireplace and sank into a half sleep. The atoms flitted before my eyes . . . wriggling and turning like snakes. And see, what was that? One of the snakes seized its own tail and the image whirled scornfully before my eyes. As though from a flash of lightning, I awoke. I occupied the rest of the night working out the consequences of the hypothesis."[15]

His dream image of the snakes suggested the structure of the benzene molecule. In a later speech at a scientific conference, Kekulé ended his presentation with a comment that must have sent a shock wave through his scientific-minded audience: "Let us learn to dream, gentlemen, and then we may perhaps find the truth."[16]

The Little People

Nature is constantly creating new life. Creativity is a natural part of life that our dreams nourish and support. One of the more famous examples of dreams providing creative inspiration is that of Robert Louis Stevenson. He relied on his dreams for story plots and developed the ability to dream in detailed narratives, often in a sequence of dreams with stories continuing for many successive nights. He credited his "Little People," or "Brownies," with creating dreams that provided many of the plots, characters, and scenes in his stories. A process not unlike author Stephen King's "muses in the basement," who help him with his stories.

Stevenson's *Dr. Jekyll and Mr. Hyde*, the dark tale that is no doubt his best known story, was developed in a dream. He explained: "I had long been trying . . . to find a body, a vehicle for that strong sense of man's double being which must at times come in upon and overwhelm the mind of every thinking creature . . . . For two days I went about wracking my brains for a plot of any sort; and on the second night I dreamed the scene at the window, and a scene afterwards split in two, in which Hyde, pursued for some crime, took the powder and underwent the change in the presence of his pursuers. All the rest was made awake, and consciously."[17] Stevenson created a classic story about the human shadow* that still resonates for people.

Of course, Stevenson's dream would still have other levels of meaning for him beyond helping him with his writing. Mr. Hyde, representing the powerful and dangerous energies of Stevenson's own unacknowledged hidden nature, might well represent creative, socially forbidden qualities that he needed to access in order to write such compelling stories. Mr. Hyde operates *outside* the rules for civilized behavior, perhaps representing a far more authentic individual than the proper, socially acceptable, civilized Dr. Jekyll.

7. Relevance

Dreams are relevant to what is now happening or what is about to happen in our lives in the future.

This means that our dream last night about Julius Caesar *does* have something to do with our life *right now*—it *is* relevant. The dream of setting fire to my childhood home and burning it to the ground occurred just as I finally felt free of my mother's constant career advice: "Whatever you do, John, be sure it's something that makes a lot of money." Similarly, still dreaming about an ex partner who left years ago often means we are yet caught in some behavioral pattern from the past: We are continuing to do something to ourselves that we did back then, in that relationship.

While on a recent early morning walk, I passed a house with a family loading up their car in the driveway. All of a sudden, a large black dog, clearly excited at being outside and temporarily free to run around, ran

---

*The shadow, as used in this book, simply refers to anything we are unaware of about who we are. This also includes unknown influences from society and our culture. The shadow side of human nature can contain hidden genius as well as unpleasant aspects of our nature we would just as soon not look at. The *Radical Dreaming* approach exposes those "shadow" elements that do not belong to the Authentic Self.

up to me, tail wagging and apparently quite friendly. I was just about to stop and pet this dog when a painful memory reached out of the past and stopped me: I remembered a traumatic event that occurred when I was about three years old. My mother and I had just left the grocery store. Right outside the door, someone had tied a dog to a bicycle rack. Thinking how cute the little dog was, I proceeded to bend over, giving the dog a hug and a kiss on the top of its head. The dog let out an ominous growl, and before I could react, it bit me on my forehead, drawing blood.

I was stunned and hurt. On that day I probably lost a pretty good chunk of my trust and innocence. At least I learned a painful lesson about strange dogs. The point being that memories, particularly dreams that leap into our awareness from the past, do so for a reason. Our psyche uses memories of dreams to help us understand and explain some present circumstance or feeling.

8. Non-literality

For the most part, dreams speak to us in a language using symbols and metaphors. They are *seldom* literal.

Is It Junk Food? or Is It Really Junk Food?

It's sometimes difficult to get ourselves out of a literal interpretation because our minds so often use elements of our waking life—people, friends, situations, and events—to create our dreams, as in this example of a young college student who dreamt that "he was out in a shopping center on Saturday night. He went from place to place, and everything went badly for him. He found 'junk food' that made him sick, superficial acquaintanceships, things to buy that left him unsatisfied."[18]

He interpreted the dream as referring to his "Saturday night syndrome," which included "going out with the guys," drinking a lot, eating unhealthy food, getting into adventures and relationships that felt empty afterwards.[19] While understandable, his interpretation creates two dilemmas: It requires a literal interpretation and it implies that his dream is telling him something he no doubt already knows. The interpretation at first *seems* to fit because of how dreams gather their raw material from our everyday life.

But what if his dream is using his "junk food" Saturday nights as a metaphor for stuffing himself with "junk": worthless attitudes, beliefs, and self-defeating *collective* ideas (selling himself worthless things in the "shopping center") that leave him empty and unfulfilled? Suddenly we have new information, potential insight into his nature that has a serious connection to his ability to live his own life.

There are occasional, rare exceptions where a dream *appears* to be literal or precognitive. However, even with the unusual possibility of a literal meaning, the literal face of a dream might be a synchronistic daylight world event that the dream, which operates beyond our waking world of linear time, may be using as raw material for its story. This timeless characteristic of dreams would explain why with some dreams we have to live our life forward in time, live *into* the dreams in order to fully understand them.

Here's another, more subtle slant on the issue of literality: Wilhelm Stekel developed his well-known interpretive abilities by way of his intuition. He compares the difference between a "material" and a "functional" dream interpretation with this illustration:

> *I break open a locked door, and in so doing I destroy the lock, so that the door can no longer be closed properly.*

Here is the "material" interpretation:

> The dreamer has become acquainted with a girl, a virgin. He intends to seduce her. Defloration is symbolized. . . .

Here, on the other hand, is the "functional" interpretation:

> I am forcing my way into my own interior. To do so I must destroy something precious. The new knowledge annihilates a fiction, which has hitherto served as a safeguard (self-protection).[20]

Stekel's "material" interpretation still relies on literal events in a dreamer's waking life: "seducing a girlfriend." Do I smell cigar smoke from Dr. Freud? In contrast, his "functional" interpretation does not put any assumptions on the dream images, like the material view which makes a leap to a sexual situation. Much of what passes for contemporary dreamwork is totally stuck in the material aspect of dream interpretation. Hence dream dictionaries with pat answers for every dream image.

Then there are those rare dreams that are more aptly called visions, or spiritual experiences, which appear to be straightforward directives, prophecies, or warnings. I once had a startling dream experience in which a godlike voice commanded in no uncertain terms, "Study the work of C. G. Jung!" Those words lit a fire under my *ordinary life* and inspired me to return to graduate school in psychology, which then enabled me to begin a new, much more fulfilling career as a psychotherapist.

Still, looking back, even with such an obvious, literal directive, the experience contained other levels of meaning, perhaps to find the "Jungian *depth* psychologist" in my own nature, a part of my unlived life that wanted out, a part that wanted space in my waking life. The dream certainly did not want me to become another cloned "Jungian," but it was a powerful push into the ocean of depth psychology, a field of study that I have always loved. And Jung has proven to be an invaluable mentor for me in my own inner work.

Dreams have inspired countless wars resulting in the massacre of millions of people, most of them innocent victims. In this sense, dreams can be extremely dangerous when they are taken literally. In fact, a literal interpretation often places an individual in a *fundamentalist* mind set, similar to religious or political extremists who interpret the Bible, the Koran, and other ancient texts *literally*. Dreams of killing the enemy are acted on literally instead of looking at the dream as a metaphor for overcoming an *inner* enemy. It is mind-boggling that people continue to kill themselves and others based on literal interpretations of dreams and scriptures.

Changing History

History is replete with disasters of literalisms. For example, the angel Gabriel appeared to Muhammad in a dream and encouraged him to leave the city of Medina, where he had been in exile, and lead an army to Mecca. Muhammad *literally* followed the dream and conquered Mecca, which resulted in the rapid spread of Islam throughout the East.[21] Good if you're Muslim, not so good if you're suddenly a "heathen."

But, let us look at this dream as symbolic of an inner drama: Muhammad's work on his own nature. Then his dream suggests that he needs to use all his capacities to return to what Mecca would have represented to him as his *birth place*; a return to his origins, a return to his essential nature. *Exile*, the enforced absence from his *native* land, would mean he had become alienated from his *native*, innate, authentic nature. Such a dream might actually mean he needed to get back to his center, his core, his *native* self. The consequences of Muhammad's dream interpretation have dramatically changed the course of history.

Starting a War

In 49 B.C., a politically skewed dream interpretation prompted Julius Caesar to cross the Rubicon with his legions, enter Rome, and ignite a civil war. Caesar dreamt that he was sleeping with his mother, which was interpreted as the "mother city of Rome."[22] What if his dream was really about sleeping with his mother's influence and ideas? A different interpretation would have again changed history and perhaps prevented a war.

Empire Building

In a similar scenario, Genghis Khan had two particular dreams that he credited with inspiring his military conquests. His first dream told him that he was destined to reign over the Mongols. Of course, his acting on the dream literally made the dream a self-fulfilling prophecy. But had the dream been taken as a message to "reign over" an inner empire, then a very different outcome would have ensued, not only for Genghis Khan, but also for the lives of the conquered peoples. In his second dream, he was told that heaven wanted him to conquer other kingdoms and countries.[23] As a metaphor, "other kingdoms" in a dream would likely refer to unknown parts of the dreamer, other unexplored territories of the individual psyche.

If a dream suggests we need to "conquer" another land, it may actually be saying we need to get control over some out-of-control area of our lives. Threatening *foreign* armies in a dream often mean we are faced with the impact of some *mass* movement, an ideology, "uniformity"—collective forces armed with destructive ideas that threaten to overrun the individual life.

Foreign Invaders

Laurens van der Post, a prolific author and master storyteller, was convinced that "[a] dream is never false. Every detail is there for a reason, and has a meaning."[24] He gives this example of a young South African girl's dream: "She dreamed that her tribe (the Amacoza) needed to sacrifice all their material possessions, to eat up all their cattle, which was the greater part of their wealth. The dream said that on the day they consumed their last worldly goods, their ancestors would come out of the sea and drive out the white man."[25]

Laurens explained, "The tribe took the girl's dream literally. As they began to slaughter their cattle, the area's governor, Sir George Gray, tried desperately to persuade them to consider other interpretations. But they wouldn't listen. The girl told them, 'It's another trick of the white man to keep you in [his] power.' The Amacoza kept faith with the dream, and hundreds of thousands died as a result. They didn't see the dream's symbolism."[26]

According to Laurens, the girl's dream really meant "that they mustn't be preoccupied with the material world and its values but rather turn back to the spiritual values of their ancestors. You've got to see imagery both literally and symbolically. Only then will the dream never betray you."[27] Her dream also plainly says that she, the dreamer, and perhaps her tribe, need to "drive out the white man," expel those ideas and influences that are not a part of their original spiritual values. The dream is really an alarm, a warning that the dreamer and her people have probably *put up with* another culture's ideology and views. Again, taking a dream literally had tragic consequences.

In this sense, our dreams hold a valuable key to creating a more civilized society and a world where people respect and value all life. Dismissing dreams as unintelligible nonsense may well be one of the modern world's greatest tragedies—a tomb filled with a priceless storehouse of unimaginable riches sealed with ignorance and arrogance.

The social and political implications of *how* we interpret our dreams can not only transform *our* lives, it can, and has "literally" changed the world—creating horror, promoting inhumanity, and fragmenting the world into hostile camps—or it can inspire constructive change and ennoble the human spirit.

Over and over, our dreams prove to be potential peacemakers, healers, wise counselors—trying, with eternal patience, to return us to ourselves, to guide us home to our *essential character* and our Authentic Lives.

9. Synergy

Dreams strive for *integrity*, a holding together of disparate characteristics, an integration of different elements—a synergetic combination that gives birth to something new and *unpredictable*.

Dreams uniquely enable us to integrate different aspects of who we are that then become necessary ingredients in the creation of an authentic, original life. Working with dreams helps us cultivate the ability to *hold the tension between opposites*, to tolerate ambiguity and some chaos. Dreams tell us over and over that the human spirit abhors one-sidedness and identification with any one fixed ideology, attitude, or viewpoint. In this regard, dreams tend to zero in on opposites. Our dreams steer us away from an either–or approach, a black and white world view. Our dreams want a *both–and* world. They strive for balance, not necessarily *fifty-fifty* but a place of *just-rightness*.

10. Contradiction

Our dreams break down the walls of our often limited views of others and ourselves; they open our vision to our unexplored potential. They love to contradict our egos' self-imposed limitations.

To accomplish this, dreams use exaggeration, nonsense, and graphic, disturbing images to get our attention, to dismantle our faulty perceptions, and to propel us into a world without boundaries and unnecessary restrictions.

Jung believed that most dreams were attempting to *compensate* for some erroneous conscious attitude. I am convinced that our dreams intend far more than "compensating" a conscious attitude. We ought to ask *whose* attitude might be in conflict with the dream's intent; it usually turns out to be the parts of our waking persona that are focused on survival and adaptation in society. Dream researcher Gordon Globus suggests, in contrast to the theory of compensation, that, "During waking there is intense attachment to one way of being, so that the alternatives are not available. The dream does not compensate for waking excess but expresses a more balanced presentation of all of our possible ways of Being."[28]

Intent and Purpose

Using dream imagery as the well from which we will draw the life- and world-saving elixir, we will explore boundaries, edges, spaces in between things, the anatomy of collisions, of opposites, the nature of relationships: between the individual and her/his own interior nature, between individuals and others, between individuals and their surrounding world—between *individual authenticity* and collective/familial/societal/ political "shoulds."

We can work with our relationships to our community, to our natural world, and to our group through dream symbology and imagery. Our dreams reveal that each of us is connected and implicated in our institutions and systems, both inwardly and outwardly, whether we are aware of it or not. And a large part of our suffering can be attributed to destructive collective influences.

Living a life dragging the immense weight of commonality and sameness, of lost passion, will show up in our dream world, where the psyche attempts to alleviate our one-sided involvement in the masses. As group ideologies and collective systems increasingly become our "outer garment," we become more and more disconnected from the world around us and from our own authenticity.

It is my intention to awaken the rebel, the revolutionary, the "Radical Dreamer," the Authentic Self, the adventurer—your *natural* genius and your innate creativity. I want to set loose the spirit of the dreams in this book; I want to let the dreams dance through your life and your imagination, burn down obstacles, topple prisons of conformity.

PART 1

PREPARATION FOR THE JOURNEY

Humanity is estranged from its authentic possibilities.
—R. D. Laing

CHAPTER 1

Inner Revolution

Tell me, what is it you plan to do with your one wild and precious life?

—Mary Oliver[1]

Pulling the Sword from the Stone

And where we had thought to find an abomination,
we shall find a god;
where we had thought to slay another,
we shall slay ourselves;
where we had thought to travel outward,
we shall come to the center of our own existence;
where we had thought to be alone,
we shall be with all the world.

—Joseph Campbell[2]

A long time ago there was a kingdom that had fallen into a place of misery, suffering, and decay—a land torn apart by the beasts of war. The people longed to find their true king who would restore the kingdom. One day a great, foursquare stone miraculously appeared in the churchyard. Embedded in the center was a steel anvil a foot high and therein was stuck a sword on which, written in gold lettering, were the words: "Whoso pulleth out this sword of this stone and anvil, is rightwise king . . ."[3]

Only the rightful ruler of the kingdom (the *authentic* individual), the *Self*, can extricate individual power and real authority—the "sword"—from the stonelike grip of family, social, and cultural expectations, from authoritarian-structured groups, elitist, extremist ideologies, and from the anvil's steel grasp, its pounding and shaping of our identity into a socially approved role. In restoring the "rightwise king," the center of gravity of our existence returns to the individual Self, out of which our unique life blossoms.

I first met Lilly as a client in my psychotherapy practice. She wanted to work on understanding her dreams, which she hoped would provide some of the answers she so desperately sought. She complained that her life felt miserable, that she had "lost her soul." A striking brunette in her early thirties and recently divorced, she described feeling overwhelming and uncontrollable emotions, from intense anger and bitterness toward her ex-husband, who had walked out on her and their two girls, to grief and hopelessness about the formidable task of raising two young children as a single mother.

In addition, she had worked for most of her adult life in the family business—now owned and managed by her mother—as the office manager of a busy suburban carpet and tile store. Lilly not only thoroughly hated her job, she felt economically trapped in it with a salary just barely enough above average to feel somewhat secure. With no other job skills or experience, she explained that to get a different job in a similar position she would have to take a pay cut, a scary proposition for her in her present circumstances. Still, she could barely make ends meet. Even worse, she and her mother had never gotten along and fought constantly. Working with her mother on a daily basis and having to "follow orders" made even thinking about going to work stir up a sickening anxiety that seemed more like a recurring nightmare. Lilly felt she was indeed "living someone else's life."

Lilly and I launched ourselves into what became a year-and-a-half of dreamwork using Radical Dreaming techniques. Gradually, dream by dream, she began to separate herself from the intricate web of outside influences and attitudes that were not a part of her true Self. Eventually, a powerful part of her true identity emerged from her dreams: she called it her "Free Spirit Self." She described her Free Spirit Self as a risk-taker, a rebel, an adventurer, and "not liking rules." She connected this important aspect of her Self with her first visit to Hawaii many years ago—a place where she felt grounded and completely at home. Lilly had begun to "pull the sword from the stone," to free her unlived life from the stone of her outer circumstances. And her dreams then began to focus on the obstacles impeding her Free Spirit. She started exploring different work options and began developing friends and connections in Hawaii.

Step by step, she began changing her life and her circumstances. Her Free Spirit Self freed her from what before had seemed to be an insurmountable predicament; it liberated her to think about new possibilities.

Lilly now lives in Hawaii where she operates her own flourishing gourmet catering business, fully living her lifelong passion and talent for preparing great food. And she has married a "very different, wonderful man" whom she deeply loves. Such is the awesome power of dreams to transform and change our lives.

Through working with her dreams and applying what she learned from them, Lilly radically changed the nature of her relationship to her surrounding world. Her personal transformation has been an inspiration to her children and to many other people. Her life now impacts society in a positive, creative manner. But she first had to break free of the restrictive social stereotyping and negative attitudes associated with being a single parent. Lilly's dreams helped her to separate herself from these limiting outside influences and reconnect to empowering aspects of her real nature.

Living a "Radical" Life and Making a Difference

It is not society that is to guide and save the creative
hero, but precisely the reverse.

—Joseph Campbell

I chose "Radical Dreaming" as the title for this book because the word *radical* comes closest to characterizing the inner and outer revolution that takes place when we have the courage to live authentically, to follow our dreams. "Radical" literally means "going to a root or source, departing markedly from the usual or customary," and it means "*effecting fundamental or revolutionary changes in current practices, conditions, or institutions*," and also, "one who seeks to overthrow the social order." The Latin root of radical, *rādīx*, means "root." To live a distinct, original life, we need to go to the source, into our roots, our *original* nature. We need to "overthrow the social order," which has been implanted deep within the human psyche with all its attendant rules and expectations heaped upon the individual. Radical Dreaming implies leaving the stagnation and servitude of an "ordered," common life, a deadly, soul-numbing status quo; it is the ultimate rebellion!

Using Dreams for Personal Transformation and Social Change

As we move deeper into the twenty-first century, we find ourselves in the midst of a tremendous and extraordinarily difficult transition from a world fragmented into often hostile groups and ideologies to a world where people are united by their common humanity, not divided by boundaries of race, religion, identity, or geography. Our dreams hold the potential to transform the archaic, medieval mass-mindedness that labels and judges others not as unique individuals but instead as members of a particular group or belief system.

Certainly many groups are supportive of the individual and are constructive, helpful forces in society. Support groups, religious and spiritual groups, common interest groups, and community groups can be invaluable, provided they maintain a healthy balance of power between individual, creative expression, and group ideas and influence.

The balance of power in our present age is heavily weighted in favor of the outer world, the collective* arena where popular influences are more likely to determine the course of an individual life. We may believe we are living "our" life, but powerful, often unacknowledged social forces push and pull, shape what we do and how we live. We find ourselves following a set of implanted "shoulds": getting the career our family and society approve of, getting the house in the suburbs, having kids, saving for retirement—ending our working life at sixty-five because that's what everyone expects us to do. So people have dreams about death, about people at the end of life, incapacitated, in wheel chairs, dreams about returning to high school or being in some classroom setting preparing for or taking a test. We begin to feel insignificant, that our life could not possibly matter or make a difference. We give up before even trying.

The Exam

Ted had reached a crisis in his life. "What am I doing in this world?" he asked at our first meeting, slumping forward, his eyes fixed on the floor. Should he continue with a career in the medical field that would promise him financial security and a comfortable life style, or should he follow his passion, step into unknown territory, disappoint his family and friends? He brought this dream to our next session:

---

*I use the term "collective" in a generic sense, to refer to outside influences: family, society, the culture, religion, politics, economics, the media, or any group-based belief system.

I am in a big classroom with other students. It reminds me of my college. We are all surprised when someone announces there is going to be an exam. I feel panicked and unprepared to take this test.

Ted's dream coincided with his serious consideration of a new career path, a path that meant he would be stepping outside the "plan" for his life. In theory, a good education prepares us to live a productive, responsible life. However, education can also limit and sometimes smother our real nature. "Examination dreams" and back-to-school themes in dreams often warn us that some aspect of our emerging potential is colliding with collective conditioning to obey the rules, to play the game, to follow tradition, to "fit in," to be "normal," and to conform. Ted realized that his examination dream represented a challenge, an "exam" from the establishment, from powerful, implanted influences that could keep his authentic life depressed and entombed. These conformist pressures from his college experience collided with his choice to follow his passion.

When we encounter one of these examination dreams, we need to ask ourselves:

- How am I not measuring up to some societal or cultural standard?
- How might I be judging, examining myself as a success or a failure based on outside expectations?
- What have I been trained to be and to do with my life that feels alien to who I really am?
- What have I been telling myself that represents outside ideas and attitudes? And which particular ideas feel self-defeating?

Social responsibility then depends upon being true to ourselves, not becoming a clone and living someone else's life.

We desperately need a new way of looking at ourselves, others, and our environment, a way free of the deadly, dehumanizing judgments that a group-oriented perspective often places on life. Seen through a collective mind set, being black, brown, or white becomes a label that overshadows individual character and identity. We see the group, not the individual and we tend to judge or assume things about individuals based on what we have been told or conditioned to believe. When the collective view dominates, it's nearly impossible to see a *human* being. Instead we see a "Jew," a "Republican," an "Arab," a "Protestant," a "Liberal," and so on. Our dreams rarely address this labeling of people but they do focus on images of containment and entrapment within soul-killing influences from all types of "group-think."

We need to become much more *conscious*, more aware of who we are and of our particular destiny, our true vocation. This dilemma requires a spiritual, psychological, and sociological reorientation, a new way of perceiving ourselves and others, a way of living and experiencing life that combines inner and outer consciousness—a way of living that includes *dreamwork* not only as a social responsibility but also a profound summons to our authentic life—a priceless resource that we all have access to. Indeed, our dreams are screaming solutions for the imbalance, injustice, and social chaos that permeates our present age, but almost no one is listening.

After years of dream research, Montague Ullman, professor emeritus of clinical psychiatry at the Albert Einstein College of Medicine in New York, and the founder of the Dream Laboratory at the Maimonides Medical Center in Brooklyn, New York, concluded that "Dreams are nature's way of trying to counteract our seemingly unending compulsion to fragment the world. Unless we learn how to overcome all the ways we've fragmented the human race, nationally, religiously, economically, or whatever, we are going to find ourselves in a position where we can accidentally destroy the whole picture."[4]

Why Your Dreamwork Is So Important

Why try to understand our dreams? Because our contemporary world urgently needs the intervention of a perspective that brings greater soulfulness and compassion into our experience and actions; qualities that our dreams help cultivate and develop. And because our dreams have a profound purpose: the creation of distinct, integrated individuals who will add vitally needed qualities to our collective life as well as encourage the development of mutual respect, interconnectedness, and empathy for each other and for our natural environment. Understanding dreams and incorporating their meaning into our waking life makes individuals a source of creativity, a wellspring of insight, character, and integrity, renewing society and reinvigorating culture.

Our modern world increasingly suffers from a variety of symptoms that may well be the result of potent societal and cultural influences that increasingly dominate the individual life. Might we be in the throes of a pervasive "collective neurosis," a deadly condition that only individual authenticity can cure? Psychologist, author, and Auschwitz survivor Victor Frankl described one of our more common modern maladies as an "existential vacuum," which, Frankl observed, results from not existing within the context of one's Authentic Self. This "non-existence" is particularly relevant to our exploration of how dreams portray the effects of living a life based upon outside influences and authority. An existential vacuum is what we more often experience as a barren emptiness or a lack of meaning and purpose. Maslow, the founder of humanistic psychology, termed a similar condition "metapathology," which he characterized as a sense of alienation and disconnection.[5]

An Identity Crisis

Rob, a forty-six-year-old contractor, complained of feeling depressed, lost, and hopeless, as though he had never lived his own life, but instead had followed in the footsteps of his parents. "I'm terrified of becoming just like them," he said. He had this dream in the midst of this crisis:

> I was walking around feeling angry and frustrated because one moment I had my wallet and the other moment it was gone. I started frantically looking for it. I felt that I was going to have a breakdown.

Rob's actual wallet, flawlessly organized, always contained seven business cards, his identification, his driver's license, at least $200, credit cards, insurance information, and a faded snapshot of his wife and two daughters. I asked Rob, "If you are your wallet, who are you?" He explained that his wallet represented his identity, his individuality, and his way of relating or fitting in to his world. And it had disappeared. This made sense to Rob. He told me that he felt as though his old life, his former identity, was collapsing, "breaking down." His dream now felt reassuring to him, implying that he could find and live his own life.

Rob had begun to experience what William Bridges, author of *The Way of Transition,* calls the "neutral zone." Bridges describes it as "that in-between time, after you've let go of your old life and before you have fully discovered and incorporated your new life."[6] Marilyn Ferguson puts it even more succinctly: "It's not so much that we're afraid of change or so in love with the old ways, but it's that place in between that we fear . . . It's like being in between trapezes. It's Linus when his blanket is in the dryer. There's nothing to hold on to."[7]

In my psychotherapy practice, I consistently encounter individuals in an identity crisis that usually accompanies a crisis of meaning. They find themselves struggling to understand who they are, why they are here in this world, and what their particular role is. They have lost their sense of Self and often complain that they feel powerless and insignificant in a world that appears to be increasingly complex and indifferent. They muddle through their lives with anxiety, hopelessness, and depression, feeling like failures. We could say they are suffering from an encounter with "non-being," a bone-chilling meeting with the deathlike predicament of not knowing themselves, of not knowing or acknowledging their innate potential.

This separation from the Self often creates a haunting emptiness, a troubling angst—an estrangement from our own essential nature and potential, a deep, gnawing disconnection, a feeling of homelessness. But individuals, persuaded to follow the dogma of popular social values that emphasizes "having" instead of "being," adopt a way of life that can obliterate individual uniqueness while reinforcing conformity. As a result, people find themselves living in a wasteland of adaptation to what others think they should be doing and an unquenchable desire for more. The accompanying loss of human dignity and individual integrity goes hand in hand with a loss of self-respect and respect for others. T. S. Eliot called this disconnect from our true nature, "the dissociation of sensibility"—the chief spiritual dilemma of society.[8] Nothing is more dehumanizing than living someone else's life and a dehumanized—*non-human*—person has no empathy for others or the environment. Our dreams work to heal this tragic loss of soul and Self.

Holding Life at Arm's Length

Gene, a man in his late thirties with two small children, complained of debilitating anxiety and stress. He brought this dream to his first psychotherapy session:

> I am holding a king cobra snake by its head, at arm's length. It takes all my strength to keep it from biting me, it is so strong.

Gene's harried suburban home life involved a never-ending "list" of things to get done around the house and a high-pressure job that he described with a pained expression: "It's like being trapped in a hanging wire cage and poked with sharp sticks." He explained, "There's only one or two percent of me left."

We explored Gene's dream cobra. What or *who* is the "king cobra" that wants to bite him, inject him with its venom? Is the cobra a god in disguise, or is it perhaps his *unlived* life he continues to hold at arm's length? Gene realized that the king cobra was actually a powerful part of his authentic, natural identity, that he indeed *needed* the "bite" so that his ninety-eight-percent, desperately-held-together, impossible, activity-jammed life could die. When I asked Gene to become that *king cobra* and describe what it's like, he explained that from the cobra's viewpoint Gene represented his "harried" life and *that* impossible life was what the cobra wanted to kill.

His dream shows how the *dreaming ego* closely replicates the waking ego—an aspect of our personality structure that attempts to "hold things together," which often means maintaining the status quo even as it slowly destroys us. His "nightmare" had become a valuable image of change and transformation, an encouragement to stop holding on to circumstances that put his life out of balance and were slowly destroying him, leaving no time or space for his creative life or his life-long interest in public service and politics.

Gene's subsequent dreamwork focused on the devious mechanisms his waking ego had devised to enable him to maintain his grip on the life he thought he wanted but which had become so stressful and unfulfilling. He explored the intricate web of defenses he had built against living his own life. For him the *king* cobra represented a powerful aspect of his real Self—the "rightful ruler of the *king*dom" that he could no longer "keep at arm's length." The work to extricate his authentic life had begun. And he now had a powerful new ally.

Swallowed by Conformity

> *The greatest danger before you is this: You live in an*
> *age when people would package and standardize your*
> *life for you—steal it from you and sell it back to you*
> *at a price. That price is very high.*
>
> —Doris Haddock

Rollo May suggests in *The Discovery of Being* that we need to confront our own lack of authenticity or non-being: "Perhaps the most ubiquitous and ever-present form of failure to confront nonbeing in our day is in conformism, the tendency of the individual to let himself be absorbed in the sea of collective responses and attitudes, to become swallowed up . . . with the corresponding loss of his own awareness, potentialities, and whatever characterizes him as a unique and original being."[9] In my research I have found that our dreams provide a potent tool to reconnect to our original Self because our dreams are constantly working to illuminate those outer dynamics that are "swallowing up" our true potential.

I find, especially among younger people, a tremendous fear of slipping into socially approved, stereotypical roles. They want desperately to do something in their lives that gives them a sense of significance and value while also making a difference in the world. They are justifiably suspicious of our institutions, our political and economic systems. Perhaps much of their rebellion from tradition, their attempts to be different, their desire to stand out from the crowd, represents an expression of "not being" a participant in the collective status quo. But far too often, people find that they have ironically become part of yet another subgroup that in turn overwhelms individual authenticity. And not understanding ourselves or our particular calling in life certainly becomes a major cause of both boredom and low self-esteem, which have become immense issues among children and teens.

Why Most Psychotherapy Doesn't Work

"Three Aliens Land": Dreams and Drugs

Peter, a computer programmer in his early forties, hated his job and the company he worked for. He had just begun taking a new prescription drug for anxiety and depression when he had a scary dream he called a nightmare:

> It was just getting dark and I was standing outside and realized that there had been a nuclear war. Everywhere I looked I saw blackened remains, a burned-out landscape. It was horrible! Then three white Atlas rockets landed like space ships, the kind that carry nuclear warheads. As I watched, three alien beings came out of the rockets' doors. A strange green glow came from the doorways. I woke up really frightened wondering how aliens can be in U.S. ICBMs.

After working on his dream using the Radical Dreaming approach, Peter understood the true impact of his devastating bout with depression, how it had effectively wiped out his world—the "burned-out landscape." He realized, with a look of real shock, that the three white ICBMs in his dream represented the *outside world's remedy* he had chosen as well as the actual *three white pills* he took each day—a powerful, synchronistic allusion to the gravity of the pharmaceutical establishment's attack on his "depression"—a quite real "alien" invasion of his psyche.

From this dream he began to rethink his approach to his depression. Instead of chemically altering his brain chemistry so that he would not feel depressed, Peter began to consider other alternatives including exploring what his depression wanted and using his depression as a catalyst to change his life and his career, to stop *depressing* his hopes and dreams and his *unlived life*. Peter's dream helped him redirect his life by illuminating foreign influences that ironically were preventing him from getting to the heart of what his depression really intended.

A compelling, unnamed longing for our own life and identity often motivates us to join some group or seek out a psychotherapist. Unfortunately, many contemporary therapies, while well-intended, focus on social re-adaptation and continuing conformity, leaving persons in the same or worse circumstances. I remember Julie, a client who told me, "I'm sick of being labeled with one of those personality disorders from that horrible big book and then having the therapist try to fix me."

To address this therapeutic compulsion to fix us so that we fit back into society, whether in a group context or in individual psychotherapy, we need to create space for an inner revolution, a radical reorientation that supports the emergence of our individual, unique nature, which must by definition be essentially *different* from what everyone else expects us to be. Of course this reorientation requires an obvious focus on understanding the reality of each person's existence and experience, a task that many groups do not address at all, particularly when we find ourselves part of a group that places the group's agenda above the individual.

In the context of individual therapy this perspective suggests that therapists rid themselves of as much theory and technique as possible. Consequently, psychotherapy ought to concentrate on ways to help individuals connect with their own genius, their own distinctiveness and way of being in the world. This book provides a *radical* way to look at our dreams and at life; it explores this remarkable process of reconnecting to our essential nature, to our authenticity; and shows us how our dreams respect individual differences and promote the process of freeing the real Self and living a genuine life.

More and more evidence points to the conclusion that following the path of conformity, not living out of one's Authentic Self, is a major culprit in what has become an epidemic of clinical depression, which, in turn, promotes the mushrooming use of mood altering drugs to keep us feeling "good" and "normal." When we *depress* the real aspects of who we are in order to conform to outside rules and expectations, we then feel depressed because we have pushed aside and pressed down our passion and creativity in favor of adaptation to what we believe we should do and be, based on family and social pressures. Depression then becomes a very real consequence and symptom of an unlived life. As Martin Seligman, head of the American Psychological Association and professor of psychology at the University of Pennsylvania, concluded, "the United States is in the throes of an epidemic of clinical depression. An American today is significantly more likely to suffer clinical depression at some point in his or her life than at any other time in the last hundred years."[10]

Depression, however, may well be one of our most valuable signposts, a red flag, a symptom of spiritual distress, a deep inner protest to free ourselves from expectations and unattainable goals imposed upon us by society or family. To mindlessly obliterate our depression with drugs, shutting down our natural alarm system and numbing our innate human sensibilities, is nonsensical and perverse.

Maintaining an Image

> But the first step is to realize what the "real" thing is we're searching for. And it isn't a can of Coke.
> —Richard Wainwright

Never in history has there been a greater saturation of the individual psyche with images of idealized lives that equate meaning and fulfillment with "having" *things* and maintaining an image and life style reinforced and promoted by powerful economic, political, and social forces. With an unrelenting persistence, dreams point to this invasion of the soul by alien forces, not unlike what epidemiologists call "diseases of civilization." Hence we dream of Britney Spears, Madonna, celebrity "images," authority figures, priests and presidents, dilapidated cities, infections, schools, and invading armies—dream images that often represent the effects of intrusion from negative outside influences.

While dream images must be placed in the context of the dreamer's life and experience, in our Western culture certain types of images are red flags: dreams of apartment complexes, machinery, highways, and all sorts of *mass-produced* materials, public structures impinging on the natural world. As my friend Jane dreamt: "A housing development had overwhelmed an old growth forest." She felt her natural life was disappearing, replaced by what Jane described as "living in a place that's just the same as everyone else's." When she imagined being one of the homes in the development, she commented, "I feel really insignificant." Connecting her experience with her everyday life, she observed, "It's my job, it's swallowing up my life. It's not at all what I really imagined doing with my life." And when Jane imagined being the old growth forest, she remarked, "I feel really threatened, as though something unique and extremely rare is about to be lost."

The Oasis

Here's another example that illustrates the potent influence of collective ideas: Connie, a woman in her early forties, was working on plans for a new kind of equestrian center, a project that would fulfill a lifelong dream. One evening after despairing of ever starting the venture because of her concern over raising enough money, she had this dream:

> I am driving along a road in a desert. It's a nicely paved road winding its way toward a city in the distance. We approach the city and I think to myself, This is a very wealthy city, probably the wealthiest per-capita city there is. We pass a splendid house on a hillside that looks new, but fashioned after a castle with two simulated turrets. I somehow know this house is owned by the wealthiest individual in the town: a man—the wealthiest of the wealthy.

"A part of me is seriously considering dropping my passion. Am I self-deluded?" Connie asked, sighing and slumping back in her chair. After working on her dream, she likened the wealthy city to an "oasis of money in the desert." The splendid hillside house reminded her of an actual country home belonging to a wealthy horsewoman she had once met. Working with the image of the paved road, she described it as "easy, comfortable, smooth going—the only way into the city. But it takes everyone in the same direction."

The wealthy man in the dream exemplified, for her, a symbol of power and control that reminded her of her father's influence and attitudes about money. Through his example, she had learned to place money first in life, that before undertaking any project, money and a detailed business plan had to be in place. Her dream eloquently shows her that this money-based view of life was colliding with her creative side. As a result of this dream, she reconnected with the true spirit of her project and plunged back into her plans for the equestrian center. From her dream she felt free to let money issues become a part of her creative process as her center developed.

Medicating the Loss of an Unlived Life

Psychologically, an unlived life, relegated to the unconscious, tends to get projected onto outer objects, other people, certain groups and "stuff." Consequently, we become fascinated with our own projections captured by those images that mirror some aspect of the Self: celebrities, gurus, religious and political movements, fancy cars, homes, vacations in "paradise," exotic places, wilderness, money, endless self-help seminars that promise wealth and contentment. We turn to insatiable consumption and consumerism—all temporary self-medications for the alienation and disconnect from our inner treasure. We escape confrontation with our own potential through TV and a myriad of electronic media that promotes our popular addiction to constant entertainment.

As psychologist Roy Baumeister observed in *Escaping the Self:* "I am a burden—escape into masochistic behavior such as alcohol abuse. I am empty—escape into compulsive eating or conspicuous consumption of other goods. I can't measure up—escape into rigorous spiritual disciplines or exercise regimes. I am repugnant—escape into binge eating or binge drinking."[11] Are we, as Swiss author Max Frisch maintained, "so arranging the world that we do not experience it"?[12] The outer world then has really got us, holding the Authentic Self captive in the most intractable illusion.

Added to the above we have the gradual disintegration of our cities, social and political stagnation, essentially a lack of any real innovation and creativity, spreading urban, commercial, and residential sprawl. Potent marketing persuades many individuals to choose mass-produced, neatly cloned life styles so that they can spend the remainder of their lives in collective servitude to the gross national product, measuring success by accumulating more of everything and anything regardless of the consequences for ourselves or the planet. Our dreams, by returning us to ourselves, function as a way to *deprogram* our life, a way to free ourselves from destructive outside influences.

Dreamwork, by its very nature, connects us to what it really means to be fully human; to ignore our dreams, to silence their wisdom, has profound consequences not only for the individual but for society and our planet as well.

Our dreams want us to break free of "isms," popular political, social, and economic systems that often overshadow our capacity to act from our own innate humanity. Most dangerous are those groups and belief systems that are both anti-Self as well as divisive, fragmenting forces in the world—one of many examples being religious fundamentalists around the world who spread hate, prejudice, and often terrorism. As we break free of these nefarious influences that have taken up residence in our psyches, we contribute to greater real freedom and integrity in society at large. Our supreme initiation into an authentic life does not come from any group, but from within the individual soul.

Like the biblical Exodus out of Pharaoh's Egypt, we need to extricate ourselves from outer authoritarian forces which imbed their expectations, values, and demands deep within the individual psyche. In this context the "promised land" equates to living an authentic life out from under the influence of the negative aspects of our popular culture. In collective hands we cannot fully realize our individual passions. Overwhelming and powerful exterior influences abort the individual's soul-making process, depriving society of precisely what it most needs—individual genius, innovation, and creativity. Not only does an outside-in orientation dehumanize individuals, it has created societies in which people are disturbingly lacking in self-responsibility, individual integrity, dignity, humanity, and character—qualities that no "ism" can ever provide.

Unnecessary Suffering

In fact, many of our so-called personal problems may actually be the result of social and cultural problems that have been internalized in the individual psyche—suffering that does not belong to us, yet ironically our un-consciousness helps to perpetuate it. Dreams directly address this dilemma, tirelessly redirecting individuals into their own unique life. But this singular track must also wind its way through the collective world—each is indispensable to the other.

Following the Herd

Kathy wondered why she had recurring dreams of flying in jumbo jets. I asked her, if she were a jumbo jet, what would her job be? "My job is to take everyone to the same place—the route's all planned out.

Oh! I get it," she replied, smiling and suddenly realizing she was following the herd, going along with the crowd instead of finding and following her own path.

Going Down

When I first met Tony, he was a gaunt, depressed nineteen-year-old. He told me about a disturbing dream: He was walking in a forest, one of his favorite places to hike as a kid. Suddenly he noticed a large commercial airliner flying high overhead. Unexpectedly it turned sharply upward, rolled over, and crashed into the trees, bursting into flames. Hundreds of people were running everywhere and he woke up in a panic.

He explained, "I would walk in that forest and daydream about what I really wanted to do with my life. I felt connected with my dreams in that place." When we explored the passenger jet using the Radical Dreaming process, he immediately sat straight up, a sparkle in his eyes. "That's it! That plane represents what everybody else thinks I should do. It already has the destination picked out. I've been studying computer science for all the wrong reasons—I hate it. It's not me." With a tremendous sense of relief, Tony felt free to begin exploring his dreams once again, to begin living his own life and following his passion. Tony had been *depressing* his authentic life.

Avoiding Dead-End Roads

Our dreams work to integrate two worlds: the divine and the human, or the imaginal and the physical, as I prefer to look at it. While necessary and valuable, the scientific, linear, rational side of modern life tends to disconnect us from the divine or inner worlds—the realm of the gods, of myth, image, and symbol. Our attempts to enter the inner world through a group system or ideology are at best a partial initiation. A group-directed journey often provides leftover, meager nourishment for our true nature and authenticity.

Most important, when a collective orientation dominates our life, it more often than not diverts our inner journey, sending us off on dead-end roads and unnecessary detours. Ironically, the particular *ism* we expect to show us "the way" frequently turns into a life-consuming diversion preventing us from reaching our own life. I spent fifteen years of my life on such a detour in a spiritual group that I thought had all the answers to my search. Even though I learned many valuable lessons there, I also wasted many precious years absorbed in the group's mission.

The Rip Van Winkle Syndrome

Taking a detour away from our own life is similar to the story of Rip van Winkle, the returning hero who entered the inner world unconsciously, just as most of us do each night in sleep, waking up in the morning with nothing but whiskers to show for the experience. By consciously committing to discover our real existence, entering the inner realm, and working with our dreams—a *willing introversion*—we open the door to an entirely different experience: A transformation and integration of these two kingdoms gradually takes place. The apparent split between two very different types of consciousness gives way to an awareness of both at once, to a sense of being grounded in our essential nature, out of which our genuine life unfolds.

Concealing Your Essential Nature

In his seminal book, *The Hero With a Thousand Faces*, Joseph Campbell describes myth as ". . . the secret opening through which the inexhaustible energies of the cosmos pour into human cultural manifestation."[13] We encounter the gods in dream images: mythological themes common to all persons, *but*—as the Radical Dreaming process makes clear—*cloaked in our specific historical and cultural beliefs and stories*. Hence, in dreams and in the waking state, Christians experience the Self through Jesus, Mary, Yahweh, and other images imbedded in their belief system, while Buddhists experience the Self through Buddhist imagery and various Buddhist spiritual teachers, past and present. Moslems dream of Muhammad, disciples dream of their guru. The many faces of the Self appear in a multitude of projected forms and images throughout the world.

If Horses Could Draw

When the well-known Indian philosopher Krishnamurti was a young boy, Charles Leadbeater, a prominent figure in the Theosophical Society, selected him out of a crowd of other Indian boys to be the vehicle for the World Teacher (the Christ). Mary Lutyens, in her book *Krishnamurti:*

the Years of Fulfillment explains, "Most Theosophists at that time (1910) believed that the Lord Maitreya would soon manifest in human form, as two thousand years ago he had manifested in the body of Jesus."[14] Many years later, Krishnamurti rejected the Theosophists' plans for his life and renounced his title as the World Teacher.

As part of his training, his teachers taught the young Krishnamurti about each of the major world religions. He soon observed a curious pattern that contributed to his decision to abandon his appointed position. When he studied and absorbed himself in Hinduism, he began having dreams of Krishna and other figures found in the Bhagavad Gita. When studying Buddhism, he began having dreams of Buddha. When he studied the Moslem faith, he had dreams of Muhammad, Islam's prophet.[15] It reminds me of the saying, "If horses could draw, they would draw their gods as horses."

A Dying Guru

In a current example, Terri, a thirty-seven-year-old member of a New Age spiritual group, had repeated dreams of her "enlightened" teacher and guru over a ten-year period. She joined the group hoping to "change her life." At first her teacher often appeared as an authority figure, a wise old woman. Realizing she had put her life on hold in order to "serve God"—doublespeak for the group's agenda—she decided to leave the group. Her recurring dreams then changed. She began dreaming about her teacher having trouble breathing, almost dying. She realized her belief in the system represented by her spiritual teacher was dying along with many of the group's ideas, rules, and values.

That night when Terri actually got up and walked out of the chapel for the last time, she thought, "Oh God, have I just made the biggest mistake of my life?" But later, sitting alone in her car in the chapel parking lot, she described herself as feeling calm and confident with her decision: "I felt peaceful and resolute, like when you somehow know you've done the right thing."

After leaving the group she worked with the dreams that correlated to her group experience. Terri identified and eliminated from her thinking those group ideas and attitudes that had prevented her from living her own life, for instance "art is no longer a viable way to make a living." And she also realized that something about her guru and the spiritual ideas that she represented had "hooked," pulled out important parts of her inner Self. Meanwhile, Terri repressed her creativity and her gift for fashion design. She had projected her own unacknowledged insight and wisdom onto an external figure who paradoxically became a mirror for her own unseen Self. The recurring dreams ended with a vision of her guru in a large boat. She was dead. Terri's experience is an excellent example of a dream image, her spiritual teacher, that represents an exterior collective influence controlling a person's life. But the image of Terri's teacher also carried valuable information about her own authentic nature.

Saving Bill Gates

Once we discover our particular way, we face a new challenge: how to find a way to place our inner treasure, our authentic nature, into the collective world—this becomes our soul's ultimate challenge and our highest adventure.

Sara, a talented but starving artist, refused to even think about money issues. "It's commercialism and would distract me from my work," she explained with indignation. Finally hitting rock bottom, with no funds to pay rent or buy food, she seriously thought about giving up her art. She then had a dream of rescuing Bill Gates from drowning in a deep lake. This dream shocked her into attending to practical money matters and to begin brainstorming ways to earn more money with her art. She had to rescue her inner entrepreneur in order to save her creative life.

Collisions

The meaning and intent in many dreams at first collide not only with the directions and attitudes that our conscious ego has assumed but also with the expectations of family, society, tradition, and culture. And it is precisely this inner versus outer life conflict that sends most would-be dream enthusiasts running from their own insight and real inspiration. As a result, many individuals tend to interpret their dreams on the trivial, self-centered surface of mundane life issues, forgoing the soul-making, life-changing potential of real dreamwork.

Trying to Get In

Kate had just begun to take her dreams seriously, wanting to explore ways her dreams might help her live a more creative life that felt meaningful. She brought this "nightmare" to a group session:

I'm in a house and people are trying to get in. I'm in my bed-room—all the rooms are bedrooms. The people trying to get in are like people from Uganda. They are native people and they are trying to get in and they have their arms inside the window and I'm trying to get the window closed and their arms out and I can't. This goes on for a long time. I try to push them out and even try to slam the window down and nothing works. I finally get them out but they are all around the house. There are people sleeping in all the bedrooms and I say "Wake up! They're trying to get in"—and they don't do anything.

Kate's dream presents her with a terrifying collision between two forces: her contained, dreaming ego, *once safe* within its house, and her dangerous "native people," those aspects that Kate described as "scary, chopping people up, less rules and structure." The word "native" means "existing in or belonging to one by nature; innate: *native ability.*"[16] And the natives want *in* to her house through the *windows*, perhaps a refer-ence to Kate opening her psyche to the dream worlds, to potential change and transformation.

The natives not only want in, they intend to get the dreamer, or to be precise, the *dreaming ego*. They want to chop it up, *dis-member* it—a horrific possibility for the dreamer's ego. To dismember something means to take it apart, and in dreams, dismemberment usually precedes putting things back together again but in a way that creates a new syn-ergy, incorporating elements of the Authentic Self. It's as though her dream explains that she needs to look at and reflect on the structures, the dynamics of her waking life, take things apart, break things down—examine the "rules" that define and limit her life.

Kate realized her dream was graphically informing her that she must first integrate the natives, bring "less rules and structure" into her life in order to reconnect to her *native* self. Of course this is the polar opposite of her waking ego's desire for safety, structure, and comfort. Her dream prepared Kate for the struggle that was just beginning, and her dream told her this struggle for her Authentic Life would indeed have its terri-fying moments. The battle had begun!

Chewing Time

Crumbling teeth or teeth falling out is a common dream theme most of us have experienced in some form. Popular dream interpretation books usually view these dreams as a result of some anxiety in the dreamer's life or a fear of aging or being toothless, or difficulty getting a "bite" on something. You recall Terri's dreams about her guru. When she was a dedicated disciple and the group's activities were consuming nearly all her spare time, she had this dream:

> I was trying to chew or eat my wristwatch and my teeth were crumbling apart in the process. I woke up feeling relieved I still had all my teeth.

In Terri's dream her teeth, natural (original equipment: bones we use to take in nourishment, to work with the tongue to help form words) aspects of her Self, are trying to consume her watch—how she keeps track of time, time that she had allowed her church to monopolize and control. "My watch ruled my life," she explained. "It was always 'time' to go to a service, time to go clean the grounds, time for something going on at church." As a result, something natural and unique is crumbling. For Terri, her dream explained the effects of spending all her time on church activities and projects; parts of her authentic nature, her teeth, were falling apart. And the one-sided way she had been spending her time was the culprit.

In the example above, teeth as a dream image point to a dramatic collision between Terri's life as a dedicated member of her church and real damage to her genuine Self as a result of too much dependence and focus on an outer authority figure.

Dreams, when at odds with what we think we should be doing with our lives, often terrify the waking ego—an ego highly adapted to our collective world, often quite competent at surviving in it, and intent upon maintaining the status quo. In this efficient, adapted way of being, even the uncomfortable aspects of life often feel safe, because they are known and familiar. However, a state of comfortable conformity and adaptation, when at odds with our true purpose for being alive, becomes a subtle trap, a spiritual and psychological death for real individuality.

Lost Passion

On this subject of conformity and adaptation, Carl Jung once met an older military officer while on a trip. Seated across from him, the general unexpectedly told Jung about one of his dreams:

> I am on parade with a number of young officers who are being inspected by the commander in chief. When the commander in chief reached me, he surprised me by not asking a technical

question but instead demanding a definition of the "beautiful." I was embarrassed that I was not able to give a satisfactory answer. The commander in chief moved on to a very young major and asked him the same question. The major gave an excellent answer, and I felt I would like to have given that answer. I felt great distress at this point and woke up.[17]

In the discussion that followed about what the dream might mean, Jung asked the general if he had noted anything peculiar about the young man's appearance. He replied that the major looked just like the general had looked when he was a young major. Jung suggested that perhaps his dream was asking him to look at something he had possessed when he was a major which had since been forgotten or lost. Listening intently, the general burst out with the explanation that he had loved art as a young man, but his interest had been overwhelmed by the rigidity of military routine.[18]

The general's dream provides an excellent example of an authentic life inundated by outside forces—"military routine"—and the relentless inclination of our dreams to recover our lost treasure, to live our potential to its "beautiful," fullest brilliance.

Evidently the human soul does not like this conformist state of affairs at all. Once you begin applying the Radical Dreaming process, it will become apparent that dreams address not only our relationship with our own inner nature; equally important, they address *how we influence and are influenced by the world around us*. Our dreams are social activists. They intend to derail the status quo, to dynamite the careening train of a routine life.

Hidden Treasure

This is a good place to clarify what I mean when referring to the individual "Self," since it plays a vital role in the conflict between individual authenticity and pressure to make our lives fit into the world's demands and expectations. First, I use "Self" primarily for two distinct meanings: In using the lower case "self," I refer to the waking ego attributes, attitudes, and characteristics of the personality such as self-responsibility, self-loathing, self-improvement, etc. When I capitalize the word, I intend a reference to the creative and unique work in process that shapes and moves the individual life—those particular, distinctive characteristics that define our authentic nature at any given point in time.

The Self *is* the "hidden treasure" but it is also a *continuing process* of discovery and creativity in contrast to an ultimate, absolute goal to attain in some distant future. We can look at the Self as holding our unique fate and destiny, the seeds of our vocation, our calling in life. Working with so many dreams and individuals over the years has convinced me that what we are attempting to describe as the Self is a cooperative venture between our waking consciousness and something that defies description or even naming—more of a creative process of movement towards incorporating and being more *authentic* and creative.

I have also come to look at the Self as an inner Gestalt, as a state of being, of potentials comprised of a synergetic set of relationships between different parts of our authentic nature. Our dreams are masterful helpers in exploring and developing a conscious relationship with the Self so that we can live our own life and create meaningful relationships with others and our world. Dreams draw the waking ego into an experience of itself as an integral part of something much larger. As author and dreamworker Marc Barasch puts it, "In dreams our narrow selfhood is loosened."[19] And so we dream of breaking through a ceiling and rocketing into space, walking into a magnificent, unknown mansion, opening the door to a great ballroom, riding an elephant through the ancient streets of Rajasthan.

Author Edward Deci describes this larger Self as the "integrated, psychological core from which a person acts *authentically*, with true volition."[20] Deci adds, "Various aspects of a person's psyche differ in the degree to which they have been integrated or brought into harmony with the person's innate, core self. Only when the processes that initiate and regulate an action are integrated aspects of one's self would the behavior be autonomous, and the person, authentic."[21]

Dreams do much more than provide, as Freud suggested, a "royal road to the unconscious." They return us to ourselves, they take us *home*. And in so doing, they reconnect us to all life.

Foreign Rulers

But, as we shall see in our *Radical* approach to dreamwork, without understanding how outside influences contaminate our self-image, the Self can take on a dangerous, deceptive aspect, more a "false Self" *cloaked* by popular ideologies. I like Marie-Louise von Franz's description of how this works. She refers to this corruption of the Self as a form of possession: "Some individuals become possessed by the Self instead of being realized and related to the archetype* of the Self." She adds: "These people cannot relate to their material but get possessed by it. They speak 'out of the archetype' and 'announce' archetypal material like an old medicine man, but they do not link up with their modern level of consciousness, and they never ask themselves about it."[22]

Many of us have witnessed extreme cases of such "archetypal possession" in individuals who believe themselves to be a god or goddess, an infallible guru, or a representative of God, ministers with an exclusive connection to God who know what *their* God thinks you should do with your life. Or even a certain celebrity, politician, or public figure can capture our attention, causing us to follow them or be just like them. In extreme cases, an outside influence or ideology can assume complete control of the entire personality and even modify individual behavior. Our dreams focus on these "social intrusions" into our personal lives and also on what Ullman calls "social myths," which appear "inevitably and of necessity"[23] in dreams. So people have dreams that intend to *contradict* our waking, ideal image of someone: gurus in demeaning situations, people drugged, buying drugs, stolen babies, bees attacking a house, a dead tree, someone else driving our car.

Faces of the Authentic Self

Aspects of the Self appear in a multitude of images and symbols in our dreams. People have dreamt of: Florence, or some unknown city, a large Greek temple by the ocean, an exquisite oil painting of George Washington, an unknown "singer," music, a gift of three diamonds shaped like Buddha's head, jewels, stones, space and stars, spacecraft, an exquisite landscape, supraordinate figures such as a hero, king, queen, goddess, prophet, savior, a guru, and certain symbols, for example the circle, square, cross, or sphere.

Over time we will identify our own unique set of images that provide deeper and deeper insight into the real nature of our Authentic Self, but equally important, we also need to recognize those particular "self" images that relate not to the individual but to implanted attitudes and influences.

---

*I use "archetype" to refer to an "original model or type after which other similar things are patterned; a prototype: "'Frankenstein' . . . 'Dracula' . . . 'Dr. Jekyll and Mr. Hyde' . . . the archetypes that have influenced all subsequent horror stories." An ideal example of a type; quintessence: an archetype of the successful entrepreneur. It is derived from the Latin, *archetypum,* and from the Greek, *arkhetupon* and *arkhetupos,* meaning *original*: arkhe-, arkhi-, archi- + tupos (model, or stamp).

Ultimately, the Self, as we will explore it in this book, is that unique representation of one's individual spirit at any given point in time, first and foremost distinct yet also interconnected, an integral, inseparable part of the human spirit and the greater cosmos.

The Self and its *natural* authenticity and originality are portrayed in an immense range of images we will discuss throughout this book, but I have found a particular set of natural, environmental images to be significant and worthy of our attention when they appear in dreams. These images often represent the beginning of our journey and the expansion of the personality. Our journey will take us into unexplored territory in our psyches that collective forces have not yet compromised. This natural, environmental imagery includes dreams about: wild, uncivilized places; forests; oceans; lakes; particular geographic areas; exquisite, beautiful landscapes; finding treasure; digging up jewels or gold; untamed, dangerous, threatening creatures. Wild, hairy humanoid figures sometimes portray *natural*, nonconformist aspects of the Self. Many dreams portray some sort of violation of these natural images, which is one way our dreams warn us about the effects of what we are subjecting ourselves to. Of course each dream image must be kept within the context of your life and never interpreted without *your experience* of your own dream.

Pursuing the Dreaming Ego

Our unlived life challenges and often attacks our familiar, adapted, dominant ego-built structures. The Authentic Self challenges and provokes our often limited self-concepts: who we think we are or are not.

Gods and Demons

While working on this book, I recalled a particular dream from a book I read some years ago by the Jungian scholar and analyst Marie-Louise von Franz. I think the dream is an excellent example of how terrified we can be of our own potential and also how an organized religion can inadvertently demonize aspects of the Authentic Self. In her book *Projection and Re-collection in Jungian Psychology*, von Franz reported this remarkable dream of a pastor's son who viewed God (from the context of organized religion) as an exterior power and authority. The man's nightmarish dream recurred for many years into his late forties.

He would dream that he was walking through a vast wasteland. He heard steps behind him. Anxious, he walked faster, but the steps also became more rapid. He began to run, the terror still behind him. Then he came to the edge of a deep abyss and had to stand still. He looked down: deep, deep down, thousands of miles below, he saw hell-fire burning. He looked around him and saw—or rather sensed in the dark—a demonic face.[24] He would awaken terrified of being caught by this demonic pursuer. Then the dream recurred just as before, but instead of the demon he saw the face of God. Finally he had the dream for the last time when he was nearly fifty years old. But now the dream changed. His panic and fear drove him to jump off the cliff into the fiery hell below. As he fell, thousands of little square white cards floated down alongside him. On each card a different mandala had been drawn in black and white. The cards then floated together, forming a floor beneath him on which he landed safely about halfway down. Then, looking back up to the edge of the abyss he saw *his own face*![25] "The pursuer in the dream was the Self, which first appears as 'the uncanny,' then as God, then as the dreamer himself," observes von Franz.[26]

At first the dream portrays the fiery hell and the demon representing his father's religious belief system. But his dream goes on to show him that what appears to be a demon* is in fact his own face and the face of God. Most important, his abyss dream dismantles his religious concepts of an outer, authoritarian God and reconnects him to the Self—a Self that his religious views had demonized. Such dreams are terrifying to the ego—that aspect of the personality that believes *it* is the center of the psyche and for the most part bases its approach to life on influences from the exterior world.

The Self *intends* to *get* the ego, to put it in its proper place. From dreams such as the above we can begin to differentiate ourselves from inherited, implanted ideas that are erroneous and anti-Self. Each dream removes a little more stone from our hidden authentic nature. Dreams tell us that what at first appears to be frightening and reprehensible may be a part of our genius and our real nature. But we have to make a leap, leave behind familiar ground and plunge into the abyss of our own being.

---

*Demon, also *dae mon*, means an attendant spirit; a genius. From the Latin *dæmón* or spirit, and from the Greek *daimōn*, meaning divine power. From: *The American Heritage Dictionary of the English Language, Third Edition,* 1992, Houghton Mifflin Company.

On Language and Meaning

By speaking, by thinking, we undertake to clarify things, and that forces us to exacerbate them, dislocate them, schematize them. Every concept is in itself an exaggeration.

—José Ortega y Gasset[27]

In our Radical approach to dreamwork we want to unwrap the dream images, remove the collectively defined limits, influences, and authority, and we also want to promote meaning, get a clear understanding and definition of our own authenticity. Consequently, our use of words and language becomes deeply significant.

Radical dream interpretation depends upon understanding the meaning of certain terms. This presents some problems when working with dreams in that any definition involving the human psyche will of necessity fall short. Words can only approximate any psychological phenomena through the lens of our current understanding. Simply because we have defined a psychological term or concept, we must still be careful not to limit its meaning or character. Instead, we ought to allow definitions to be open-ended, without concrete edges. This is particularly important when dealing with dream images. The logical, rational side of human nature wants to put everything into neat boxes—concretize definitions and therefore destroy the possibility for increased consciousness and awareness. We can literally kill an image when we attempt to explain it or define it in absolute terms or throw a wet blanket of formal theory over it.

Language and Dreams

Because our dreams speak to us through images, symbols, and metaphors in contrast to our waking world's language, we are always in danger of reducing a dream's meaning in order to fit it into linguistic containers familiar to our waking ego structure. Hence the danger of sealing a dream figure inside any *label*: The child in our dream becomes an "eternal child," another figure becomes the "wise old man," while male and female are labeled as "anima" and "animus" in Jungian psychology. Or we force the dream's feet into mythological shoes, saying *that* dream is about your *Aphrodite* nature.

The Silver Dagger

We need a way to bridge what at first glance appears to be a collision between two separate operating systems: our waking life and the night world or what some call the unconscious. However, as we delve more deeply into our house of dreams, we find that these two realms are not actually disconnected at all. In fact, they are profoundly interconnected. But we need to rethink and expand our notions of meaning and language. For example, an articulate, professional woman who had just been diagnosed with rheumatoid arthritis dreamed of walking through a dark underground tunnel made of iron. Standing immediately outside the end of the tunnel she saw a dark, menacing man holding a silver dagger, its mirrorlike brilliance shining in the moonlight.

For her, the tunnel's structure represented something stiff and inflexible, something the collective, public realm had built. And she related the tunnel's stiffness to the growing inflexibility in her hands. But her dream also helped her realize that her inflexible approach to her life, which had its origins in society's and in her family's ideas about women's roles, did not represent a part of her Authentic Self. Instead, some-"thing," a collective idea, had gotten into her psyche and, according to her dream, was contributing to (if not the actual cause of) her illness.

Shortly after working on understanding her dream, she became acutely aware of how she had always avoided conflict, which made it difficult to express her real feelings and ideas to others. She recalled how her parents, particularly her father, would ridicule her ideas and always insisted on "no conflict." To cope and survive, she learned to cover up and withhold her own feelings and opinions.

Now, as she gradually began to speak her mind, tell others how she felt and what she thought, her dream image of that "dagger" exploded into her awareness; she exclaimed, "My God! It's the dagger! I'm holding it—I can feel it in my hand." The dagger represented her own power to speak directly about what she thought and felt, to use her "silver-tongued" eloquence, her powers of fluent and persuasive speech that she had suppressed for so long. She had taken hold of an invaluable part of her Authentic Self.

Being Authentic

"Authentic" means "conforming to fact and therefore worthy of trust, reliance," and of "verifiable origin or authorship; not counterfeit or copied."[28] Authentic comes from the Latin *authenticus*, and from the Greek *authentikos*, and *authentês*, meaning "author."[29] It is the "author," the original Self, our authentic—not "copied"—life that our dreams help us access.

The Paradox of Integrity

The Radical Dreaming process helps reconnect us with our innate integrity—another important term we need to explore. The dictionary defines integrity as coming from the Latin, *integritas*, meaning "soundness," and from *integer*, meaning "whole, complete." Literally, the word *integrity* means the state of being *untouched*; but its Sanskrit root, *tag*, means *to touch* or handle, while *integ* means *not touched* or handled. Thus we can look at integrity as embodying a paradox of two opposite qualities: one involving connection, touching, and the other original and untouched.

The Roman emperor and philosopher Marcus Aurelius (121–180 A.D.) described integrity as coming from the individual, not the state: "A man should *be* upright, not be *kept* upright."[30] We can think of integrity as embodying both an innate sense of authenticity that outside influences have not touched or contaminated, and a connectivity to the outside world. Integrity, it seems, holds the idea of unique individuality as well as the importance of meaningful relationship.

Without integrity, we do not hold together as a whole individual. Without integrity, we fall apart, *dis-integrate*; we lose touch with our own center. As Emerson observed, "Nothing is at last sacred but the integrity of your own mind. Absolve you to yourself, and you shall have the suffrage of the world." Emerson seems to be saying that the very universe itself supports integrity. And, in his book *Integrity in Depth*, author John Beebe draws this conclusion: "Integrity implies an ecological sense of the harmony and *interdependence* of all the parts of the whole, a felt sense of the entirety of the situation."[31] This brings up an important question: What about the integrity of a city, community, or place? Can inanimate objects have human characteristics? Ask any engineer, architect, artist, or designer. I think you know their answer would be a resounding yes!

The idea of integrity residing in both the animate and inanimate worlds opens us to a logical and fascinating application of individual dream images to our outer, physical world, an aspect of what I call the *dynamic imagination*.[32]. What if we created imaginal dialogues with a city, a building, a forest, a river? What if we asked a city what it most needed? It might say, "More green space, less concrete, no more exhaust fumes, less traffic, please." Or, "I need elevated sky trails for bicycles suspended above my buildings." Or, "Would you please put all these asphalt roads underground when they pass through my center."

Ten Thousand Masks

Without our dreams, our inner work, our individual soul work, we cut ourselves off from the animating center of our life, enabling the ego to build its empire by default. In this twenty-first century, Pharaoh wears ten thousand masks: power, authority, wealth, celebrity, exclusiveness, separateness, arrogance, control—and he builds his palaces in the human heart as well as on Wall Street.

Dreaming and the Unconscious

The Swiss psychiatrist Carl Jung's concept of a *collective unconscious* evolved from his work with patients whose dreams, artwork, fantasies, and images could not be explained only as products of their personal experience. Jung realized that some of these images represented themes from world mythology and religious ideas; hence a "collective" unconscious in which we all participate.

When we take Jung's collective unconscious and add concepts from quantum physics, some quite remarkable possibilities emerge. The first is a universe in which all forms of consciousness are infinitely interconnected, where, despite appearances, we are participants in all of life. As physicist David Bohm observed, "Deep down the consciousness of mankind is one."[33] Bohm also stresses that this interconnectedness does not mean we are part of a giant undifferentiated mass; individual consciousness can be a part of an undivided whole and still possess its own distinct qualities.[34] In a similar vein, Jung saw the unconscious as the source of all creativity, a primal matrix out of which our individual capacity for consciousness evolves.

In our waking life, we often experience the unconscious when we have a sudden insight, a curious word or phrase "slips out," or we are driving along on our way home, but some unknown part of us is turning in the other direction. We have all experienced the sudden appearance of a creative idea or inspiration—where did it come from? Artists, writers, composers, any person in a creative mode will tell you that they experience and often go into "another world" where time seems to stop, where they feel connected to a deep source of creativity and inspiration. Who is it in me, what unknown part of me reacts with such emotion at this seemingly trivial event? Why did I, just this instant, remember that particular dream image from years ago? Why do I keep recalling that terrifying dream I had over and over as a child? These are but a minute sampling of our daily experiences of the unconscious.

Some Dangerous Ideas

This book will provide ample evidence that what people like to call "archetypal" images or ideas often are, in the hands of any organized "ism," gigantic snake pits for the unwary. These archetypal images represent basic structures, types, motifs, and images of a universal nature which reoccur around the world, often as constituents of myths.[35] Some of these so-called "archetypal" images represent potentially dangerous ideas. We will look at this aspect of dream symbolism and how to understand its implications in the context of activating our true existence.

The tendency of individuals to identify with and conform to some group's expectations and demands presents the most dangerous and subtle of obstacles, and effectively enables individuals to escape confrontation with their own demons and their own genius. In his essay "From the Prison of the 'Isms,'" journalist Jonathan Alter wonders how the 21st century will cope with destructive "isms." Alter observed that the 20th century "was beset by . . . grandiose fanaticism, and it became the bloodiest in all of human history. Will we see a sequel in the century to come? Communism and Nazism are gone, but their suffixes remain. The biggest of the big political questions is whether other malignant 'isms' can be held in check. The health of our new century hinges on the answer."[36]

Entering the "Zone of Magnified Power"

This collective/organizational gravitational pull on the individual psyche demands our thorough examination, since, as Joseph Campbell describes, it stands as one of the most fearsome "threshold guardians at the entrance to the zone of magnified power."[37] Campbell's "zone of magnified power" represents the individual's *unlived* potential that makes each life a priceless value added to the human spirit and to our natural world. Many dream images and symbols allude to the approach to our own zone of unlived potential.

Our dreams summon our authenticity and creativity with a gnawing persistence, telling us that our world needs something from us. Dreams inform us over and over that life is far more than taking up space, far more than rote existence under the tyranny of collective conformism; they ask us to be authentic—*now*.

Our dreams can protect us from wasting priceless time and energy as a result of making choices and decisions that take us away from our life instead of into it.

Falling "Toward the Glassblower's Breath"

This book is dedicated to you, the reader; to showing you how to use your dreams and your *dynamic imagination* to plumb the incredible, limitless depths of the human psyche, and in so doing, resurrect not only your own unique life, but add a vitally needed quality to the human spirit. For ultimately, individual uniqueness is the essential treasure we are each responsible for bringing into this world. As Thomas Merton puts it: "How do you expect to arrive at the end of your journey if you take the road to another man's city? How do you expect to reach your own perfection by leading somebody else's life?"[38]

So prepare yourself for a remarkable journey, and as the Sufi poet and philosopher Rumi advised: "Here's the new rule: Break the wineglass, and fall toward the glassblower's breath."[39]

CHAPTER 2

𝓓

Approaching the World of Dreams

And he turned his mind to an unknown art.
—Stephen Dedalus[1]

Entering the Garden

Dreams have a poetic integrity and truth. . . . These whimsical pictures, in as much as they originate from us, may well have an analogy with our whole life and fate.

—Ralph Waldo Emerson[2]

"Do Be Sensible—You Know You Mustn't Do That"

A middle-aged, married man reported this dream, which shows how a collective authority figure often appears in a dream, challenging our attempts to cross the threshold into a creative new life:

> I dreamed that I wanted to get into a wonderful garden. But before it there was a watchman who would not permit me to enter. I saw that my friend, Elsa, was within; she wanted to reach me her hand, over the gate. But the watchman prevented that, took me by the arm, and conducted me home. "Do be sensible—after all!" he said. "You know that you mustn't do that."[3]

If we could talk to this garden we might ask, "Who are you?" and "What is your job?" The garden might answer, I provide space to contain, protect, and nurture the transformation of seeds and their growth into a magnificent variety of flowers and plants. This inquiry of the dreamer's "wonderful garden" results in an explanation from the garden that corresponds to a secret or unusual garden as a classic symbol of the Self, of Paradise, the soul, and the qualities cultivated in it.

In our example, the "watchman" will not let him in. Traditional dream analysis would view the watchman as a part of the dreamer's psyche. But what if we look at the watchman as an invasive influence depicting ideas and attitudes from the outer world which have been internalized—not unlike a computer virus that attacks the integrity of a system. The watchman then represents a threshold presence: an aggregate of self-imposed restrictions standing between the dreamer and his Authentic Self. Moreover, it is "Elsa," the feminine, his creative soul nature that tries to reach out to him in the dream. Related images in dreams include uniformed police, soldiers, officials, and other authority figures, particularly those representative of the public or organizations. As we work with our dreams and identify each of these restrictive, outside influences, the Authentic Self will begin to emerge in all its elegant distinctiveness.

Most of us have evolved a way to approach life, a technique or method through which we encounter and engage our world.

From the Outside In

Some live their lives from the *outside in*—less an approach and more a reactive way to live; life becomes a *fundamentalist*, concrete existence. Life solidifies in all its hard reality and inexorable pressures to conform and adapt. Such people are likely to feel like victims of circumstance, helpless and disempowered. Outside-in people interpret life literally, dogmatically. They don't remember many dreams. When the occasional dream manages to crawl out of the basement, they dismiss it as nonsense or bury it in the concrete tomb of literalism. Outside-in people are much more susceptible to nightmares, to violence, and to the influence of violent individuals. Image is more important than the environment or other people.

This outside-in, fundamentalist approach to life also chains persons to rigid rules and outside authority; making individuals vulnerable to mass ideologies, political movements, and to cult-like groups that thrive in an *either or, black and white* world where some outside enemy must be wiped out. Or media hype, celebrity images, fads, popular life styles, stereotypes—all combine to chop the hands and feet off the real individual, turning life into a completely inauthentic, cloned existence—a life lived on the shallow surface.

Radical Dreaming facilitates a *radical* reorientation—it implies living life "off grid," disconnecting from an unbalanced adaptation and dependence upon the established *outside* power structures, reversing the flow of power and control to the individual.

Until we find our own treasure, we will gravitate toward living outer-directed lives subject to collective impulses—an existence consisting of moving with the herd, first this direction, then that direction. We will certainly miss living our own life and the world around us will lose the unrealized, innate value and potential of a genuine, creative life. And we will spend our lives living in a state of projected illusion, chasing rainbows, pursuing a certain life style, imagining that our life is "out there" in this or that group, mass ideology, or following some guru. Outside influences will relentlessly turn the gold of our essential nature into something flattened and ineffective.

From the Inside Out

In contrast, a creative, symbolic, allegorical, psychological approach suggests living life from the *inside out*, from the authentic core of our being. Life then has depth. It becomes a creative work of art. *Inside-out* people tend to rely more on their intuition, their feelings, and they somehow know that dreaming and the imaginative arts, like deep wells of life-giving water, are necessary ingredients in creating a complete life, ingredients that nourish the garden of an authentic life. *Inside-out* people know how to walk in the stream without getting soaked; they know they must be involved in life, in the community, in the world, yet they also intuit that they must forge their own life, carve out their own path, live their own life no matter what the cost.

The outside-in people and the inside-out people are often quite uncomfortable with one another. And inside the human psyche, we often find an inner war between these two forces, these two ways of being in the world. Ultimately we must choose, not to eradicate the outside-in people or ignore the inside-out people, but instead to walk a golden mean—finding the right mix of the two worlds while remaining careful never to compromise our authentic natures.

Tools: Setting Up Your Dream Journal

If you don't already keep a dream journal, you will need one to record your dreams. Get a book you really like, along with a special pen if you plan to write your dreams by hand. Many individuals find it easy to record their dreams into a cassette or other recorder and later transcribe it either into a journal or onto the computer. You will find that recording dreams by hand seems to sustain a better connection to the dream material and to the unconscious than immediately going to a computer, since a mechanical device tends to disconnect you more rapidly from the dream experience.

Consider setting up your dream journals with the right-hand pages left blank for future comments and interpretive notes. In the process of researching my own dreams for this book, I compiled a chronological dream log with dates and a brief description of each dream. This has been a tremendous aid in locating specific dreams as well as an excellent way to see how dream patterns and motifs change over time. In any event, use the method that works best for you. You can leave space in the back of your journal for the log.

Establishing Your Creative Space

To facilitate your inner work your psyche needs work space: to be precise, a special, sacred space you carve out of your environment that you use only for your inner work, your dreamwork, and related creativity, art, writing, and reflection. It might be a separate room, a desk, a private corner, or a particular chair. Don't use it for anything else. Keep the things that you love and that inspire you in and around this space: your favorite books, talismans, art, pictures, your journals, a candle, fresh flowers—whatever helps you feel inspired and excited about life. Joseph Campbell calls this "an absolute necessity," and he explains, "You must have a room, or a certain hour or so in a day, where you don't know what was in the newspapers that morning, you don't know what you owe anybody. . . . This is a place where you can simply experience and bring forth what you are and what you might be. This is the place of creative incubation."[4]

Some Helpful Tools for Your Journey

You will need to begin with some basic tools: For starters make sure you have a good dictionary, one that includes *Indo-European* roots, which will help find the meaning of any unusual words or even portions of words that show up in dreams. Access to a comprehensive encyclopedia is important. Fortunately, the internet as well as many computer software programs also provide easy access to these resources. Looking up the origin of words and names that occur in dreams often yields surprising and valuable information.

You will find a good symbolic encyclopedia useful in your dreamwork. J. C. Cooper's *Illustrated Encyclopedia of Traditional Symbols*[5] is an excellent resource that describes the origin and history of many common symbols that show up frequently in dreams—not to interpret a symbol in some generic fashion, but to understand how different cultures and societies viewed a particular image. For example, we encounter a terrifying image in a dream, but discover that the image frightens us because some group has impressed upon us the notion that the particular image represents "sin" or "evil." A "black cat" in a dream can appear to have evil implications when seen through some religious perspectives, but the same black cat, devoid of outside religious ideas, can have a very different meaning. Dreams clearly illustrate the fact that most of the time the dreaming ego views the dream drama in part through collective-colored glasses, through the lens of some popular or theoretical point of view, and then reacts in the dream accordingly. So it's important for us to free dream images from popular labels so that we can understand what an image actually represents and what it wants to say to us.

Starting an "Images and Symbols" Workbook

In the process of working with my own dreams, I have found it helpful to keep a workbook of those dream images and symbols that keep showing up in my dreams. I started my workbook with images that represented aspects of my authentic life and then worked on images that represent obstacles in my life.

Find a large blank book, at least 8½ by 11 inches. Certain images and symbols begin to stand out as we continue to work with our dreams. As you identify your own symbolism, make it a part of your *Images and Symbols Workbook*. Use this workbook to draw and write about your personal images as well as the images you feel represent outside influences. Consider making an index in the back of your workbook so you can easily find particular images and symbols. Awareness of our own dream symbolism for both our individual life and our collective world helps us know when we are stepping off our own path, straying from our authenticity. You can then make course corrections in your journey, preventing wrong choices and wasted time.

Keeping an "Insights, Synchronicities, and Ideas" Notebook

Get a small, pocket-size notebook that you can carry with you wherever you go. In this notebook, make a note of any ideas, synchronistic events, or realizations you may have. Flashes of insight often happen when we least expect it: on a walk, on the way to meet a friend, or at work. I carry my notebook on long walks. Not only do I get some good exercise but my psyche is free to talk to me and it usually does. I get lots of ideas for my writing and often some new insight about a particular dream.

Recording our creative ideas or an unexpected "Aha!" about a certain dream is part of respecting our psyche. You can file the ideas later or add them to a permanent journal. You'll notice that dreamwork creates aftereffects in your waking life, and fully understanding a dream often entails being alert for subtle images, moods, feelings, and thoughts that are still coming from the dream.

Dream Structure

Most dreams consist of four basic structural elements: first, the setting or introduction to the dream, which consists of location and characters; second, a statement of the central problem or dilemma; third, the drama of what happens—the response to the struggle, the conflict, the ups and downs; fourth, the solution or resolution. Sometimes we only recall a dream fragment, a single image. However, even a single image can yield a wealth of meaning when approached through the process of Radical Dreaming. Keep in mind that the deepest meaning, the peculiar and unique "resonance" from your dream occurs when placed within the context of *your* own life experience and circumstances. The black stallion in your dream will have a very different meaning from that of a black stallion in another person's dream. And this basic characteristic of dreaming renders books that give set meanings to dream symbols essentially useless in pulling out meaningful information. The Authentic Self does not follow the herd or any predetermined road maps.

We will never find a distinct, absolute division between our dreaming awareness and our outer or waking consciousness; both are present whether we are awake or sleeping. Dreamwork enables us to integrate these two seemingly divided realms of the psyche while in the waking state. As you work with your dreams, you will notice, usually when you least expect it, that you suddenly remember a particular dream or dream image. Something or someone in your waking life has been a catalyst to pull up the dream memory. When this happens, we need to reflect on what we were just thinking, saying, or feeling, because two worlds have just connected and some meaning or lesson in that particular dream is relevant to our current waking situation. This is an excellent way to fur-ther expand and understand a dream's meaning. You will find your awareness of your dreams and their meaning in your waking life deepening and expanding as you practice working with this approach to dreaming.

Attitudes and Dreaming

Before going through the actual steps of the Radical Dreaming process, it's important to look at some particular attitudes that will make a big difference in the depth and transformative effects of dreamwork. Dreams are connected to oceanic depths and universal dimensions far beyond anything our conscious ego or our dreaming ego can comprehend. Our attitudes, motives, expectations, and desires determine the depths we are able to access as well as the response from our psyche.

In fact, most dreams contain complex, interconnected levels of meaning. What we glean from a dream has a direct correlation to our attitude toward and respect for our inner world. Both accommodating and remarkably efficient, our psyche will respond to and make use of our particular approach much like a wise parent would respond to a child's questioning, making the best of our attempts to understand ourselves.

Ego-Centric Dreamwork

While there are a number of important and valuable dreamwork techniques, much of what our popular culture refers to as dream interpretation occurs on a shallow, superficial level, what I call "ego-centric" dreamwork—methods dominated by a conformist, outer-world orientation. On the ego-centric level, people attempt to control or program their dreams in order to get what they believe they want—power, wealth, love, sex, or promotions at work. An ego-centric approach tries to manipulate dreams to fulfill what are essentially the waking ego's desires and ambitions, which nearly always involves greater and greater adaptation to social expectations with decreasing or nonexistent connections with our Authentic Self—the exact opposite of what our dreams want to accomplish.

This ego-centric approach limits our inner work to playing in very shallow water. Working with dreams in order to get something—self-gratification for the waking ego—exploits and rapes the psyche. You need only ask yourself, *Who is it* that wants to direct my dreams? Of course it's the waking ego that wants to stay in control and maintain its position of authority. If we think of slaying the ego in this sense, it is precisely this ego-dominance and underlying fear of the unknown that blocks our path. Such pseudo dreamwork is actually a defense against real dreamwork. This getting-stuff-for-the-ego also makes certain aspects of our own ego structure a daunting obstacle in our quest for our authentic life. The waking ego and the Authentic Self must ultimately become a dynamic, creative partnership.

However, in appropriate circumstances, confronting frightening figures in a dream can have therapeutic effects, particularly in overcoming fear and past trauma.[6] But even in these circumstances, we may still need to confront and integrate a fearful dream image into the psyche in a way that supports our real individuality.

Entering Sacred Ground

Once, while listening to a client describe a dream, I had a particularly difficult time connecting to her experience. I suddenly had an image of myself kneeling at the edge of her dream, and knew that I must ask permission to enter her dream. I was not sufficiently respecting her dream. I am six-feet-two and tend to tower over most people, so for me, kneeling meant putting myself on an equal level with her. Now, particularly when working with others' dreams, I imagine myself kneeling at the threshold of the dream and I ask the dream's permission to enter. When we enter our inner world, the unconscious, a dreamscape, or approach an image, we need to do so with a deep sense of reverence, gratitude, and respect, for we are in many ways entering sacred ground. Reverence means profound awe and veneration. We need to mentally remove our shoes at the entrance—leave the soil and cares of the outer world outside.

Humility

The root of the word humility comes from the Latin *humilis*, meaning lowly, and from *humus*, ground or earth. It's wise to approach dreams and the unconscious with humility—particularly intellectual humility, with a sense of childlike wonder, a state of not-knowing.

Many times, I have felt sheer panic upon first hearing a dream, thinking, Oh my God, what's this all about? Robert Bosnak, author and Jungian analyst, gives an excellent description of this reaction: "Generally I have no idea how to start on a dream. At such moments absolutely nothing comes to mind. Then a painful feeling of inferiority develops regarding the dream, and in this way my rational consciousness begins to sense its limits and my other faculties get their chance. Thus a wretched feeling at the beginning of work on a dream is completely normal."[7]

In approaching our dreams, humility enables us to be open to unexpected and often pretty blatant course corrections from the unconscious. Humility makes it less painful to admit we took the wrong path or had the wrong goals.

Again, it's the waking ego that believes it knows the answers, and it often takes some serious crashes for our egos to realize a little humility. Mary Watkins, author of *Waking Dreams*, cautions: "Try to take the image as a given and as completed rather than a play which you, as ego, must rework and finish."[8] We ought not to get caught in the attitude of *having* to figure each dream out in its uttermost details. Often a dream's images along with our experience of exploring the dreamscape need time to circulate through our lives. And we need time to mull it over, think about potential meanings, explore some what-ifs. Sometimes we need to live our life into the dream's meaning in order to understand it.

The Reality of Dreams and the Imagination

Dreams are the facts from which we must proceed.
—C. G. Jung

William Wordsworth once wrote: "[Imagination is] reason in her most exalted mood."[9] Because we cannot yet scientifically identify the dreaming state other than to locate areas of the brain that are active during dreaming does not mean that random firings of assorted neurons explain dreams and the dreaming process. In fact, aspects of quantum physics may soon provide our first scientific understanding of the "stuff" of dreams, the imagination, and the unconscious. Anyone who has undertaken a serious exploration of dreams, however briefly, quickly discovers that whatever dreams are, they connect us to another world and to a deep, often unexplainable, extraordinary wisdom.

For most people, even to think about working with dreams evokes stereotypical attitudes of unreality and fantasy. Unfortunately, we live in a modern world that has essentially lost its connections to fantasy, mythology, the imagination, and the transformational wisdom contained in images and symbols. Indeed, the clinical, scientific, psychological establishment has demonized the imagination, as have most mainstream religions, resulting in such mass-produced cliches as "You're such a dreamer," "It's just your imagination," or "You're in fantasy." Most of the scientific establishment reduce dreams to physiological dumping—random, meaningless neural discharges. But we can also look at neurons firing as the physical manifestation, tracks of the dreaming process, scientific evidence of the way our brain interfaces with another level of consciousness. But this would never explain recurring dreams. With random firings of trillions of neurons, it would be beyond the wildest probability that any dream could ever repeat itself.

Cold science and logic often prompt us to condemn our own imagination, labeling it as meaningless. It's worth noting that the word "fantasy" comes from the Latin *phantasia*, and from the Greek, *appearance* and *imagination—to appear*, and from *phantos*, visible. So "fantasy" implies the *Dynamic Imagination* appearing, bringing something into our conscious awareness—a necessary first step for the creative process or any new endeavor.

Radical Dreaming means looking at dreams, symbols, and images as meaningfully interconnecting each of us, not only with our own psyches, but with everything, with all life and with the cosmos. Radical Dreaming proceeds with the understanding that dreams and the imagination, with its images and fantasies, are quite real—that they do indeed have profound value, meaning, and intent.

Dreamwork—Spiritual Art and Natural Science

The Radical Dreaming process utilizes experiential information based on your observation and your experience of dream and imaginative images.

From my experience, I have found that we don't need to concern ourselves about a subjective or objective perspective as long as we are careful to avoid literal assumptions about our dreams. An actual literal dream is extremely rare. In traditional dreamwork, the "subjective" approach *assumes* that everything in your dream is a symbolic part of the your psyche—personal images existing only within an individual's mind, while the objective side refers to "reality," to a literal interpretation, to actual material objects uninfluenced by individual emotions or personal prejudices. This subjective prejudice tends to split dream interpretation into two separate worlds: one entirely subjective with all dream images interpreted as part of the dreamer's psyche, another where people take the dream content literally: If I dreamt that my brother had cancer, I would interpret the dream literally to mean that he must actually have cancer or soon will have it. Subjectively, the dream would require me to look at cancer as a metaphor, cancerous ideas, something eating away at me, something out of control and self-destructive in my life.

I believe that assuming that everything in a dream belongs to the dreamer, that the dream is our "private property," creates a one-sided, self-alienating position: it attempts to lock up our consciousness in a neat little box, ignoring the possibility of dream elements belonging to their own world—a world we can enter and participate in, but certainly not a world limited to the individual psyche. Dreams will always astonish us with exceptions to any rules or assumptions we try to impose upon them.

Going back to our example, I suggest there is a *third*, significant possibility: Cancer may represent the self-destructive growth of some influence or a way of life that has invaded one's psyche. Cancer, in a dream, could be a job that's eating up our life, or something eating away at us. The Radical Dreaming process does not lock up dreaming in any subjective box that requires you to make everything in your dream a part of your psyche. In fact, most dreams contain a complex mixture of subjective and objective personal meaning as well as subjective and objective outer influences. The process itself will make it quite clear what your dream represents.

Radical Dreaming also focuses on the nature of the relationship between the dreamer and a particular image, and the relationship between dream images and our outer, objective world. When we focus on relationships instead of labeling something as subjective or objective, we free our dreams from splitting the objective, outer world from the observer, which can result in ever-increasing fragmentation in society and within individuals. This either-or split tends to assign "reality" or "truth" to a detached, objective, presumed reality. Consequently, outside influences are reinforced, which then dominate individuals who gradually succumb to greater social and political adaptation often at the expense of living their own distinct lives.

The Time Bomb

Here is a dream, one that appears to have a literal warning: Aaron, a soft-spoken young man in his late twenties, was struggling with what to do with his life when he had this frightening dream that, at first glance, appeared to be a literal warning about a terrorist attack:

> Someone keeps showing me a map. I notice it's a pie-shaped area and realize it's somewhere around the Great Lakes area, maybe Chicago. An unknown man's voice tells me that a nuclear bomb is going to be detonated there on November 1 and I should make sure that I'm at least fifty to a hundred miles away from there.

Aaron's family, particularly his mother, wanted him to follow family tradition and go into the medical field. But he had always loved art and architecture and felt a frustrating split between giving in to his family's expectations and following his own passion.

A new aspect of the Radical Dreaming process involves a technique for exploring images that clarifies what belongs to the dreamer's Authentic Self and what symbolizes outside influences. I asked Aaron to describe what it would be like to imagine *being* that part of the country, and, as the land and the waters, what had happened. "The water has been polluted," he replied. "And if I'm that land, I've been overrun by civilization, covered up." Then I asked him to describe what it would be like, from the land's viewpoint, to experience a nuclear explosion? He explained, with a sudden smile of realization, "Everything that's been put on me is gone!" A few days later I received an excited call from Aaron, who couldn't wait to tell me that November 1 was the final deadline for him to enroll in dental school and that he had just decided not to register.

Aaron's dream, one week before the school deadline, dramatically showed him the power of this decision on November 1. It had the potential to clear away all the attitudes and expectations from his family that were preventing him from living his life—everything that had been "put on" him, that had "overrun" and "polluted" his original, natural landscape. His "nuclear" family's influence was about to be exploded. Moreover, atomic fission, a nuclear reaction, promised to release tremendous energy, energy that would now be available to begin a new life—energy no longer tied up in the exhausting effort to conform and to live someone else's life. And his dream also warns him to keep his distance from this event, to be aware of the "fallout"—the reaction from his mother and his family to his decision.

When we explore the collective meaning of our dream images, in particular the *collective cloaking* of our images and symbols, we begin the crucial step of separating and freeing our Authentic Self from our collective persona and the collective-oriented or false self.

Instead of thinking through the traditional dream interpretation method that divides dream content into subjective versus objective meaning, we will approach dreams from a spherical, inward-outward perspective, thinking of the individual, Authentic Self as a center without a defined circumference, a state of being and becoming comprised of an intricate web of relationships.

Courage

To say that it takes considerable courage to undertake the exploration of the psyche would be an understatement. Our waking ego has built its structures based on what it believes to be necessary for survival in the world, and to encounter long-submerged parts of our authentic life surging up from the depths of the unconscious takes courage and trust—trust that life is more than survival, consumption, and entertainment.

And herein lies one of the chief difficulties in dream analysis: effective interpretation necessitates that we face our outside-dominated, ego-built structures as well as our shadow side: all the unknown, hidden, repressed aspects of our nature along with all the unrealized potential and genius lying dormant and unacknowledged in the unconscious. Understanding our own unique shadow images and qualities helps us to understand who we really are as participants in the drama of life—an important part of knowing our own authenticity.

Taking the Plunge: What to Expect

> We must be willing to get rid of the life we've planned
> so as to live the life that is waiting for us.
>
> —Joseph Campbell

Contemplating this greatest of all adventures, the quest for our Authentic Self, evokes initial feelings of excitement and adventure. This initial romance with the unconscious can quickly give way to darkness, misgivings, and doubt as our dreaming psyche does what any wise and logical intelligence would do: focus directly on the enemy—those obstacles that are preventing us from living our own original lives. We may have been persuaded to pursue the wrong career; we may be in a destructive relationship; we might have low self-esteem from parental influences; we might be under the influence of political, economic, or religious ideas that are preventing us from fulfilling our own potential. This focus on obstacles stops most would-be adventurers into the inner worlds in their tracks. The waking ego thinks, "Why stir up this pot? I'm doing ok. I'm surviving."

Surviving Your First Collision

At this stage we often experience a real collision between our waking ego structure and our Authentic Self, which relentlessly seeks to move us into our own unique life. Consequently in dreams we find ourselves, as the dreaming ego, encountering what appears to be a frightening array of figures, caught in impossible circumstances and fleeing from all manner of beasts and brutes intent on doing us in. Most of these apparent enemies represent qualities that we actually need, but from years of neglect *appear* to be bent on our destruction. Paradoxically, it is precisely our suppressed, unlived potential that often attacks the conformist, outer-world-dominated ego in our dreams.

Hitting Authority

Our dreams also show us collisions with authority figures, usually representing *implanted* rules, *shoulds* and *should nots*, that become road blocks to our essential nature. Kate, raised in a religious Catholic family, presented this recurring dream in one of our group sessions. "The intensity of this dream," she explained, "wakes me up. I'm exhausted from crying and explaining it to the policeman. It's very, very frustrating to me, at a very deep level. I am very tired and depressed all day." Here's Kate's dream:

> Four times I am driving the car and I put it into gear—I'm getting away from parking places—and each time when I put it into gear to go forward, it goes backward, and each time it hits a police car—four times. My brother is with me and he doesn't really help me and I think in my mind, "Well, why doesn't he help me?" I tell my story and the policeman isn't mad, but he says, "Well, what are you going to do about it?" and I say, "Well, I have to go back to my old car."

Kate said that she really liked her brother, that he was "very sweet," a quality that does *not* help her dilemma: her "sweetness." And what is Kate's dilemma? After exploring the images in her dream, Kate realized that her life was "parked," not going anywhere, and each time she tried to move forward—pull out of the parking *spot* (an unfulfilling life) she was in—the car (not her actual car) ends up going backwards and "hits" *authority*, the law, the collective rules of the road. For Kate, Catholicism was the police department that had surrounded her life with concrete walls of *thou shalts* and *thou shalt nots*.

Her dream offers a solution: She realizes in the dream that she has to "go back to [her] old car," the dream's way of telling Kate that she needs to retrieve her *original* way of moving through her life, starting with a different career. She loved her old car, a special car she had owned for years that felt like "her" car. "I'm doing what others say I need to be doing and it's not working," she said. From her dream, she developed a new resolve to listen to her own heart and follow *her* passion, to stop conforming to others' expectations about how she *should* live her life.

She also thought about her "sweetness," an endearing side of her personality that would sometimes come out in inappropriate circumstances by trying to please others. She would then find herself doing things she did not really want to be doing. And she began to watch what she told herself about what she "should" or "should not" do—her internalized police department. Kate had begun to pull her sword from the iron jaws of social and religious pressure to conform.

The "Garborator"

The judgmental side of the intellect often chews up the insights and help we glean from our dreams, often before we pull our treasure into the daylight world. Laural, a participant in a *Dream Therapy Group,* told me about a dream she had after a particularly inspiring group session.

> I have discovered beautiful, ornate silverware in my sink in soft, sudsy water (the correct way to clean and preserve silver). I am thrilled (since in real time I ruined my beautiful silver by washing it in the dishwasher). As the water is draining away, I am bringing up fistfuls of this beautiful, sparkling silver. When the water is gone I see that someone turned on the garborator and was trying to garborate the silver! The garborator is off at the moment of the dream, but I fear this person will turn it back on in a moment and I am proclaiming aloud both my joy and appreciation at discovering this treasure in the sink, and my warning to the unseen vandal that trying to garborate the silver will only ruin the disposal apparatus itself.

Laural realized that the "garborator" was her tendency to immediately critique a dream with her intellect, a classic, left-brain logic and scrutiny of a symbolic world. We have all felt, usually just upon awakening, our "garborators" spinning into action, their deadly blades disposing of what some "unseen vandal" sees only as garbage and nonsense. Her dream helped her realize the seriousness of a pattern that had been affecting her for years: a critical voice that automatically ruined her ideas and inspiration.

Raped

Carrie, a twenty-eight-year-old architecture student, was struggling with low self-esteem when she had this dream:

> I realized I had been violently raped by an evil man. I can't seem to get away from him. There's blood all over me. I'm horrified and afraid I've been infected with AIDS.

"I don't know who the man was," Carrie said. "He felt more like an evil presence. In the dream, I was unconscious for it—the rape." I asked her to explain the meaning of "rape." She described rape as "a violation of power, giving others power over me. I'm making myself subservient." For Carrie, her dream brought back the impact in her life from her father's constant demeaning, crude comments about women in general. She also saw this "evil man" as representing negative stereotypes about women in our society coming from a male perspective. A lethal virus—negative influences from her father and society—had "violated" her essential nature. Outside influences were "drawing blood," robbing her of her vital life spirit, her essence.

Carrie began to eliminate the negative self-talk that she had been "unconscious" of, things she told herself that kept these outer influences alive. Her self-esteem improved, she felt empowered and more confident. Carrie's dream is an excellent example of how our dreams zero in on a boulder, often a collective one, that stands as an immense obstacle in our quest for our own true nature. Acting on her dream immunized her from these nefarious influences that had infected her thinking and her self-image.

Much of this scary intensity in the initial plunge into our dreams stems from long-repressed and ignored aspects of our authentic life that have, over time, evolved into apparently fearsome forces and images—parts of ourselves that are really upset that they've been ignored. Additionally, as the deep reality of our authentic life begins to emerge into our waking consciousness, we find that the supposed reality, the life we have been living, is more ego-created illusion, a comfortable prison, a sweet poison to our soul and our true nature. Thus our conscious view of life, now under attack from the *real* nature and character of *our* life, resists and struggles to maintain its grip on the status quo, even though we sense a deep, gnawing unrest, a troublesome suspicion that we are indeed not living our own life. At this point in our inward journey, we are quite likely to quit in disgust, despair, and apathy, for both inner and outer worlds now seem to be all that Shakespeare's Hamlet observed:

> *How weary, stale, flat, and unprofitable*
> *Seem to me all the uses of this world!*
> *Fie on't! ah fie! 'tis an unweeded garden,*
> *That grows to seed; things rank and gross in nature*
> *Possess it merely. That it should come to this!*[10]

We must consciously will ourselves through this initial encounter and let the dysfunctional, "otherated" aspects of our waking ego die a natural death so that our potential and authenticity have space to live and grow. Interestingly, in this beginning phase, people dream about problems with buildings and structures: a house burning down, childhood homes, new construction, old structures falling apart, large ships sinking, etc., representing various stages of ego disintegration and reconstruction.

Dreams and a Self-Responsible Life

Ironically, irresponsibility is one of the disastrous side effects of living a life of conformity. A outside-in standpoint maintains a parent-child attitude of dependence upon outer authority. Hence we live our lives feeling more like victims, looking to the prevailing outside powers and institutions to provide solutions, to make our world "safe," to be responsible for us and to protect us from what the masses perceive to be dangerous. Going along with the crowd, the latest poll numbers, we depress our real nature, flatten the psyche in the dull gray world of "average" and "normal," and lose our real freedom and authenticity in the process.

Our dreams can return us to a freeing, natural, empowering self-responsibility whose core embraces our ultimate responsibility to the world we live in. This approach to life and to our dreamwork evokes a potent sense of existence, interconnectedness and participation with the world around us—*not* because we are like everyone else, but because now we are *distinctly different*, *extra-ordinary*, embodying new qualities that society and our world need.

Dreams Say: "Truth Is a Pathless Land"

Carl Jung expressed a particular attitude toward beginning work on a dream that I have found to be extremely helpful; he said, "I avoided all theoretical points of view and helped patients understand dream-images by themselves, without the application of rules and theories."[11] This rule-free stance suggests that we enter the dream world free of institutionalized, ideological viewpoints, or at the very least, acutely aware of our religious, political, or other group-based persuasions, which will inevitably color and contaminate our dreams.

Dream images constantly refer to influences that stand between us and living our own life: the rapist in Carrie's dream, the "watchman" who would not let the dreamer into the "wonderful garden," the three "Atlas rockets" in Peter's dream which represented the medical establishment's attack on his depression. Or, as one person commented about her dream, "I've caught something that is going around."

Our essential task will be to separate out these outside influences, see through them, so that our original, Authentic Self emerges. Consequently, we need to enter each dreamscape with a *blank slate*, with *no* preconceived ideas or agenda, as though, as Jung once commented, "we had just arrived from another planet."

Don't Mess with My Hair!

In many dreams, the "Devil *is* in the details." In this example, the dream points out a controlling group dynamic and its repercussions for the dreamer. The dreamer is a fifty-year-old woman who was searching for a spiritual philosophy. Here's her dream:

> I was with my Course in Miracles study group and the minister, the one who led the group, fiddled with my hair, putting my falling-out-of-place hair back in place so that it looked right.

For the dreamer, her hair had a lot to do with how she looked, her appearance to others, and it also represented her ideas and thoughts—things that "grow" out of her head. In her dream, the "minister," an authority figure, rearranges her appearance, her thinking, and her ideas so that they *look* "right." This "resonated" for the dreamer and she realized her dream meant that the group's ideas were causing her to "rearrange" her thinking so that she would *appear* "right," please the minister, and fit into the group. It is precisely her "out-of-place" hair, her uniqueness and authenticity, that does not fit into the group mind set.

We could look at the "minister" in her dream as a paradoxical figure representing a masculine aspect of her psyche that inflicts conformity on herself. But he also represents an *outside* influence that has gotten into her head. When I asked how her "out-of-place" hair felt, she replied, "Angry! It feels like I'm disappearing, like I can't be seen, I'm being like all the other hair that looks right."

Trusting Your Dreams

We need to enter our dreamwork with an attitude of trust in ourselves, in our own unique inner process of unfoldment. You can trust your psyche; you can rely on the integrity and intent of your unconscious. Making this statement, I can imagine your response: "What about psychosis, mental illness, or hallucinations?"

Multiple Births

I am reminded of a gifted writer who had completely suppressed her creativity and eventually began to experience psychotic breakdowns, suffering with what the medical world calls a Bipolar disorder. Just before one of her "episodes" she had this nightmarish dream:

> I am pregnant and have gone to a clinic to give birth. Suddenly there are several women all giving birth at once. I frantically scream for help. In spite of several midwives they are overwhelmed and cannot help. Then our babies are born, about twenty, all at the same time—they shoot out and splatter on the clinic wall. All are killed. It's horrible!

Her dream accurately predicted the onset of her psychosis, but it also clearly explained that it is her tremendous creativity—creating new life—that has been "killed" *in* the "clinic." The "clinic," which she said looked like the hospital where she went for her medications and treatment, represented the medical establishment's attempts to fix what they perceived as a serious mental illness. It's interesting to look at the word "clinic," which comes from the Greek *klinikē (tekhnē)*, or method; her suppressed creativity "overwhelms" methods and techniques that cannot contain or cope with her creative life.

When we are inside a structure, it often means we are under a particular type of influence, under the *supposed* shelter and protection of a theory, method, or technique. After working on this dream she realized the clinic represented a cluster of medical techniques and treatment methods that she had accepted and sincerely hoped would help her, but "the clinic" was *not* a part of her Authentic Self. Instead it represented outside influences that tragically aborted her real vocation—poetry and writing. Only by extracting her own unique creative spirit from the "clinic" could she save her authentic life.

One of many examples, the dream described above illustrates that no matter how bizarre or frightening, we can trust the healing wisdom in dream images, in our imagination and fantasies —*as long as we do not literalize and concretize images and symbols or act them out as though they were literal*. We could even say that strictly literal interpretations of dreams, imagination, and mythology is pathological and often dangerous.

Turning Inward

A dreamwork-centered approach to life requires a "willed introversion." An important aspect of creative genius, willed introversion is a *conscious choice* to undertake the exploration of our psychic depths, a deliberate activation and linking up with the unconscious. However, as with life in general, we must balance our inner work with creative involvement in our outer world. Otherwise we risk falling into the trap of a one-sided retreat from life, which in its extreme results in psychological splitting and the disintegration of consciousness.

Joseph Campbell distinguishes willed introversion from an answer to a specific calling: "Rather it (willed introversion) is a deliberate, terrific refusal to respond to anything but the deepest, highest, richest answer to the as yet unknown demand of some waiting void within: a kind of total strike, or rejection of the offered terms of life, as a result of which some power of transformation carries the problem to a plane of new magnitudes, where it is suddenly and finally resolved."[12]

If the "offered terms of life" emanate from family or society's expectations or "shoulds," we need to be especially suspicious of those terms and their implications for our life.

In chapter 3, we will explore each step in the Radical Dreaming process.

Truth is a
pathless land.
Man cannot come
to it through any
organization,
through any
dogma, priest or
ritual.
—J. Krishnamurti

PART 2

EXPLORING THE DREAMSCAPE

I have learned this at least by my experiment: that if one advances confidently in the direction of his dreams, and endeavors to live the life which he has imagined, he will meet with a success unexpected in common hours.

—Henry David Thoreau

CHAPTER 3

☞

The Process—Breaking the Dream Code

Listen. Make a way for yourself inside yourself.
Stop looking in the other way of looking.

—Rumi

Choosing Your Adventure

Jump!
—Joseph Campbell

In this chapter we will explore the six steps for interpreting your dreams in detail:

Step 1: Walking through the dream—direct observations
Step 2: Awakening the dream—dream alchemy
Step 3: Linking dream images and symbols
Step 4: Freeing the authentic self—pulling the sword from the stone
Step 5: Summarizing the dream
Step 6: Integration

The Dream of "The Pit"

In my thirties, with a successful business, a wife and two small children, a home in the suburbs, I thought, "There must be more to life." I had become aware of what some people call the "God Hole," an unfulfilled, empty feeling that psychologists ofter describe as an "existential vacuum."* So, I began to search in earnest for the meaning of life and somehow I intuited that dreams would hold important keys to understanding life and why we are here.

Shortly after my search began, I found a spiritual group that blended Eastern and Western philosophies and seemed to support my dream research. But the group gradually demanded more and more of my time and energy. Eventually group events, projects, meetings, and weekend conclaves completely swallowed up my life. I did not realize it at the time but I had jumped off the edge of the ordinary, familiar world into what became a collective pit, a pit that would prove to be extremely difficult to leave. Looking back, it has proved to be a priceless exploration into the nature and purpose of dreaming. In fact, my own dreams eventually got me out of the group, freeing me to begin living my own life. Here was a real paradox: Without that experience I would never have understood the *radical,* life-changing potential and creative power of dreaming. Since that time I have worked with countless dreams from individuals who have found themselves "under the influence" of a vast array of social and cultural forces: familial, economic, the media, institutional, political, religious, and spiritual. One of the more remarkable features about our dreams is their ability to wake us up to the reality of what we are doing to ourselves and to others.

For an example of the Radical Dreaming process, let's apply the steps to an actual dream from my journal which helped me realize the group's real impact on my life. About three months after finally leaving what I had at one time believed was my spiritual home, I had a dream that I named "The Pit":

> I'm outside, standing on the edge of a large, cylindrical pit dug in the earth hundreds of feet deep with perfectly smooth vertical walls. As I peered down into the pit, I saw maybe thirty people at the bottom with their hands joined together, slowly moving in a circular fashion around a man standing in the center. As I watched I realized, with a great deal of relief, that I had somehow, only seconds before, been lifted up out of the pit. I thought to myself, They (the people in the pit) remind me of our Saturday prayer ritual in the group.
>
> Suddenly I'm standing with a woman in the middle of an

---

*John D. Goldhammer, *Under the Influence: the Destructive Effects of Group Dynamics.* (New York: Prometheus Books, 1996), pp. 50–51. See *"Trapped in Paradise"* in this book for a detailed account of my experience in the group.

enormous bridge high above a vast river that extends to the horizon, so wide it's not possible to see the other side. I noticed a small current of water rushing back into the main current to my left far below and under the bridge. It had come back from a side channel that was a dead end. The woman on the bridge turned and said to me, "We have been working for a long time to get you out of the pit." I then experienced a most indescribable and exquisite sense of freedom!

Step 1: Walking Through the Dream—Direct Observations

Nothing exists until or unless it is observed. An artist is making something exist by observing it. And his hope for other people is that they will also make it exist by observing it. I call it "creative observation." Creative viewing.

—William Burroughs[1]

In the first step, you concentrate on recording your initial, direct observations about the specific images and symbols in your dream. By "direct observations," I am referring to your view of the image from the outside, from different angles, the way we would walk around an artifact in a museum or walk through a movie set. You simply describe each element in your dream. Be careful to stick to a descriptive observation of your dream contents; don't use any "associations" at this stage. We also want to know what is *known* or *unknown* in the dream. For example, ask:

- Is the car in your dream your actual car or one you owned in the past?
- Does the house in your dream remind you of your childhood home or is it an unknown house?
- Are the people or creatures in your dream known or unknown?
- Is the setting familiar or does it remind you of a place you've been or heard about? Or is it new and unfamiliar?

Here are my direct observations, my "walking through the dream":

The setting: Bright sunlight, in a country setting with gently rolling green hills.

For your dream:

- Describe the basic landscape, surroundings, time of day, etc., in your dream.
- Remember to note if the setting is familiar to you or unknown.

The dreaming ego: I am my present age in the dream. It's not clear what I'm wearing.

For your dream:

- Describe how you appear in your dream. In some dreams we experience the dream as an observing mind, a disembodied awareness.
- Begin with yourself as you are in the dream. How old are you?
- What are you wearing or not wearing: textures, colors? Anything odd about your clothing?

The pit: It's about 100 feet in diameter, very deep! It's like looking down from a twenty-story building. Seemed impossible to get out of it with its perfectly perpendicular walls of dirt. Nothing I have ever seen before.

People in the pit: Members of my former spiritual group. Very small and distant. Could not see their faces or clothing details—men and women.

For your dream:

- It's important to note the gender and approximate age of dream figures.

The ritual: Looked like our regular Saturday ritual in the group, which I had begun to really dislike before I left the organization. It involved paying homage to our "spiritual teachers," one of whom was standing in the center of the circle.

Being lifted out of the pit: Felt like some unseen force or power suddenly extracted me.

The woman on the bridge: Unknown, in her late twenties, stood on my right side. She had dark or black hair and was wearing a flowing, light blue gown.

The bridge: Also unfamiliar, enormous, shaped like a great arch, carved stone, waist-high railings, very high above the water—maybe five stories up? I did not see any cars or anyone else on the bridge.

The river: An unknown river. Its vastness impressed me, an immense current moving toward the horizon.

The side channel: Really small compared to the main river—water returning into the main stream from a dead end.

Woman's comment: "We have been working for a long time to get you out of the pit." I recall wondering who the mysterious "we" were that she referred to.

For your dream:

- *Censoring dreams:* The waking ego sometimes has a tendency to adjust a dream's content, or omit something embarrassing or shocking from the details. That is why it's important not to censor or edit any details in your dreams.
- You want to get at the authentic dream, not images the waking ego has altered or defined. At this point you want to have an accurate understanding of your dream's actual, *uncensored* content.
- Be alert for *resonance,* chills, or "It clicks," or a "That's it!"—something about your dream just feels right; you suddenly know that you are getting at the real meaning and intent in your dream. I like to think of it as connecting with our *deep intuition.*

Step 2: Awakening the Dream—Dream Alchemy

> *Where is a foot worthy to walk a garden,*
> *or any eye that deserves to look at trees?*
> *Show me a man willing to be*
> *thrown in the fire.*
>
> —Rumi[2]

With this step, you will begin to experience the awesome power of dream images and symbols to unfold their wisdom and meaning in the most remarkable and unforeseen ways. By "Dream Alchemy," I mean your experience of *being* the image, imagining yourself as the image, and your process of forming and transforming as the image.

The setting: When I imagine being the landscape in my dream, I am natural, green, fertile, expansive, gentle, soaking up the sunlight, lit up, warmed, relaxed. Inside, I am dark, rich earth, layered with history—increasingly ancient and mysterious as the depth increases. I contain hidden seeds yet to reach the surface air and light. As this place, I give birth to unplanned, wild growth on my surface; I am un-civilized, not fenced or walled in. But something machine-like has created a deep wound, a pit, a gigantic bullet hole, and that hole feels like an invasion, a violation.

For your dream:

- Explain *your* experience *as* a dream element in contrast to describing it as we did in Step 1. Your point of view changes from outside observations to an image-based perspective.
- To facilitate your experience of being an element in your dream, begin by asking yourself these questions:

  – Who (what) am I? What do I do?
  – What is my job?
  – What is my purpose?
  – What is my role as a tiger, as this place, as this house?
  – What is my life like as a tiger?
  – Who/what are my enemies? My friends?
  – How did I become what I am now?
  – What has happened to me that I am in this state?
  – What is the nature of my relationship to my surroundings?

- For example, if you explored the image of a dilapidated house, you would want to know what it was like to *be* that particular structure in relation to the neighborhood, the city, other cities. You would also want to know, from the house's perspective, how it fell into a state of neglect.

The pit: As the pit I am immense but strangely empty, cold, and unfeeling. I am a perfect cylinder with perfectly vertical walls; solid earth surrounds me yet I'm not the earth; I am the space, an odd emptiness. I am open on the top to a small circle of sky but I see my world horizontally, straight at myself, my walls. Beneath me I am aware in a detached way of movement, objects revolving—that's how I grow, deepen. And I am space slowly revolving. I have no interest at all in the surface or the surrounding landscape—almost no awareness of it. I got this way by utter self-absorption and focus on perpetuating my ever-turning ritual—I am mindless repetition.

People in the pit: When I imagine being one of the people in the pit, I am obediently following our prescribed ritual. I feel childlike, infantile, regressing back in time into mother earth, into a womb state—strangely comforted but utterly trapped at the same time. I can't see out. It feels very difficult even to tilt my head back to look up—like breaking the ritual, the rules. A part of me feels like I'm dying, like I'm helping to dig a mass grave deeper and deeper, more and more impossible to get out of.

The ritual: When I imagine being this ritual, I am a two-dimensional, flat, circular movement like a recording disk, and I'm played over and over and over—the same song. I have a smooth, chrome-plated, metallic, reflective surface but I have jagged teeth underneath, hidden from view. I am digging myself deeper into the earth. My power and danger are in my digging, and even the person standing in my center, the minister, is in danger but does not see it. I am a force unto myself and the people standing on my outer circumference perpetuate my movement. I see them as non-human, automatons, but as necessary for my survival.

I would define "ritual" as an act or ceremony intended to represent a spiritual or religious principle. But also, ritual alludes to a detailed format repeated or followed with regularity: like my morning cup of coffee to start the day. Types of rituals span a range of events from a singular, spontaneous, just-created ritual to commemorate an important life event or transition, to dogmatic, repetitious, obligatory routines. In my dream, the ritual in the pit clearly belonged to the latter variety.

For your dream:

- *Symbolic inquiry:* Ask yourself, "How would I describe an image in my dream to someone who had arrived from another planet, who had no concept of what it is or what its name means?"[3] This way of inquiring, which I call symbolic inquiry, propels us into reality-based, experiential definitions of images and it also requires us to stay with the image.
- For example, a dream tiger might be described as a four-legged, warm-blooded, wild animal who lives in the jungle, untamed, a meat-eater, a predator, powerful, cunning, beautiful, deadly.
- Symbolic inquiry brings dream images to life. The moment we step into the symbolic world, we step outside the walls of our waking ego's containment, confinement, and limited awareness.

The woman on the bridge: As this woman, I feel a profound sense of accomplishment that "we" have got him out of the pit. A feeling of magic permeates the scene, of having saved a fallen hero from a tragic, deadly dilemma. As the woman, I am a part of those connected with the openness and the infinite possibilities that real freedom introduces into life. I embody the untapped potentials that have saved the person in the pit from a slow death. "We"—all the dreamer's unfulfilled creative passions—have "worked a long time" and have at last resurrected our lost brother from his grave, removed the stone from his tomb.

- The "we" element of a dream occurs frequently and points to the plural nature of the psyche: that many different aspects combine and participate with each other to make up what we think of as the individual Self—a polytheistic, networked reality as opposed to monotheistic hierarchy.

The bridge: I would define a bridge as a structure that connects two places that are divided by water, a chasm, or some impassable obstacle. As this bridge, I provide a safe way across; I connect things to each other, and I am the in-betweenness, the third element beyond duality. I provide an overlook, a new perspective. My strength comes from an arched, bow-like tension between opposites, a just-right balance for this particular place. I am also a life span, a transition, and the dreamer has reached my mid-point.

The river: As the river, what am I? I am water, fluid, expansion, movement, depth, purpose, strength, unstoppable—on my way to the ocean. I have come from many tributaries in the high mountains. Uncountable rivulets of water as well as great storms have combined to create what I now am.

The side channel: I have hit a dead end and am now returning to the main stream. As this side channel I feel like a diversion, an exploration, a sideline from the main stream. I also feel childlike and naive compared to the bigger stream. I was trying to flow uphill, against nature, and I was fated to fail eventually; it was unnatural.

Step 3: Linking Dream Images and Symbols

> *I listened to the earth-talk,*
> *the root-wrangle,*
> *the arguments of energy,*
> *the dreams lying*
> *just under the surface . . .*
>
> —Mary Oliver[4]

Once you have explored the elements in your dream, you need to link the information your experience of *being* the dream element or image has provided with your waking life experience.

Linking the setting: When I made this self-inquiry regarding my dream, I immediately connected the setting—the rolling hills and the bridge—to the freedom I felt after leaving the group.

For your dream:

- *Ask yourself this question:* In my waking life, what circumstance, situation, person, experience, or part of myself, *past or present*, feels like or reminds me of my experience as the image? Imagine walking on thin ice in a dream. You might feel unsafe, uncertain, threatened, likely to slip. You then ask yourself what circumstance or situation feels unsafe and threatening in your waking life.
- In linking your image experience, pay special attention to your choice of words, the language and phrases your experience of being the image evoked. They often open obvious connections to circumstances in your waking life.
- Note if *you* are in any way different in your dream: wearing unusual clothing, or perhaps you are a different age. For example, if you were twelve years old in a dream you might feel innocent, not grown up, full of adventure. You would ask yourself where you see those qualities or the lack of those qualities in your life.

Linking the pit: The pit clearly felt like my experience as a member in the group—a deep wound in my psyche that I had helped to dig. In my dream, the "pit" and the landscape above became metaphors for what it was like being in and out of the group. Even now, writing about this dream, the "pit" image wants to unfold additional meaning. I am seeing all the rituals we religiously and repetitiously performed in the group as a revolving, human drill, deepening the pit and making it more and more difficult to get out of what had become a Self-destructive organization. The spiritual leaders "drilled" their rituals and dogma into me. Contained in the collective "pit," I could not see the world above, its rich expanse. The more I worked at being a "dedicated member," the deeper the pit became. I was indeed digging my own grave. The perfectly cylindrical nature of the pit reminded me of the absolutist, perfection-seeking dynamic in the group, which allowed for no variance from their viewpoint and their "system."

Linking the people in the pit and the ritual: They were obviously members of my former spiritual group. While I did not recognize particular individuals, I knew they were performing a ritual we had done in the group each Saturday for a long time. We actually did join hands and walk in a circle surrounding the minister, all the while repeating prescribed prayers. My dream image of the pit emphatically illustrates the deep impact this repetitive ritual had on my psyche. My waking ego would rationalize: "It's no big deal, just go along with it. You're not *being selfless." But my waking ego had become an accomplished expert at conforming, at fitting in, at wanting to be liked, admired, thought well of.*

Looking down from the top of the pit, I realized how impossible it would be for anyone to get out. This felt very much like my exhilaration and amazement when I realized that I had actually, finally left the group, an extraordinarily difficult undertaking. I felt as though I were deserting my family and friends of the last fifteen years, not to mention the fear that had been *drilled* into me about leaving the "spiritual path." The people in the pit represented a collective spiritual orientation that I had put myself into, that had trapped me and taken fifteen years of my life.

Linking the woman on the bridge: I found linking this woman difficult because she did not remind me of anyone in my waking life. But she does remind me of unlimited possibilities, hope, freedom, liberty, beauty, aesthetics, creativity—reconnecting with all those qualities (the "we") that had never succumbed to the group, had never fallen into the pit. It's as though she had been waiting patiently for me to return from being lost at sea for years.

Linking the bridge: This feels exactly how I felt after leaving the group—that I had a new perspective, a vastly expanded view of my life; I could now see much farther and I could see a world that had been invisible to me from inside the pit. Suddenly I had choices and options available that I had not seen before. And like the bridge, life now feels solid, substantial; I found new strength standing in the center of life in contrast to being totally absorbed in one particular religious viewpoint. My standpoint had changed dramatically!

Linking the river: For me this links more to my feeling state after leaving the group—that I have rejoined life, returned to my own life, the "main stream." And I felt real joy at simply being able to connect with and appreciate everyday people. In the group, we had become superior, exclusive, judgmental, and withdrawn from society. This "main stream" felt like a combination of my natural Self and also humanity—that I had indeed rejoined the human race in the Buddhist sense of "joyful participation in the sorrows of the world."

Linking the side channel: This clearly represented my group experience as a member and participant in the group. This was my naive excursion away from living my own life and following my passion. An excursion that removed me from my own life and my surrounding world as well.

For your dream:

- Keep in mind that *everything* in a dream needs to be explored including feelings, moods, emotions, smells, colors, sounds, sensation, touch, elements of the landscape, buildings, the sky, daylight, darkness, dusk, etc. Skipping anything would be equivalent to not reading a chapter in a novel yet expecting to understand the complete story.
- Linking and Free Association—What to Avoid

  - Don't let yourself slip into any "free association," sometimes referred to as "chain" association or "word association," which actually takes you away from the dream content.

    Free association would go something like this: *The parking garage*—concrete—a cement truck—Uncle Chuck (who drives one)—my cousins. In the latter example, free associating takes us *away* from the original image and away from the dream.

  - Imagine you have a dream in which you find yourself in a public parking garage. Linking your experience might be as follows:

    Linking the parking garage: The concrete parking garage reminds me of my job at Giganticus, Inc. When I'm at work, I feel like I am in a massive, public or collective structure where rigid (concrete-like) company rules and authority govern everything. I feel trapped, confined, lost, in a monotone world without color—I'm not living *my* life at all!

Step 4: Freeing the Authentic Self— Pulling the Sword from the Stone

There lies the hoarded love, the key
to all the treasure that shall be;
Come fated hand the gift to take
And smite this sleeping world awake.

—William Morris[5]

A critical point in the Radical Dreaming approach, in this step you clarify exactly what your essential nature has been released from. In my dream, I freed myself not only from the group as a whole, but from repetitious, mindless, group prescribed rituals. We can understand why Arthur's sword was named "Excalibur," which comes from the Irish "Caladbolg," the name of an ancient sword used by heroes in Irish legend and derived from *calad* (hard) and *bolg* (lightning).[6] Radical Dreaming enables you to wield these powerful elements in defense of your authentic life: *lightning*—brilliance, illumination, *natural* flashes of insight; *hard*—sharp, intellectually penetrating, astute, able to cut through, to separate the real from the unreal.

Step 5: Summarizing the Dream

> *"Dreams that have not been interpreted are like letters that have not been opened."*
>
> —The Talmud

By now, your dream and its images have essentially interpreted themselves. And this self-interpretation is one of the immense advantages of the Radical Dreaming approach: you do not have to "figure out" your dream with just your waking intellect, or be trained in mythology, symbology, psychology, or philosophy. Your dream's images, characters, and content will unfold their meaning to you in surprising ways you could never have foreseen with only the waking ego consciousness.

Step 5 consists of simply recording in your journal a brief summary of your dream's meaning for future reference. Writing a summary of your dream will seal it in, make it official, and help reinforce your resolve to act on the dream's message in your everyday life.

For my pit dream, I wrote this summary:

> Represents the freedom I am experiencing after leaving the group, and impressed upon me the impact of what I had been subjecting myself to—how the rituals in the group became damaging and dangerous for me. Must watch out for ritual-like non-thinking or future religious or spiritual practices that in any way feel like the ritual in the pit. A real miracle that I got out! When I think of joining some group, I will ask myself: Am I stepping into some hidden pit, some group mind set that will be next to impossible to get out of?

Naming Your Dreams

Coming up with titles for your dreams helps not only to clarify a dream's focus, it also becomes a quick reference for finding a particular dream in your journals as we described earlier.

Step 6: Integration

Unrealized consciousness becomes a burning fire.
—Marie-Louise von Franz[7]

Step 6 in the Radical Dreaming process focuses on integrating both personal and collective symbolism from your dreams into your waking life, which in turn brings your Authentic Self into greater definition and clarity. It's like a gradually emerging image once trapped in a stone block; you are the sculptor and your dreams are your tools. Your work is to remove everything that is *not you* from the stone. "Integration" refers to the process of consciously applying the meaning and symbolism from your dreams in your waking life.

By *integration*, I mean something quite different from *assimilation*, which we ought to be careful to avoid. Assimilation refers to an incorporation of something back into a central, singular identity. Of necessity, this means losing and suppressing the dream elements into a state without definition; as though the characters in a novel suddenly disappeared into one persona; the story would fall apart.

In my pit dream example, integration of the dream elements involved a still-continuing process of being aware of those dream images and symbols that refer to my Authentic Self and those images that refer to outside, collective influences. Let's review this process using images from the pit dream:

The setting: This natural countryside does refer to our real nature. To integrate what this image represents, I began to imagine myself as being in this setting, walking through it, feeling what it's like to be this countryside. And most important, whenever I found myself contemplating joining some group I would simply imagine how these green hills would feel if I placed the group among them. What would the reaction be from this natural place? What would happen to this landscape? Now I could look at a potential path from the perspective of this aspect of my natural, Authentic Self—quite a different approach than looking at a decision using only my waking ego's point of view! In this manner we integrate a dream element into our waking life; we enlarge the sphere of our awareness and suddenly our life has more depth, we have greater discernment, and we make better choices in our life—choices that support who we really are.

The pit: How do we integrate the meaning of an image like my pit? Essentially I endeavored to be aware of any thought patterns, ideas, or attitudes that reminded me of the group. Then I would ask myself: Where does this way of thinking, this attitude or this particular idea come from? Me or the group? Gradually, I have worked at separating myself from the group influences. In a more general sense, I would ask myself: What circumstance or situation in my waking life reminds me of the pit? Or: Where is the "pit" in me, in my thinking or in my life? What sort of thinking is digging a grave for my authentic life?

People in the pit: Again, I made every effort to be alert for any thought process or outer circumstance that felt like mindlessly following some outside agenda. This imagery would be a potent alarm for me regarding any tendency to follow any ideological system or theory exclusively. I would not have to actually belong to a particular group, I would only have to subscribe to a particular belief system. My dream would literally protect me from stepping into future ideological pits in my life.

The ritual: In my particular group experience, rituals were prescribed, and repetitious. Since then, I have come to value ritual on a more personal, creative level as creating a unique space that symbolizes, memorializes, and honors an important event or passage in life.

The woman on the bridge: This woman presents a more difficult, more subtle figure, one that I now look at as representing my unlived life. For me she *is my life*, the reason I am here. When I contemplate changes or new directions in my life, I can go to her inwardly and ask for her help, her ideas. For her, the greatest tragedy would be for me to step into another collective pit, be diverted or sidetracked.

The bridge: I use the bridge image whenever I want to reconnect to the ecstatic sense of freedom I felt after leaving the group, and at those times when I feel I need a different perspective, an overview about my life—what really matters to me in the long run. As with any meaningful dream image, you can ask the image about your life and the choices you are about to make. We will explore this powerful aspect of Radical Dreaming thoroughly in chapter 4, *The Language of the Dream*.

The river: I use the image of this river to connect myself to the flow of life, the flow of my life, to my own particular destiny, which derives its meaning and value from participation in the flow of life in the world. This great river also reminds me of the inexorable flow of all life into the sea, returning to the ocean, the unconscious.

The side channel: Like the pit image, this side channel represents distractions in my life, time wasted on unnecessary detours. So anything I'm doing that brings to mind the image of that channel enables me to stop and reexamine what I am about to do or am doing in my life. Have I unconsciously embarked on another side-channel?

The woman's comment: Her comment, "We have been working a long time to get you out of the pit," has become like a verbal lightning bolt to awaken me from any notion I may ever have in the future about allowing some *collective ism* to shape or control my life.

Here are additional ways to help you integrate the elements of your dream in your waking life:

- When making choices and decisions, ask yourself if what you are considering brings to mind any dream image or experience.
- In your imagination, go to a particular dream image and present your dilemma to that figure and wait for a response. This can be done with any image, a person, an animal, or even an inanimate object (see *Dynamic Imagination* in chapter 4).
- Be alert for any dream image that appears spontaneously. Notice what you were just thinking, what someone just now said to you, etc. This is a powerful way to link and integrate dream imagery with specific events, circumstances, or decisions in your waking life.
- When you are in the process of making a choice or decision in your life, take time to imagine a landscape you are walking through that represents making that particular choice. One way to initiate this process is to imagine there are two or three doors, each one representing a specific choice. Open each one and step into that world, notice what is there and where you are. Record your experience as you would a dream.
- When experiencing a difficult time in your life, go into a dream image that you find reassuring and hopeful about your life and who you are. *Be* in the image, or with it, and let it speak to you.

Getting to Know Our "Selves"

As this integration of dream material occurs, we will begin to feel more connected not only with our inner world but with others, and with our outer world as well. We will feel a deepening sense of Self in knowing our many "selves." And we will begin to feel more in control, less a victim, more self-responsible for our lives as we begin to sense what real freedom is like, perhaps for the first time. We have begun to *hold together*, like a diamond, as a distinct human being—this is the essence of "integration" that comes from releasing the Authentic Self from collective corruption!

Taking a Seat in the Back of the Bus

About two years after her mother died, a forty-year-old woman had this unusual dream of freeing the Self from a collective situation:

> I got on a bus with my mother, who went up to the front of the bus. I found a seat in the back. I'm shocked how dirty and dingy the back of the bus is—a bad place. Then I noticed that the rest of the bus did not have regular seats but instead there's this flat cord or strap that runs diagonally through the bus for the people to lean against. I have to go to the bathroom and I get off the bus.

The above dream begins in a collective situation: the bus. But the dreamer's mother is also on the bus and she sits "up front." A bus generally alludes to some collective influence as contrasted with a car, an individually controlled mode of transportation. After working through the steps in the dream, she realized that her mother's influence, which included some very outdated stereotypical attitudes about the role of women in society—highly collective attitudes—had relegated her to "the back of the bus," to feelings and attitudes of not being good enough and of feeling inferior. When she worked with symbolic inquiry about the unusual strap, she realized that all the people leaning on her had "stretched her too thin!" Her mother's potent influence had propelled her into the role of thinking she had to take care of everyone and please everyone. This dynamic was exhausting her, keeping her in a subservient position and preventing her from living *her* life, it was "taking her for a ride."

From her dream she began to separate out her own thinking and attitudes from those of her mother's. The "bus" with its "leaning on me" strap, represents the collective situation (a Self-destructive stereotype about women) as well as her mother's negative influence and judgments that she now must work to separate herself from.

The House Was Gone Except for . . .

A few months later she had another significant dream about her mother.

> We had to tear down my mother's house—a beautiful large home, but right next to a busy freeway. I knew I wanted to save a sign that had been in her garden. On the sign were the words: "Good to Love Flowers." Then the house was gone leaving a perfectly clean flat area. You could barely see a faint outline of where the house had been.

Her dream illustrates the type of dream images that reinforce the process of finding *our* life and of extricating ourselves from parental influences that are not part of out real nature. Her psyche not only confirmed that she had torn down her mother's internalized negative influences, it informed her that her mother's love of flowers and her love of gardening needed to be rescued—a part of her own passion for nature, an important aspect of her Authentic Self, and the only thing she wanted to save from the house. From this dream she felt she had reached a new beginning in her life, that she could go forward with a "clean slate."

In the following chapters we will look at many more important examples of how we "pull the sword from the stone" in our dreams.

Breaking the Mirror—Stepping Free of Illusions

Is this life I'm living the life that wants to live in me?
—Parker Palmer

Identification of our own particular collective symbolism "breaks the mirror" of our outer, conformist persona, which reflects what others think we should do and be. In this process, certain types of images are red flags and deserve our thorough exploration: public places, roads and highways (in contrast to "off the beaten path"), public modes of transportation: planes, trains, buses, large ships/boats, etc., multi-unit structures: apartment buildings (in contrast to an individual dwelling), pools in complex structures, hotels, parking garages, department stores, suburbs, office buildings, schools and universities, groups of all kinds, religions, systems, gangs, the Mafia, swarms of insects, some infectious diseases, viruses, aliens, certain materials such as concrete, cement, and asphalt that are usually machine-made and *mass*-produced. A word of caution: Do not assume an image means something just because it appears to have collective implications. You must first work through the dream, placing it within the context of your life. For example, a particular high steel bridge in my friend's dream represented an important part of his authentic nature. His dream bridge was an unusual combination of materials; it was attached to an ancient Roman stone bridge at each end.

Leaving the Herd

Rob, a forty-six-year-old contractor, had this dream in the midst of reassessing his career and trying to reconnect with his creative life:

> In this dream, I was walking around in an airport. I was trying to find the airplane and line I was supposed to be on and in. There were lots of people and lines. There were people I knew from my whole life. People from the army, school, my church, and family. I felt I couldn't decide on who or what and where I belonged.

After working through this dream, Rob felt it showed him the central dilemma in his life at the time: He was searching for his own unique life. For him, the airport represented society, group travel, a confrontation with choices—choices that would be going along with the herd. "My job is to take lots of people to predetermined destinations, to keep everyone on schedule," he said, imagining himself as *being* the airport in his dream. Rob's "airport," a public, mass transportation center, symbolized "approved routes," popular ways to get to a destination. The people in his dream represented all the accumulated influences that had, up to this time, influenced his choices in life, good and bad. Now he understood that he had to find his own way.

Dreams of the Mundane and the Ordinary

Trying to Please Everyone

Here's an example of how our dreams use what appear to be mundane images to illustrate collective qualities that help us to more clearly identify what is not part of our authenticity or creativity: An engineer in his late thirties whom I will call Robert had become disillusioned with his corporate career and wanted to reconnect with his love for music and composing, which his career demands had reduced to barely a part-time hobby. He worked with a series of dreams for about a year and he had this dream as he struggled over choosing a particular musical style he wanted to follow:

> Ellen (his fiancée) worked at Fred Meyer's (a large department store similar to Walmart). There was a couple coming to interview her. We were walking along the front of the store and saw the couple there waiting for Ellen's boss. They were supposed to meet the boss first.

When the dreamer imagined *being* a "Fred Meyer's store," he reported feeling "ordinary, middle of the road, something for everyone, trying to please everyone." Ellen, his fiancée, was a talented artist but spent all her time working at mundane, low-wage jobs. The *ordinariness* and *commonplace* feeling of the store resonated for the dreamer as well as how out of place Ellen—whom he saw as his creative side—was in that setting. A "boss" in dreams usually refers to some inner authoritarian voice, and in this case the boss is suspect as an outer, implanted authority, since the dream takes place in a collective place. He also realized that his creativity could not function in the "commonplace," that it wanted to draw him into his own *unique* musical style, a more difficult and scary path that meant going into unknown territory.

This dream illustrates two particularly deadly collective traps: trying to please everyone and attempting to fit our creativity or passion into a pre-existing style or format. Moreover, the dream refined Robert's perception of his creativity, the way he looked at it—that it wanted to be "non-ordinary."

Removing the Barbed Wire from Your Life

During this process, Robert seriously considered returning to school to get the "right degrees," jump through the collective world's hoops. He then had a dream of trying to enter Africa, but a high, barbed-wire fence built to keep people out surrounded the entire country. He noticed that there were occasional small holes in the fence and some people were sneaking through these openings. Imagining that *he* was Africa, he understood that Africa represented the origins of life for him, an exotic and mysterious land, while the barbed wire fence represented the collective world's influences ("barbs"), stinging self-criticisms that he had internalized. These critical barbs told him he had to pass through the "main gates," the socially approved ways to develop a musical career. These popular attitudes were keeping him out, preventing him from connecting (entering Africa) with his "*original* life," his own creativity. For Robert, the holes represented the fact that these outside influences were indeed weakening, that this internalized, collective barrier was no longer impenetrable.

Robert's dreams provided him with newfound confidence and the courage to risk following his own "original" music, which did not want to conform to traditional educational approaches. He felt freer, more self-responsible, empowered and passionate; and he felt sure of the direction he ought to take that would support his creativity and his authenticity. His dream had enabled him to separate himself from thoughts, ideas, and actions that did not belong to him. He felt reassured about his own peculiar artistic bent, *his* originality. And he felt a huge sense of relief at not having to make his music please everyone. A new excitement, confidence, and vitality surged into his life. Now when he thought about his music, he also felt a greater sense of his own integrity. More of his authentic nature had emerged from the stone of popular expectations and demands that were blocking his creative spirit.

Putting Up Barbed Wire

An ominous dream nailed barbed wire to the life of a forty-five-year-old German eye doctor in 1934 when Hitler was coming to power, five years before World War II began.

> Storm troopers were putting up barbed wire at all hospital windows. I had sworn I wouldn't stand for having them bring their barbed wire into my ward. But I did put up with it after all. I stood by like a caricature of a doctor while they took out the window panes and turned a ward into a concentration camp— but I lost my job anyway. I was called back, however, to treat Hitler because I was the only man in the world who could. I was ashamed of myself for feeling proud, and so I began to cry.[8]

Again, "barbed wire" represents an aspect of collective authority, and in the doctor's dream, Hitler's Nazism replaces the window panes, how we see the outside world and how we let light into a structure. An outside ideology (the barbed wire) had become a part of his ward, attached itself to his psyche. And he certainly is the "only man in the world" who can "treat Hitler," because what Hitler represented had been accepted, "put up with," internalized in his mind. Now he was being imprisoned ("a concentration camp") within Hitler's belief system. His dream also presented him with awesome social implications: If he freed himself of his internalized Hitler, he would indeed impact society—a voice of reason in the midst of mass insanity. But should he conform to this deadly outside influence, he would be an accomplice, part of the German citizenry responsible for the approaching horror. The dream also warns that by allowing this collective invasion, the corruption of his own sense of right and wrong, he becomes a "caricature," an imitation, a misrepresentation far removed from his Authentic Self and his innate humanity.

We cannot even imagine how profound the impact might have been on world events at the time had individuals taken their dreams seriously and had they been able to freely share their dreams and, most significantly, act out of their own authentic natures instead of succumbing to such a deadly, ideological plague.

Time Travel: Entering the Continuum

Time is the substance from which I am made. Time is a river which carries me along, but I am the river; it is a tiger that devours me, but I am the tiger; it is a fire that consumes me, but I am the fire.

—Jorge Luis Borges

Why Dreams Go Back in Time

Always be on the lookout for indications of time periods in your dreams. One of the more common ways dreams point to a particular time is the apparent age of dream figures. Had I been ten years old in my dream of the pit, I would need to explore what was happening in my life when I was actually ten; or the dream could be referring to some event that happened ten years ago—the birth of something that is now ten years old. Or consider a third possibility that would allude to a time span—a chunk of time that your psyche wants you to look at because it has prevented you from being yourself in some manner. Also be aware of the age of things, objects, clothing, buildings, music, etc. As you work with a particular dream, it quickly becomes clear where in time, past or future, your psyche wants to take you.

Why go back in time? Dreams show us the origin of things with un-canny accuracy—where something began that is now impacting our life in the present; this is part of "linking" dream images to other time peri-ods. Dreams use history to clarify present day circumstances and dynam-ics; they are always relevant to something we are currently experiencing or are about to experience.

Riding the Horse of Destiny

As an example, one of my clients, a university student, had this re-curring, haunting childhood dream that began when he was three to four years old, a dream he had never understood:

> I'm riding a large, white horse really fast down an ancient street between buildings that appear to be Egyptian—very old and mysteriously beautiful, covered with carved figures and faces. I'm aware that this horse has tremendous intent, that I don't know where we are going but he knows. Suddenly we stop abruptly at a precipice, right on the edge. I look down many hundreds of feet below and to my surprise I see my family sitting on lawn chairs at the beach in a typical little suburban town. I awaken terrified we're going to fall over the edge.

After working on the dream using the Radical Dreaming process, he realized that this particular recurring dream was showing him the direc-tion of his entire life, his purpose, and the chief obstacle he would en-counter. He had always been fascinated with the Middle East, with ancient cultures, and was studying anthropology and psychology. Syn-chronistically, while in the Army, he had actually been stationed in Saudi Arabia and to his surprise felt completely at home. In his dream, the horse represented his life's purpose, what he described as "powerful, pure, strong, peaceful," and "that horse has intent!" He realized that his family and especially their lifestyle—comfortable, suburban, very tradi-tional—were at odds with what he wanted to do in his life. His parents, with nothing but good intentions, wanted him to get a different degree that would get him a good-paying job, etc. Tradition, following his par-ents' influence, slipping into a comfortable, socially approved lifestyle—these outside influences stop his life (the powerful white horse) in its tracks—a potential "fall from grace," a loss of his authentic life and des-tiny. His dream now provided him with renewed resolve to follow his dreams and gave him a powerful dream image to support and guide him on his journey.

What Dreams Want from Our Personal and Collective History

Dreams portray the human spirit's inclination to use suffering and affliction as the raw material for creative transformation. To understand the depth and reach of the images in our dreams, we need to know as much as possible about our distinct history and background, along with the history of the land, the geography where we live now, and where we have lived in the past. Dreams dip into the past with regularity and with good reason. For in the sedimented layers of our history, we find the seeds of the present moments, our roots—those experiences and influences that have contributed to shaping who we are and who we perceive ourselves to be. In the Radical Dreaming process, unraveling these past influences is one of our most essential tasks in order to differentiate ourselves from what does not belong to us—those things that are not part of who we really are as unique individuals in the *present*. Not understanding or dismissing our past is not only naive, it's dangerous to our authenticity.

Regret, Guilt, and Trauma—Time Alchemy: Using the Past Creatively

The only way we can get free of the past is to know it and know it for what it really was. For example, one individual dreamt that a mummy in the basement of his mother's house was coming after him. The dream's humorous play on words—a "mummy" in mom's house—pointed out that he was unconsciously bringing back to life attitudes and influences that belonged to his mother and were best left buried. The dreamer also realized that he had been *preserving* long-dead maternal influences in his adult life, a way of "cheating nature," of thwarting his natural evolution, independence, and growing-up process.

Much of the resentment, regret, and guilt that we hang onto from our past experiences can be likened to dragging around blocks of lead—heavy, burdensome parts of our past that need to be turned into gold. To accomplish this alchemical transformation of the past, we need access to our dreaming world. Our dreams want to use everything we have experienced; they want to turn the lead in our lives into the pure gold of the true Self. Suddenly we realize, as I have from writing this book, that without *all* my experiences—the painful and tragic as well as the joyful and ecstatic—I would not have been able to write *Radical Dreaming*. Writing this book has brought new meaning to experiences in my life that have stirred up resentment and regret for many years.

It has taken me years to realize the full import of a dream I had when I was feeling pretty down on myself for what I had neglected to do with my life. I dreamt I was standing at the bottom of a mountain of rusted-out junk and old stuff when I noticed something sparkling: small nuggets of solid gold scattered in with the junk. I began climbing up on the pile to retrieve the gold. Thus do our dreams extract the gold from our life experiences to use as indestructible material in the process of freeing, supporting, and defining the Authentic Self.

Manufactured in 1972

Sometimes dreams can be uncommonly direct. I recall one member of a dream group who dreamt that she had a circular scar on her forehead about the size of a quarter. As she touched it, the skin opened like a small door and she saw one end of a *magic marker* in the hole, which she pulled out—a light blue, chisel-pointed felt marker. Stamped on the side she saw the words "Manufactured in 1972." After working on her dream, she realized it referred to a set of attitudes about her self-image that had their origins in 1972 when, as a young child, she absorbed some particularly negative parental criticisms. Dreams use nothing by accident. Note the "*magic mark*-er," which she correlated to a magical spell, a curse—something that definitely had left its *mark* on and *in* her "head"—ways of thinking about herself that were *not* part of her authentic nature. "If I *am* 'magic,' then I'm creating an illusion. I'm tricking someone," she explained. From this and related dreams, she experienced a deep sense of relief, fewer self-imposed restrictions, newfound freedom, and exciting new potentials regarding her self-image and her life. And, needless to say, she felt much better about herself as a unique person. Her magic marker dream was a key, transformative dream for her and occurred after a year of conscientious dreamwork.

Dreams of an Unknown Infant

Other clues as to time are found in clothing, the age of buildings, or the look of a place as being from the past. Many people dream of an unknown infant or small child that can represent the actual age of a new aspect of life. Often a dilemma surrounds this vulnerable new life: threats, danger, birth defects, sometimes impending death or an actual death occurs—or, the dreamer rejects the child and what it represents.

Killing the Creative Spirit

Let's look at an example: A young woman who had recently reawakened her artistic ability dreamt that she had found a baby about two or three months old—the approximate period of time she had been drawing and painting. In her dream the baby died from a "fungal infection," which deeply upset her. After working with the dream, she realized that a *mental* "fungus" was killing her creative spirit. She linked the baby's infection to the occasional fungal infections that she suffered, which would leave actual red streaks on her forehead. Her fungal infection was leaving its "mark" in her psyche, on her "head," infiltrating her thinking, which she connected to very negative self-talk, putting herself down—killing her abilities and talents.

Moreover, the fungal infection in her dream was definitely *not* a part of her Authentic Self. Instead it was a foreign invasion that was now exposed so that it could be eliminated from her psyche. She was able to do this by becoming more aware of her thoughts and identifying those that belonged to the "fungal infection." Her dream brought into her awareness a dynamic that had been operating in the unconscious. She soon experienced a welcome sense of relief and a much improved self-image. Most important, she felt a renewed passion and much less of a judgmental attitude regarding her art.

The Master and the Slave

Dreams that at first appear to be reincarnation memories may be more about protecting our authentic life and our creative freedom. When I was deepening my involvement in the spiritual group ("the Pit") that I had joined in the early seventies, I had a dream that appeared to be a memory of a death, possibly in a past life. Looking at that dream as a reincarnation memory was interesting and certainly an ego trip for me, but I could find no particular relevance to my current life. Moreover, treating the dream as an actual memory would require looking at the dream as *literal* and factual, which is most unlikely. Here's the dream:

> I'm observing an older man who lived in one room with a dirt floor attached to the rear of a large estate situated just outside of a town. The time period appeared to be in a medieval era somewhere in Europe. As I watched I saw that the old man was an artist and was a servant or slave to the master of the estate. He had nothing but was happy because he was allowed to paint and

that was his life. I saw paintings on many canvases standing in vertical wooden compartments.

On a trip to the nearby village, a gang of youths attacked, beat, and stabbed him. He managed to return to his room but was mortally wounded and died a short time later. At the instant he died, I became the old man and I could even feel the rough, worn garment he was wearing. From the feeling of his garment, I sensed the extreme poverty and lack that the old painter had experienced in his life. As he died I moved out of his body in spirit form, like a vapor, and was again watching the following days' events. He apparently had no relatives or maybe no one was notified about his death. I saw the master of the house going through the painter's room with a group of people from the village, selling all the paintings.

Looking at this dream many years later, it makes sense as a *symbolic* drama about allowing my creative side—my writing and my dreamwork—to be placed in a state of enslavement under the control of the "master" of that *estate*. Finally, a "gang of youths" ends the painter's life. The old painter's death occurs *after* he subjects himself to his "master," someone who has control over everything and everyone within the boundaries of his land.

This dream paints an uncannily accurate picture of my life at the time: I had forced my creative side into a restrictive space. I continued to write but only to prepare sermons and lectures for the group. Everything I wrote supported and promoted the group's ideology. The group's dogmatic approach to dreamwork overwhelmed my own research and ideas about dream interpretation. So, while I continued to work with dreams, trying to understand how to interpret them, I forced my dreams and dreams of others into the group's shoes.

The master's estate is a perfect analogy for my spiritual group. The leaders had everything: luxurious homes, travel, plenty of money, and complete control, while most members had nothing. And, although difficult and embarrassing, I must take responsibility for all that the "gang of youths" represents: As a member of my spiritual group, I became arrogant, disrespectful of others' beliefs, believing that "we" had all the answers, that "we" were special, and that *we* knew everything.

When I looked at this dream symbolically, I realized it was showing me that by so severely restricting my creative life, I had moved my creativity into a state of old age and death. While the group supposedly encouraged creativity among its members, that creativity had to support and follow the group's ideology. Anything outside that context was un-acceptable. Hence the " . . . canvases standing in vertical wooden com-partments," in *storage*, contained in small compartments, inside a room, "attached to the rear of a large estate"—a very limited, confining expression of the old man's art.

And what about the "rough garment" that impressed me with his poverty? I now feel that I put on that garment when I joined the group—my vows of spiritual poverty, my naive, idealistic "selfless" dedication to *someone else's* God. A well-intended but self-deceived part of myself locked up my creative life in that small back room with the dirt floor.

But why "medieval" times? Perhaps my dream was showing me that I was regressing, moving backwards, placing my creative life in a state of bondage so typical of artists in those times who, in order to survive, had to find a wealthy sponsor, who would often direct and control their artistic life. Or maybe I was really in a *mid-evil* place. The term "me-dieval" comes from the Latin, *medius,* meaning *middle,* and *aevum,* meaning *age.*[9]

Thus the dream selects its images from our collective stories, from our history, even from actual events, like some wise old time-traveler walking through the vast archives of human experience.

Tension and Authenticity

Life depends on tension.
—Joseph Campbell

Many people misunderstand the idea of reconciling opposites as having to do with balance, but maybe it's not quite so simple. We constantly en-counter opposites, polarities, differences, contrasts, and inequality in our dreams. Our task becomes one of holding the tension in-between opposites until a third thing begins to happen, a third something not bound up with one side or the other. This "third something" will be a deeper, more profound insight, a new standpoint, an expanded aware-ness, a new understanding. We will feel as if our psyche has increased its circumference; we will realize the import of Heraclitus's words: "The unlike is joined together and from differences results the most beautiful harmony, and all things take place by strife."[10] So the "differences," the "strife" in our dreams, become extremely significant in our search for the Authentic Self.

The images and figures we encounter in our dreams connect us to values far beyond the human scale. Indeed, dreamwork links us to a depth of insight that moves us through and beyond the dogmatic side of virtue, a dark side of virtue reflecting a collective, relativistic, educational interpretation of goodness. Such virtue can be a balm to the self-centered ego, and in our culture it remains trapped by pairs of opposites: vice or virtue, good or bad, impure or pure, pain or pleasure.

The Tendency to Take Sides

The collective world of conformity reinforces the tendency to take sides, to adhere to *one* viewpoint, *one* ideology, *one* solution. In our dreams, the psyche zeroes in on any duality in our thinking and in our outlook on life. It is far easier to align oneself with *one side* of things than to hold the tension between a pair of opposites. Just as plants barely grow in space under zero-gravity conditions, a tensionless state of being prevents natural growth in the human psyche—and by "growth" I mean increasing self-awareness of who we are, which requires a tension between who we *think* we are and our innate creative potential, a primary characteristic of the Self.

Many people are caught in a basic pair of existential opposites: extreme individualism or dedication to a group, organization, a particular belief system, or religious orientation. Both are egocentric in that utter individualism places total emphasis on the individual, while a destructive group orientation creates extreme ego inflation through identification with group ideals: We are "special," exclusive—*we* have knowledge others do not have, *our* God is the only God. Thus fundamentalist cults in mainstream religions and particularly a group-dominated mind-set frequently create dangerous opposites such as social fragmentation, hate, and separation in a far more lethal manner than rugged individualism. Terrorist groups who supposedly want to expand their religious beliefs try to exterminate Jews; Americans in turn want to convert the "unsaved" masses of the world to Christianity. Our dreams work to thwart and expose influences from these shadowy ideological swamps now proliferating within the human psyche and throughout our collective world.

Instead of self-responsible inner work that enables us to contribute to society in a creative way, the group-think zealot tries to reform the outer world—the fault lies in the other, other groups, other races. Our "in-group"—racial, tribal, economic, political—becomes a missionizing cult enlarging the ego rather than integrating the ego into a whole individual. As a result this deviant side of group dynamics has created a global aberration, a mutant, group-based hysteria that flies in the face of all that it means to be human. Our dreams will without fail expose any such collective dynamics that threaten our authentic life.

In the next chapter, The Language of the Dream, we will explore the roles *Symbolic Inquiry* and *Dynamic Imagination* play in understanding and deepening our dreamwork.

> *I know that I love the day,*
> *The sun on the mountain, the Pacific*
> *Shiny and accomplishing itself in breakers,*
> *But I know I live half alive in the world,*
> *Half my life belongs to the wild darkness.*
> —Galway Kinnell[11]

CHAPTER 4

✍

The Language of the Dream

You must give birth to your images.
They are the future waiting to be born.

—Rainer Maria Rilke

Images and Imagination

when deep in the tree
all the locks click open,
and the fire surges through the wood,
and the blossoms blossom.

—Mary Oliver[1]

The Authentic Self, the soul, the spirit, nature, God, the unconscious—however you look at the transcendent character of the human spirit—speaks to us through dreams and the imagination. And dreams, for the most part, speak to us with images, weaving their meaning into our lives through metaphor and simile. Hence, a dream of a storm at sea may be showing the dreamer that her life is moving through a "a sea of troubles."[2] When we *are* that sea, we can imagine feeling tremendous turbulence, being at the mercy of forces far beyond our control, perhaps in danger of being overwhelmed.

Dreams also use similes or comparisons: the grizzly bear with his fur on fire is *like* the dreamer's rage, terrifying and dangerous. These comparisons through simile and metaphor are critical keys to translating and integrating our dreams' meaning into our waking lives. In order to accomplish this integration of our dream material, we must *experience* the dream by putting ourseves into the experience of *becoming* the meta-

106

phor, of *being* the images in our dreams and in our waking imagination, of moving and feeling the world through the eye of the image.

The Mountain Lion

Thus, when I imagine *being* the mountain lion in my dream who has come down the mountain to help me with this book, I am allowing a wild, natural, powerful, authentic, instinctual part of myself *into* my waking life. As the mountain lion, I can see in the night, I can sense things, feel my surroundings, hear a twig fall a hundred yards away. And I have teeth and claws. I can imagine words and images that *bite*, dreams like claws that tear apart my inauthentic persona.

This *experiential* process of mining the gold from our dreams makes it possible for the dream to interpret itself; the dream images will tell us who and what they are and what they mean.

Dynamic Imagination

Images are magic. They have the power to change perceptions, even lives.

—Thomas McKnight

Our imagination becomes a powerful way to draw water from the same well of inner wisdom and guidance that gives birth to our night dreams. When necessary, I can imagine being the mountain lion, seeing through his eyes, feeling how he might react to a situation, how he would move through my life.

A Waterfall of Numbers

By calling on our imagination in our waking life, we are creating dreams and images that we can interpret just as we would a night dream. Another example: Many years ago, in what now feels like another lifetime, I earned my living in the business world as an accountant and financial consultant. On a walk one morning, during the period when I was writing this chapter, I asked for an image that would represent that corporate life I used to be a part of. I immediately saw cascading black numbers against a stark white background, like a waterfall of numbers instead of water. I was struck by what it would be like for me to go back into that world, step under the waterfall; it would be a powerful *black and white* world, no color, all about numbers, the bottom line, absolutes, success or failure. For me, the lack of color symbolized a world without depth, without feelings, and without emotion—cold and calculating, overwhelmed and obsessed with *the numbers*, that would and did rule my life.

Such is the awesome power of the imagination with its deep connections to the unconscious; images become our own inner teachers and we do not have to be schooled in any theoretical framework, or even understand rudimentary psychology to access our own innate, natural wisdom.

Exploring and working on dreams releases the living life essences in images, symbols, and language into the physical body, waking life, and then out into the world. The importance of working with dream imagery in one's *waking* life to allow and give space to the transcendental, the creative spirit carried within dream images—to let them actualize themselves in our outer life and circumstances—is obvious. This requires an integrative approach to life and to the unconscious. That is why just analyzing dreams without applying them in one's life creates a psychic indigestion, sustaining the status quo and eventually leading one into greater disillusionment with life and one's outer world.

Active Imagination

I am sunlight, slicing the dark. Who made this night?
                                                    —Rumi

I have found Carl Jung's method (called "active imagination") for working with images very helpful, particularly with difficult dream images and as a way to better understand images in waking dreams.

Using our imaginative powers helps us to integrate images into our waking life that represent valuable aspects of *who we really are*, images that resonate with our distinctive, authentic nature. Through our imagination, we allow this "special world" to have space in our waking life.

The Islamic scholar Henry Corbin coined the term "imaginal," in order to describe this *other world* and to distinguish it from the "imaginary." Corbin described the imaginal realm as:

> An intermediate world, the world of idea-images, of archetypal figures, of subtle substances, of "immaterial matter." This world is as real and objective, as consistent and subsistent as the intel-

ligible and sensible worlds. It is an intermediate universe "where the spiritual takes body and body becomes spiritual.". . . It is the scene on which visionary events and symbolic histories appear in their true reality. The organ of this universe is the active imagination.[3]

I like Corbin's description of the imaginal world because it helps us begin to appreciate our imagination as a wonderful tool for further exploring dream and image. I find that it also helps to look at our imagination and its images as an "intermediate" realm connecting our day and night worlds. Corbin does not mean to imply any literalisms to his imaginal world and also makes a point of saying that in dreams, in active imagination, and in waking dreams, we must look at things symbolically.

Jung said the object of active imagination is to access the unconscious in the waking state, giving a voice to unacknowledged parts of the psyche, establishing a conscious linkage and dialogue with the unconscious.[4] What I most appreciate about active imagination is its profoundly important feature as a meditative, spiritual process that provides us with a non-directive, *dogma-free* approach to our inner work, which thrusts us back into finding *our own way* outside and beyond the influences of the collective world. It is a self-responsible, meditative tool to help us excavate our authentic life.

We can use our imagination to create a conscious *dialogue* with the imagination, the soul images, the dream figures, even moods—holding the tension between where we are and where the images beckon us to go—letting ourselves fall *inward* into deeper and deeper depths of understanding and meaning. Working with a multitude of images and feelings promotes the reality of the human psyche as a polytheistic dynamic—many gods and demons. Moreover, this polytheistic inner dreamscape strikes at the root defect of the collective: its monotheistic, totalitarian structure.

When we make these connections with our own images and symbolic worlds, we encounter a deeper wisdom, a profound level of insight and knowledge that is a part of who we are and yet is also connected to something much bigger—what Jung referred to as the "collective unconscious" or "objective psyche," containing the "whole spiritual heritage of mankind's evolution, born anew in the brain structure of every individual."[5]

Creative Imagination?

When we inject some preplanned intent into our imaginative explorations, we put ourselves in dangerous territory. For example, in my church group, we were taught to police our imagination to keep negative or bad thoughts out. When we meditated, we used prescribed prayers and mantras; the group's agenda and belief system was hard-wired into our heads. Author and psychologist James Hillman cautions against this whitewashing or directing of our imaginative process: "Our approach to imagining is predetermined by our idea of it. Disciplines of the imagination turn into a disciplining of the images. And active imagination becomes subverted into mind control, gaining knowledge, strength, and wisdom at the expense of the images of the soul."[6] So people have dreams of: electrodes attached to a child's head, Nazis breaking into the house and arresting one's parents, working for the boss one had ten years ago.

Thus the necessity to engage our imagination *without any predetermination*. We have tremendous pressure placed upon us to make our inner dream world conform to popular images and ideals—to make our inner life "fit in" to some organized system of prayer or meditation or other practice. Trying to "fit in," people dream about: shoes or clothing that no longer fit, rooms that are too small, being back in school, returning to high school, preparing for exams—we should be doing what we were "trained" to do with our lives. We need to "fail" those tests!

I learned the hard way that we are killing our own creative potential when we place any *agenda* on our dream images or on our imagination. Any pre-planned agenda means we are not doing *our* true inner work but instead are simply perpetuating some collective/ideological system's needs at the expense of our souls. This implies that we ought not to work with images from the perspective of any organized belief system. If I see a snake through a Christian mind-set, I condemn it as evil, Satanic. If I see the same snake through some Eastern teaching, I might say that snake is the kundalini, my serpent power. In either case, we are in danger of entirely missing the real meaning of that powerful cobra the dreamer is desperately holding at arm's length, the cobra intent on biting him.

Dreams and active imagination provide a crucial orientation to life: The significance of our own "inner" wisdom and counsel as opposed to an outer-world authority figure means the difference between following *someone else's* path and fulfilling *our own* life's potential. We can essentially trust our own psyche, *but* we have to learn how to differentiate all the *implanted* ideas, images, and attitudes from the Authentic Self. James Hillman, in his book *The Force of Character and the Lasting Life*, writes about these potent exterior forces: "Of these conditionings none are more tyrannical than the convictions that clamp the mind and heart into positivistic science (geneticism and computerism), economics (bottom-line capitalism), and single-minded faith (fundamentalism);"[7] all of these "conditionings" and many other similar tyrannies keep our unlived lives imprisoned, institutionalized, and hidden away.

Technology as God, the solution for everything that ails humankind, robs us of our innate humanity and interconnectedness with all life, as does "bottom-line capitalism" when it becomes the dominant guiding authority in one's life. Fundamentalism, in particular its literalizing of myth and image, is perhaps the most dangerous and potentially destructive of these group conditionings, and extreme fundamentalism is now an ominous gathering storm in many of the world's major religions.

Accessing the Remarkable Power of Images

Chased by a Dignified Elephant

Over a period of time certain images emerge from dreams and sometimes the imagination, images that we can use in our everyday life, images that hold aspects of the Authentic Self. Dream animals in particular often are the equivalent of the canary in the mine shaft; dilemmas or problems with animals in dreams usually mean that we are injuring or blocking a natural, authentic part of ourselves. Or we may be afraid of our own wildness, our uncivilized, non-rule-following Self who lives *outside* our "civilized," village life.

For example a woman had several dreams about an African elephant. In the first dream, the elephant was chasing her. In a later dream, she was running after the same elephant. Intrigued with this dream elephant, she began to paint images of the elephant's face, which she described as beautiful, dignified, and mysterious. A unique image and likely a potent aspect of who she really is, her elephant gradually emerged as a dream totem, an image she can go to with questions and problems about her life. The elephant becomes, as Hillman suggests, a "carrier of soul, a carrier of our own free-soul, there to help us see in the dark."[8] The "dark," whether awake or asleep, is our not knowing or seeing who we are, what our innate character is and what we must do with our life.

Stepping onto Another's Path

Norma Churchill, a California artist, uses a process of visualization similar to Jung's active imagination to create waking dreams. This example is from her journal and illustrates the danger of following another person's path. Her visualization began with a search for a god's footprint in the wet sand on a beach. When she found the footprint, she felt drawn to place her foot in it, and when she did, she felt instant pain and agony.[9] Churchill describes what happened next:

> A golden serpent comes up out of the sea and surf and wraps itself around me and drags me into the sea. We go under the waters.
>
> Still I suffer. We come to a tranquil beautiful island where the serpent lays me on a bed of cool green grass. He plucks some moss and packs it around my foot. . . . Suddenly the serpent lurches back and becomes numinous. With unhinged jaws it holds a huge faceted diamond ball which lights up the world. I am astonished, wonder-struck!
>
> He slithers forward and presses the brilliant stone into my forehead . . . like a miner's light. My light now shines brilliantly out into the void (the world). I also suffer with this weight of light.
>
> I ask, "Why am I so wounded?" nodding, toward my crippled foot.
>
> The serpent answers, "You must not step into another's path."
>
> Still I am in great agony. I realize I will remain crippled in life if I take a path other than my own.[10]

Churchill said that because of her experiences with the serpent "my life took a 180-degree turn," prompting her to explore bodywork and to create several remarkable paintings of her experiences.[11]

Dream Images and Waking Life

A Visitor from Australia

Can our natural world mirror back to us our shadow qualities? It certainly does, and here is one example from my own experience. My wife recently announced that we were going to have a visitor. A friend asked her to take care of "Buddy" while she was on a two-week vacation. Buddy turned out to be a cockatiel, a small Australian parrot with light gray and yellow plumage and a bright yellow crest of feathers standing straight up on his head, making him look like as if he just got a charge of static electricity.

Buddy finally arrived, obviously nervous and curious at the sudden change. We were excited to have this exotic visitor and for several days enjoyed whistling and talking to Buddy. One day, as I was writing, it occurred to me that Buddy might like to hear other bird calls. So I opened an encyclopedia on my computer and began playing every bird I could find for Buddy, who responded with excitement, looking around and hopping all over the place. I even threw in a tiger and some other animals. I was having a great time watching Buddy's reactions to the multitude of animals and birds.

Under Scrutiny

That evening I had a dream. In the dream Buddy was out of his cage and on my finger looking me in the eye. In fact Buddy was looking intently up and down my face and I knew he was *scrutinizing* me—checking me out. I awoke from this dream and excitedly told the dream to my wife—Wasn't it great? I had connected with Buddy's world, and of course he was checking out his new friends and surroundings. Later that morning I went for a walk and my dream came back to me, particularly the "scrutinizing" part. Suddenly and painfully memories returned of throwing rocks at birds as a young boy and even hunting trips where I shot birds as a teenager. Thankfully that part of my life was short-lived! I now knew that playing those bird and animal calls had frightened Buddy. I also remembered mercilessly teasing my younger brother when we were kids. Amazing! Buddy was showing me an aspect of my own nature that had not respected nature and its creatures—a tease that could be cruel. I felt ashamed and promptly apologized to Buddy after returning from my walk.

Here again was an example of our deep connections to the world around us and to other life forms. Not only can we learn from nature, we can do our own shadow work on a level that empowers creatures and creates a profound respect and reverence for nature and for all life. Now my work would be to find ways to integrate this young boy's cruel and teasing dynamic in a constructive manner that will not hurt others. This means being alert and aware—on the lookout for this kid's cruelty, the ways it comes out in my daily life and interpersonal relationships.

Waking Dreams

The Lost Child

Sometimes we need to use our imagination to reach a long-lost part of our essential nature. Dreamworker Ann Sayre Wiseman gives this example of extending an original dream with new material from a waking dream. The dreamer is a sixty-year-old woman in a dream group who has had a recurring dream for thirty years:

> I dream that I hear a baby crying in a room of my old house. I get up and look in every room, never finding the room or the child but still hearing its crying. It calls to me in such a deep way that I would go round and round the rooms again and never find the child, never find the room.

Wiseman explains: "I asked Cora to close her eyes, become the lost child and ask herself to find the lost room; simply see herself in the lost room. As she closed her eyes, giving herself to this suggestion, tears began to flow. She was asked not to leave the scene until she understood it. She held her face and sobbed as we waited silently. When she opened her eyes, she said the child was herself. She found it on the other side of the mirror, where it had been crying since she was seven. It wanted to be an artist and had waited all those years for her to find *room for her*."[12]

Cora's dream again points to the value of recurring dreams and their relentless knocking at the door of our waking life to get our attention. The fact that her dream kept recurring all those years shows that it's never too late to live your life to its fullest potential.

Her dream is also an excellent example of how important it is to explore all aspects of a dream including elements that are missing or lost. Cora's lost child represented her lost and abandoned artistic talent. And this inner artist wanted to be found; she wanted Cora to reach into her own depths, reach back in time into her "old house" and rescue her— that creative part of her Authentic Self, without which Cora would continue to feel like something was missing in her life, some frustrating incompleteness forever hidden from her awareness.

Using Ancient Alchemy to Understand Your Dreams and Imagination

For fifteen hundred years, alchemists plied their trade, supposedly using archaic chemistry to turn base metals such as lead into gold.

Getting the "Lead" out of Your Life

We can also extend alchemical processes from the individual psyche and dream into our society and culture. In modern times the substance we call lead has taken on new significance: literally "a soft, malleable, ductile, bluish-white, dense metallic element, extracted chiefly from galena and used in containers and pipes for corrosives, solder, bullets, radiation shielding, paints, and antiknock compounds."[13] As bullets, we "pump a target full of lead." As to toxic substances, we get the "lead" out of paint, out of our gasoline. Also interesting is the way common lead is refined. "Because galena often has other minerals associated with it, the crude lead, or pig lead, obtained from the smelting process, contains copper, zinc, silver, and gold as impurities. The recovery of these precious metals is often as important economically as the production of lead itself."[14]

This extraction of the precious elements from the crude lead is analogous to the extraction of the Authentic Self from other peoples' expectations, from social pressure, from popular stereotypes that push us into the obsessive pursuit of the "American Dream," into accumulating outer images of "success" and status. Lead's characteristics fit remarkably well with the emotional and psychological weight these influences place on the individual life. Even the actual physical symptoms of lead poisoning illustrate some of the effects of collective contamination: anemia, weakness, constipation, colic, palsy, and often paralyzed wrists and ankles, reduced intelligence, delayed motor development, impaired memory, and problems with balance and hearing.[15] We could say that by allowing the stuff out there to dominate and condition our lives, we are weakening, even poisoning our authenticity.

From this Alchemical perspective, we need to get the *collective lead*, the impenetrable denseness, the *heavy metal* out of our psyches. We need to remove the bullets of collective judgments that so wound one's sense of self—bullets that seek to kill those aspects of individual uniqueness that deviate from the accepted norm, the soul-deadening, weighted down, "averaged," and "normalized" life.

Leaden qualities—burdensome, dull, weighty, dense, lethargic—often show up in our dreams, creating an immediate dilemma. People have dreams about: metal buildings, iron structures, concrete, androids. Is the burdened feeling in a dream something we are doing to ourselves, or might it be the weight of our family's imperatives and demands that we drag along like a ball and chain? Or, does our suffering, our depression contain elements of *both*: personal issues *and* social dilemmas? Of course dreams do indeed alert us to popular ideas that have become burdens we are carrying *unnecessarily*. As you might expect, our dreams show us the effects of this contamination, this crop dusting of the individual human psyche. For instance, a person dreamt of *a lethal red tide in the ocean that prevented her from reaching the shore*. Another person dreamt that *she was buying an iron mill with an old business associate*. I once had a dream of *a poisoned stream coming from a city*.

Dismemberment Imagery in Dreams

Losing Your Head

Dreams use disturbing and graphic images to get our attention, particularly when we are subjecting ourselves to circumstances that prevent us from being ourselves. For example, a close friend of mine had a recurring nightmare while he was in a destructive religious group: He would find himself watching the group's minister chop off people's heads. His dream shocked him into realizing that an outer authority, which the minister symbolized, had severed, chopped off his mind—his ability to think for himself. By allowing the group to be the dominant voice in his life, he had become his own executioner.

The group focused on mental exercises including prayers, mantras, chanting and eliminating all "negative" thoughts, which were also *any* thoughts or ideas that did not fit into the group belief system. What at first appears to be mental self-discipline becomes the executioner's axe chopping off heads. The *minister* in his dream had nothing to do with his personality or his authenticity. His dream chose the minister as an image of mental poison that belongs to an outside ideology.

Institutional Sorcery

Dreams zero in on institutional indoctrination that can kill any creative idea that doesn't fit the way we were taught to do things. Margaret, a woman in her early thirties, had finally decided to do something about her career in teaching, which had never been satisfying or fulfilling. Years ago she had an exciting idea for a new approach to teaching dance and movement, which she never pursued. Of course, as soon as she began planning her new venture, the weather changed; dark storm clouds of self-doubt and fear moved over her life and then she had this dream:

> I see a headless person standing there silently, wearing a black gown, holding its head under one arm. I have an art piece I'm holding in my arms—it's beautiful and valuable. I'm very upset; the headless person is trying to puncture my creation.

When I asked Margaret to imagine herself as the headless person in the black gown, she explained, "I'm going to ruin her creation, kill it, and she can't stop me." I then asked her to imagine being that black gown. "I'm for a graduation ceremony, a doctorate—I'm professorial, powerful, like a sorcerer," she replied. "I'm really being hurt, maybe dying," she said when she *became* her art piece.

Margaret had always thought she had to have a degree to qualify her to do anything. As she contemplated her idea for a school of dance, she kept telling herself she *should* return to school for a degree in modern dance. These thoughts left her feeling paralyzed and putting her plans on hold until she could check out dance programs at different schools.

But her dream broke the spell, shattered the logic that said she had to jump through institutional hoops before she could follow her passion, her authentic life, her "work of art." Margaret now felt free to develop her plans and follow her own creative ideas. She stopped the self-talk about having to go back to school, those thoughts and attitudes that were like sharp knives puncturing her creativity. She felt these thoughts had their origins in society and also in her parents' well-intended promptings to "get a good education." She no longer listened to the headless magician who, like many institutions of higher learning, have lost the connection between the intellect and the heart.

Exploring the dream:

- Margaret felt that the headless person in the black gown represented society's demands. Her dream shows her that those demands have the potential to kill her creative life by institutionalizing it, by putting a straitjacket of conformity and regimentation on her essential nature.
- In any dream, be sure to explore clothing like the black gown in

the dream above. Imagine yourself *as that garment* and ask yourself:

– What is my purpose?
– Who designed me?
– How was I made?
– What sort of impression on others do I intend?
– What do I say to the world around me?
– What is it like to be a *black* (or any other color) gown?

- Notice how dreams, like Margaret's, explain the precise obstacles to living an authentic life. And how obvious it becomes that the headless person—the obstacle—is not a part of Margaret at all but instead represents outside influences, air pollution that had gotten in to her psyche.
- Once you are clear about the images in the dream, who they are and what they represent, link them to your waking life circumstances and experience. Then, with deliberation and resolve, boot these thieves out of your house forever!
- Replace those thoughts and attitudes with *your* ideas, convictions, and intuition.

Moving Through the Blackness

> No prisons are more confining than the ones of which
> we are unaware.
> —Shakespeare, *The Tempest*

Serial Murder

We also need to be alert for our reaction to buried talent and creativity, the reaction to chaining up a wild creature, suppressing an authentic life that cannot live and breathe—all potent causes of depression and anger, even rage. Consider Steven, an angry, articulate, forty-two-year-old, gifted writer and poet. He had spent most of his adult life struggling with chronic depression. Occasionally a creative idea would manage to escape the sledgehammer of his negative self-criticisms but he never let his real genius completely out of the bottle. At a particular low point, he had a disturbing dream:

I am at some sort of school or conference. Many people, including myself, are seated around a large table discussing a recent series of brutal serial murders. One of the other attendees is a young Bob Dylan. After the conference is over we go to our own rooms in a kind of dormitory. I am in a large private room at the end of the hall. Though the room is large, my bed and possessions are all crammed into the corner of the room.

I suddenly realize that I am the serial murderer, though I can't recall ever having committed any of the crimes. I also realize that Dylan suspects I am the killer. The bookshelf next to my bed is full of books on serial killers and, figuring this will give me away, I put some of the books in a hidden area next to the bookshelf. They won't all fit there, so I cover the shelf with a large piece of cloth. Dylan enters the room and begins talking with me, asking questions designed to trap me into admitting my guilt. I evade him. He begins looking at my belongings and I am terrified he will discover the hidden books and I will be exposed as the killer. This cat-and-mouse game goes on interminably.

When I asked Steven what Bob Dylan represented to him he explained: "He's an icon, the artist, a songwriter who writes obscure lyrics. He's extreme, enigmatic, hard to figure out." We talked about Bob Dylan being a unique 1960s musician who combined elements from blues, country-western, and folk music to create his own brand of protest music. The civil rights movement adopted one of his best known songs, "Blowin' in the Wind," as their anthem. The dream figure of Bob Dylan is certainly a candidate for a creative, distinctive part of Steven. In fact, Steven connected with Dylan's protest lyrics, recalling a lot of the writing he had done that was designed to stir things up. "I'm drawn to extremes," he commented.

But the real puzzler is the "serial murderer" who turns out to be Steven. However, we need to note that it is the *dreaming ego* that realizes *it* is the serial killer. Dylan also "suspects" that the dreamer is the killer and questions the dreamer, trying to get him to admit his guilt. This identification of the dreaming ego as the serial killer suggests that some aspect of Steven's waking ego is now aware of blood on its hands. But who are its victims?

When Steven explored what it would be like to be a victim and also imagined being the killer, the dream suddenly resonated. He felt each victim would represent an innocent life snuffed out along with all its creative potential. For Steven, the victims felt like his creative ideas, each with a potential life cut short. Steven's inner serial killer was like an evil composite, a dark, faceless machine that hacks each new inspiration to pieces with its razor-sharp self-criticisms, fear, and self-doubt.

Living in a small corner of a large room, he is terrified of being exposed as the killer, meaning a potent inner critic—an aspect of his "ego"—does not want to give up the safety of the status quo. If this critic allowed Steven's creative life to flourish it would potentially change everything. Steven's "ordinary world" would be transformed. Remarkably, his dream has quite likely shown him the chief cause of his depression: dead and buried creative ideas along with an unlived life.

Steven's dream shocked him into working with his self-criticism and negativity. He resolved to restart his creative life and began writing again in earnest. He gradually began to feel better. When I last heard from him he had written a complete screenplay and was in the process of looking for an agent. Naturally, it was a wonderfully creative *murder mystery*.

Exploring the dream:

- Bob Dylan represents an important part of his Authentic Self who was involved and concerned about the serial killer; a creative part of Steven who asks, "questions designed to trap [him] into admitting [his] guilt." Steven's dream illustrates the frequent dream dynamic of the Authentic Self pursuing some aspect of the dreamer's ego.
- In a dream like Steven's, where someone is killed or dies, it's important to explore the victim and the killer using these particular questions:
  - As the victim or the killer, how would you explain *who* and *what* you are to a person who had just arrived from Mars and had *no concept* of what a victim or a killer was?
  - As the killer, what is your life like?
  - If we imagine being a victim, what is life like? The answer might go something like this: "I have a life to live and that life has been aborted. I have come to birth from an act of passion and love and I am innocent; I don't deserve to be murdered. It's utterly tragic and unnecessary."
  - Then link your observations, experience, and feelings to your waking life.

An All-White World

In our dreams we encounter color: people dream of going into a *gray* warehouse, driving a bright red sports car, in the backseat of a black Mercedes, a deep blue sky.

The destructive side of the color white as a violation of the individual psyche, for example, would be the supremacy of any perfectionist, puritanical outside ideology—an all-white spirituality or theology. Consequently dreams of whiteness, white stuff, white walls, white cars, white buildings, etc. Taken in and followed as an ideal, such outside thought pollution lacks color and passion, what the Alchemists called "reddening"; we are missing the full spectrum of feelings and emotions, *both* dark and light. Perhaps our dreams are saying we are making everything look "good," including ourselves, *whitewashing* our life.

While I was in my spiritual group, "whiteness," which to me symbolized perfection, purity, and goodness, proliferated in my dreams. A friend of mine in the same group dreamt she was wearing *white* elevator shoes. I dreamt of: buying a *white* apartment building, being in a *white* car with "*Good*-year" tires with my spiritual teacher, a *white* powder covering everything at church, *white* worms in my neck, *white* snakes, a monk's robe turning *white*, a *white* briefcase, taking *white* vitamins, a *white* Mercedes with Lady Bird Johnson driving, an *all-white* house, a *white* tiger trying to get out of a *white* house, a *white* house with nothing inside, a man in *white* armor, a *white* motor boat in shallow water, church ministers teaching at a prison with *white* walls, faces buried under *white* grave markers. There are many more, but you get the idea: way too much of *one side* of something, trapped in an "abstract, ideal state," devoid of passion, far removed from my authentic life. Trying to find my authentic nature or even my own identity would have been like trying to find a polar bear in a snow storm.

As the body needs blood, life needs passion. Passion, whether an angry storm or a creative fire, adds color, redness, and vitality to life. In his book *The Dream and the Underworld*, James Hillman described this dream: "Another man dreams of standing on his head after three precise summersaults. Later, he tells me that he then tried it and experienced blood rushing into his ears. He had never imagined his head with blood in it before; . . . . He began to think in a new way and started to have what he called bloody red thoughts, that were both rebellious and also like obscene pranks." Passion—"bloody red" life—had returned to his thinking process.

Earth, Fire, Air, and Water

Water Symbolism

I Am the River

First and foremost, water is elemental, natural, and necessary for life. Water flows into our dreams in an endless variety of forms and circumstances, from rain to floods, from tears to ice, from brook to ocean. Regardless of the nature of the image or the kind of water in our dreams, we need to experience what it is like to be that particular water in our dream: what is it like to *be* the Columbia River—a powerful current carrying everything in it *into* the Pacific Ocean—and, for example, experience someone jumping from the bridge *into* you? Is it a death? Is the death suicide? Have we jumped *into* something, a situation, a group, an ideology, a circumstance so overwhelming that we lose our own volition and autonomy, carried along by forces that render us powerless?

We don't have to apply any dream theory or method. We can trust the "Columbia River" in our dream to tell us who and what it is, where it is going, where it has come from, and how it became what it is right now along with the modern world's impact on its native state.

Finally the Columbia is not only a metaphor for something happening or about to happen in the dreamer's waking life. It will help us understand how we can become more authentic and natural. Such a river might represent an aspect of society, the *mainstream*, a formidable current moving in *one* direction, a current that we can move against only with tremendous effort. But even more potent social forces shape the course of the river: A series of hydroelectric power plants control, dam, and siphon off energy to power modern civilization in the Pacific Northwest. If you *are* the Columbia, you are no longer allowed to be totally yourself. One of the major rivers that joins the Columbia in Portland, Oregon—the Willamette—is so polluted it has been designated a Superfund Site by the EPA.

Swimming in the Pool

We may find ourselves doing laps in our high school swimming pool, a manufactured container designed for a specific purpose—a very different type of water imagery. We would want to imagine *being* the container, the pool floor, and the walls in a high school environment as well as being *that water*, which is certainly trapped, not free to flow anywhere. And when we imagine *being* that pool water, we realize that we have been altered, treated with chemicals; something foreign and *unnatural* has been *put into us*.

Tidal Waves and Floods

The Sea Monster

When we are caught up in how we look to others, we can completely hide anything authentic behind our public face. Dreams help us identify what we are really doing to ourselves and show us how to extricate ourselves from the impossible task of trying to be what we believe others expect us to be. Carly, a young woman in her late twenties, was obsessed with her appearance and with "fitting in." She had this dream:

> I'm at a resort in Mexico on the beach. It's kind of overcast.
> There are lots of people out on the beach. Lots of big waves are
> coming in and we all run to escape them in a playful way. Then
> a huge wave comes that is probably fifty stories high! We all
> scream in terror and try climbing up over the sand bank into the
> jungle but we can't. Then the wave stops moving and the water
> falls down off a huge sea monster! I envision a Tyrannosaurus
> Rex stomping onto the beach and eating me. I'm trying so hard
> to get over the sand bank but I can't. I think of hiding in the
> sand; will it see me? It seems a little bewildered. It won't notice
> us. Is it bad?

Carly explained that the resort was a place she had actually visited with a group of her friends several years ago. She recalled a lot of drinking and partying and said that in spite of feeling extremely uncomfortable, she did her best to modify her behavior in order to be accepted by the group. I asked Carly, "If you are that resort, what do you do for people? What is your job?" "I make everyone feel really good. I give them an escape from the real world—that's my job," she replied. When asked about the giant wave, she described it as "very powerful, overwhelming, impossible to get away from." And when Carly imagined *being* the sea monster, she said that "it was like coming to birth—like the ocean was giving birth to me, this creature. I feel very powerful but cautious, like just stepping into a new world."

In Carly's dream it's important to explore all the dream elements including the "sand" which prevented their escape. I asked Carly what it would be like to be the sand bank or a grain of sand? She explained,

"I'm [speaking as the sand] really shifty, too soft to support someone—I could suffocate people, cover them up." Describing a grain of sand, "I'm so insignificant! I'm just like billions of others. I've been worn down into almost nothing."

The sand represented Carly's actual feelings of insignificance, feelings that her individual life did not really matter—an individual life that felt overwhelmed by the masses, that felt indistinguishable from everyone else. The sand symbolized Carly's attitudes, thoughts, and self-talk about the unimportance and irrelevance of her life. In her dream, the ocean, like a mother's womb, gives birth to a powerful, immense creature—a creature that terrifies the dreamer's *dreaming ego*, which, you will recall, reacts in the dream just as we would if we actually encountered the dream situation in our waking life. Hence the sea monster seems frightening and monstrous to Carly's dreaming ego, which, in her dream, represented the part of her personality that put her into a role of pleasing and adapting to a group of friends that she had outgrown. At the time she had the dream she was struggling with freeing herself from patterns she felt stuck in and her exhausting efforts to be someone that the group would accept instead of just being herself. Her dream enabled her to step free of this self-inflicted role-playing in order to conform to her old crowd, a group of individuals who had very negative views of life, complained about everything, spent most of their free time partying, and never did anything constructive with their lives.

Her dream shows her that something elemental, natural, huge, and immensely powerful has emerged from the depths of the ocean, from the depths of her psyche, from the source of all life—something that is definitely *after* her conforming-to-the-group persona, which it's going to "eat." Something quite unique and *authentic* had come to birth in Carly's nature. She would no longer be able to "hide in the sand" of conformity—hiding from her own Authentic Self. She felt a tremendous relief from no longer having to perform, having to put on an act for people she no longer respected or related to. Carly began living more out of her Authentic Self, she began to relax into being herself. And Carly began to feel that she did indeed have *tremendous power* to make a difference in the world. Her life no longer felt irrelevant.

Exploring the dream:

- When dreams take you back in time, it often means that something that happened back then is relevant to some situation or dynamic occurring in the present.
- Always explore each and every image in your dream, particularly any natural elements like the ocean and the sand in Carly's dream.

- When dreams exaggerate or emphasize size like the "fifty story" wave or the "huge" sea monster, your dream is saying that the meaning is big, much bigger and more important than you might imagine.
- In Carly's dream she had to be watchful for her tendency to "hide out" by not being herself. It often seems much easier to slip back into familiar patterns even when they are self-destructive instead of stepping into unknown territory of the Authentic Self.

Walkabouts:

- If you're having trouble understanding a dream, take a walk in nature, meander, reflect on your dream, and let your dream images speak to you through the natural world.

Sinking and Drowning

Pulled Apart

Dreams often use water to symbolically portray the end of something. We then need to determine what that ending means. A thirty-five year old doctor, upset by a floundering romance, had this initial dream:

> We are stranded at sea and our boat is being pulled apart. There are these connections in the middle keeping it together but our leader decides to cut one of the connections to relieve some stress. As soon as he does so, both halves of the boat separate, are upended and sink. Everyone is thrown into the water and now there are large icebergs moving erratically all around. I remain calm because I keep saying that I know that nobody will be killed because I read the book and I know how the story ends.

He realized that his dream was preparing him for the inevitable breakup of his relationship, while reassuring him that he would survive. The dream illustrates how a traumatic life experience plunges one into the unconscious (the sea). Moreover, he *knows* how the story ends. The dream tells him that he is in for a frightening experience but he will be okay.

During his therapy sessions, he explored the many connections that had proved to be self-destructive for him. Cutting the connections required understanding what was keeping him in the relationship and what he was projecting onto his girlfriend. He began to sort out dysfunctional attitudes and for the first time began to look at recurring patterns in his life that had always caused him difficulty. A big part of his dreamwork included taking back those projected qualities, which actually represented vital parts of who he was. He had seen in his girlfriend the life he always wanted to live but had never attained. He was miserable without her, and only felt whole when they were together and he could be a significant part of her life. So, you're thinking, "He's in love. What's wrong with that?" Nothing, but in this case, he could not see his own value and was unable to connect with who he really was. He was "lost at sea" in the relationship.

The erratically moving (confusion and chaos) icebergs represent *differentiated* (separated from the ice pack) unconscious material that is now partially exposed to the light of consciousness, but still only the "tip of the iceberg," meaning that a lot of work remains to be done, since so much material still remains submerged, still in the unconscious. The process of dreamwork and self-reflection will apply the required heat—the sunlight of his conscious awareness—to gradually thaw the icebergs. This dream shows how the breakup of his relationship was the catalyst for his transformative plunge into the unconscious—for a reexamination of his life and who he was.

The icebergs in this dream also illustrate how important it is to look at the *natural* state of an image. To understand the full meaning of the image, you must *become the image* in *its* world. If *you* are an iceberg you are hard, icy, frozen solid. But suddenly detached and floating, you are in movement, in a process of travel, thawing out, and ultimate reintegration with the sea. For a time, you can be seen, studied, contemplated in the light of day. But you are still dangerous, particularly at night where you are quite able to sink the *titanic* ego whose arrogance lives only on the surface of life.

Getting an Icy Intersection to Talk

> We cannot understand the dream until we enter it.
>
> —James Hillman

For example, a dream image of an icy intersection experienced as the "iciness" might become "the way I freeze up, become motionless, slippery." If you *are* ice, you ask yourself:

- How did I (the ice) get like this (the process of becoming rigid and slippery)?
- What has happened to me?
- How do I change myself from water into ice?
- What is my job description?

You might answer, "Something has changed me from flowing liquid to something hard and impenetrable. A sudden storm? My temperature (emotional intensity) has dropped—I'm playing it *cool*. I'm treacherous to approach or walk on: people should avoid me. It's my job to throw people off balance. Stay away from *this* intersection!" Ice now becomes a metaphor for how we respond when a storm hits: when an emotional confrontation with a partner erupts, etc. We begin to understand our *inner icemaker* as a part of ourselves that is simply surviving some bad weather, but in our adult relationships, this "icemaker" could wreak considerable havoc if given free rein in our life. And the *icemaker* could stop *cold* all growth and movement.

Fire!

When fire breaks out in a dream it not only gets our attention, it carries a sense of transformation: death, something ending, something being consumed, something reduced to ashes. We "burn our bridges" behind us. We are *consumed* with rage. We are on fire with enthusiasm. One person who had a serious temper problem dreamt of an angry bear whose fur would burst into flames.

Rising from the Ashes

Burning Up the Straw Boy

A teenager searching for his own identity has this dream:

> I'm babysitting a straw boy. The boy is playing and gets burned up in the fireplace and I have to go tell his mother about how I'd not been able to be a good babysitter, that the child had burned up. Then the child gets reborn. I scrape up the ashes from the hearth and re-create a live boy out of that.[16]

A straightforward dream about transformation of a "straw" boy into a real boy who comes from the ashes—from what's left when the straw is gone. We know from the dream that the *straw boy* gets burned up; something unreal, inauthentic, unimportant, insubstantial, with almost no value, ends. But the ashes give birth to an authentic, "live boy." A dream that would certainly mark an important transition for the dreamer, possibly a maturing and growing up; an end to taking care of (babysitting) something made of *straw*.

So what about the ashes? His dream says the experience of feeling like a straw boy, unreal and unimportant, provides the raw material to create a *real* boy. But the real boy emerges only *after* the fire has burned up the straw—when all the "straw boy" feelings, attitudes, and behaviors are gone. Or maybe the straw boy is a role the dreamer no longer wants to play: a younger version of a "straw man," someone who is set up as cover or a front for a questionable enterprise.[17]

Saving the Story

In some dreams fire burns up everything that is not needed for the dreamer's authentic life. For example, a writer who was trying to decide if she should continue multiple interests or just focus on her writing dreamt that her house was burning down and she went back in to save the only thing that was of real value to her—her manuscript for a novel she had been working on. But we take the dream literally if we look at her manuscript as the actual novel. Instead, odds are, the manuscript she saves is her life's work, her story, which she is writing as she lives.

She knew the house was her childhood home even though it did not look like the house in the dream. For her that house represented heavy-duty pressure and expectations about her life and her career, which had prevented her from following her creative writing for years. That structure, that well-intended parental advice, while feeling comfortable and secure to her waking ego, was a giant detour sign sending her down the wrong road.

Contact

- My dream: I was standing in the middle of a road. Suddenly a small, oval, light blue spacecraft landed right in front of me. I was told that this was my craft and ordered to get into it. As I opened the door and stepped into the ship, I stepped into space and was at once in and surrounded by stars in all directions. I felt a tremendous expansion and unity with space and with the universe. The shock of the experience woke me up.

Up in the Air

The Cement Jesus

Jeremy, a twenty-four-year-old who had just graduated from college, was in the process of trying to extricate himself from gender stereotypes and from intolerant, fundamentalist Christian attitudes when he had this dream:

> I was at the Grand Canyon with all the guys from my gay support group. Out from the sky came a cement throne and a cement Jesus. I noticed how close to the edge he was and how at any moment he could possibly fall down if he stepped off the throne. I figured he was Jesus and he could take care of himself. Then I was up on the ledge there with Jesus and we were talking and in each other's presence when I noticed a strong wind and it slowly blew Jesus away into the air and then he was gone. He was like dust particles. It was dark and almost stormy. He was very masculine and rigid, yet he delicately blew away and became dust in the wind.

For Jeremy, Jesus represented "the 'shoulds,' the right way to be. He told me, "I don't feel straight *or* gay. I feel unique." He had been feeling uncomfortable with his gay support group, commenting that they were judgmental and not very tolerant of anyone who disagreed with their ideas.

When I asked him to explain what "cement" is, his answer surprised me: "It's small particles of rock," he said. Then, hesitating, added, "It's many small individuals bound together as a religion." The wind turned all the rigid ideas and judgments Jeremy associated with Jesus and Christianity into dust. The belief system represented by Christian fundamentalism disintegrated, fell apart. Jeremy felt free of the weight of religious judgments about his sexuality. His dream said that those religious attitudes and beliefs were like concrete: unbending, stiff, and rigid. That *cement Jesus* has nothing to do with Jeremy's Authentic Self. It represents a man-made, "concretized," homophobic belief system that had been a barbed wire barrier of guilt for Jeremy.

Flying Dreams

Suddenly we're airborne, soaring through the air in our dream, levitating into space, weightless, floating, circling—an eagle gliding on the wind currents. Or we are flying but we are *in* something, *contained* by something, wrapped up in something manufactured; it's as though our dream covers us with a symbolic skin and we're left wondering what on earth it means. Or we find ourselves plummeting, falling, about to splatter on the rocks below, about to hit the "hard ground of reality." And what about *moving through* "air"? What exactly *is* air in a dream? What does the air *feel* as you move through it? If you *are* the air, what is your job? If you are the atmosphere enveloping the earth, what and who are you? What's been happening to you?

The Lost Pilot

Remember Robert, who wanted to reconnect with his love for music and extricate himself from a corporate career tomb that was killing his creative life? He brought this dream to one of our sessions:

> I was flying in a large plane and was supposed to assist the pilot who was very experienced flying the large plane but didn't know the way on this tour we were going on. I was helping him with the pre-landing checklist and the landing checklist.

When Robert role-played being the pilot, he said, "I'm very skilled and qualified—responsible and dependable. I save for retirement." Suddenly hesitating and with a knowing smile, he explained, "He helps me navigate the collective. He doesn't know how to do the tour," which Robert said felt like a "relaxing vacation." The "tour" represented a time-out from his regimented, planned life that was following a pre-approved schedule: work hard nine-to-five, save for retirement, quit at age sixty-five, find a hobby if you don't already have one, get a burial plot.

The pilot knows how to fly the predetermined routes and how to stay on schedule, but he needs Robert's help to land. The pilot, while necessary to "navigate the collective," proves helpless entering undesigned, creative space. Robert is flying; he's free of gravity, but he's *contained* in something, something designed to help him follow outside plans and expectations, not his own unique path. The plane, according to Robert, "could care less. It's just doing what it was built to do—mostly it's on auto-pilot." The plane became a manufactured, aluminum skin, a potential straitjacket that would keep Robert's life on a socially acceptable, pre-planned course.

This dream inspired Robert to carve out creative space in his busy life, to take time out for self-reflection, to give psychological space to his creative self and to allow his Authentic Self room to grow and to have a voice in his life that he listened to. And he became more and more aware of the times he was wearing his "flying-on auto-pilot suit," doing what he "should" do based on everyone else's plans.

Exploring the dream:

- Robert's dream illustrates an important category of imagery: *containment*. Whenever we find ourselves *in* something, whether a jumbo jet, a house, or a fire-engine-red sports car, we are under the influence of a cluster of attitudes, ideas, feelings, and passions that may or may not be aspects of our Authentic Self.
- In such dreams, be sure to explore the "container" thoroughly. Imagine you *are* the container in your dream and ask yourself these questions:
- Who made me?
  - Who or what designed me?
  - What is my job?
  - What am I supposed to do for people, or for the dreamer?
  - What sort of process have I gone through to become what I now am?
  - What is my life like?

Going Underground

Invasion

My good friend Naomi loved the outdoors and a natural life style. A marathon walker, she looked ten years younger than her fifty-one years. She had struggled for many years to differentiate herself from parental influences that had shredded her self-worth. She told me about one of the dreams that helped her realize what had been *put on* her inner *landscape*:

> Driving in a car with my parents. Me in the backseat . . . We seem to be on a pleasure drive looking at how housing has taken over the landscape. We're driving along the beach, but what we see mostly is houses, even garages, built into the hillsides. There are still some tall palm trees visible.

For Naomi, the landscape, the earth, represented her natural, original state. She also said that that dream landscape was "her childhood in southern California," a childhood that forced her to always take a back-seat, put her parents' issues and problems ahead of her own. She was *in* her parents' car and one of her parents was driving, meaning that she was under their control and influence—certainly a necessary state of affairs for a child. "Housing" covered the landscape of her childhood; housing comes from the Latin, *hucia, hulcia, hultia*, meaning a "protective covering."[18] In order to stay safe, sheltered, and protected, in order to survive, she had to go along for the "ride," go along with her parents' attitudes and ideas and their treatment of her.

This dream illustrates a dynamic that, unfortunately, is all too common in our society: how, as children, we often find ourselves in the position of selling out, betraying or compromising our authenticity in order to survive.

Exploring the dream:

- In any dream imagery of something manufactured or man-made, built on or put upon the land, we need to explore the dream from the perspective of the land:
  - What would it be like to be *that* landscape in Naomi's dream?
  - What has been happening to you as the landscape?
  - As the landscape, what do you need now?
- It would be equally important to imagine being the "housing," asking yourself:
  - What is my job as "housing"?
  - Who built me?
  - What do people expect from me?
- In this dream, the "housing," her parents' car, and her parents' influences that were "driving" her are *not* a part of Naomi's Authentic Self. The landscape and the ocean *are*.
- Dreams with obvious parental influences put us into a sorting out dilemma: We must keep those values and characteristics that support our essential nature—who we really are—while identifying and eliminating the poisoned food that can slowly kill the natural individual.

Naomi realized from this dream and many others with related themes, that she needed to embrace that little girl who was still in survival mode in Naomi's adult world, but operating unseen in her unconscious. Using her dreams, she successfully separated herself from those structures, the *housing*, that, like built-in software, would put her onto a merry-go-round of pleasing others at the expense of living her own life. Naomi began to feel more herself. Her confidence returned along with a healthy, independent sense of self. She made time for her creative life and overcame parental-like demands on herself that had been keeping her unnecessarily imprisoned at a job she hated. Dream by dream, she removed everything unnatural that had been *put upon the land.*

Dreams of Nuclear War

The End of the World

Over the years I have encountered many individuals who have had dreams of nuclear devastation, which can have a very different meaning depending on the context of the dream and the dreamer's life. Sometimes a nuclear war symbolizes the utter destruction of one's natural Self from powerful collective influences; nuclear weapons are, on the one hand, a creation of the collective world, the modern nation state. On the other hand, a nuclear holocaust can represent the obliterated landscape of severe depression, or it can mean exploding one's "nuclear family." Atomic weaponry has provided our dreams with a rich and powerful symbolism, a scenario that evokes images of the end of civilization with everything wiped out. Dreams have used a variety of catastrophic images for thousands of years to represent transformation—the complete end of one life and the beginning of a new life.

In my experience, dreams of a nuclear bomb or nuclear war do not have the sort of "mundane" meaning a popular psychotherapist suggests in this dream from one of her clients who decided to reduce the frequency of her therapy sessions after she became pregnant. Her client dreamt:

> A nuclear holocaust has occurred. I am in a room; I look out and see a mushroom cloud with multiple colors. I think, "Oh shit, someone finally did it." I decide I would rather die immediately than linger on with radiation sickness, yet I am attempting to survive. Then, due to the catastrophe, civilized restraint is gone in the world: I encounter people fighting, engaged in lethal combat—there were no more *normal controls.*[19]

The therapist said, "The patient's associations dealt mostly with her frightened feelings about reducing her visits to me to one time per week. We attributed this apocalyptic dream to a rather mundane and nonviolent concern: her fear of the possible symptomatic consequences of reducing the analytic frequency." This interpretation, perhaps helpful on a relatively *mundane* level, does not get into the real power and message of such a dream. It is highly unlikely that changing the frequency of therapy sessions would result in a dream about a "nuclear holocaust."

Let's take another look at this dream. It's also *extremely* improbable that this dream might be literal, a prophecy of a future Armageddon, the end of the world. But that predictable old dreaming ego reacts literally to the dream as usual. However there are important clues that point to a dream about sudden transformation: The dreaming ego's "attempting to survive" is familiar behavior for both the dreaming and the waking ego.

Then the dreamer observes that "*civilized restraint* is gone" and "there were no more *normal controls*." The basic dream is saying that the explosion and transformation have to do with removing collective *restraints* and *controls* that were keeping her authentic life *too* "civilized." And when this transformation takes place, it releases tremendous energy that was formerly bound up in the effort of restraining and controlling her life.

Finally, we have "people fighting, engaged in lethal combat," a predictable inner battle between the uncivilized, unrestrained characteristics of the dreamer and the outer world's rules, regulations, and pressure to conform. There is *nothing* "normal" about an authentic life, nor can our creative potential survive in the poisonous atmosphere of restraint and limitation.

This dream almost certainly has to do with a powerful inner transformation and the ensuing consequences for the dreamer's life. Her dream tells her that this process either has already happened or is going to happen in the very near future—it's inevitable! And we know, because it is *nuclear*, that she can expect a fireball, a flash of *illumination* like the light of a thousand suns. And you can be sure that she will experience the blast, the heat, the shock waves in her life from this event.

Exploring the dream:

- In dreams of explosions or a nuclear explosion, ask yourself, What is being exploded, blown up, wiped out?
- Look for dream puns like blowing up the "nuclear family," dropping a "bomb."
- Remember to explore *what* the nuclear bomb wiped out. In the dream above, we would also want to imagine *being* "normal controls" and "civil restraints." Then we would look for ways we might be imposing these controls and restraints on ourseves.
- Check out corrective aspects of the dream. In our example dream,

some creative chaos, civil disobedience, and breaking the rules may be just what is needed in the dreamer's life.
- Don't let literality throw its net over you. Civil disobedience does not mean you should throw a rock through that irksome neighbor's window or in any way harm others or yourself. It does say to start thinking outside internalized rules, *shoulds*, and *should nots*.
- Our dreams use images of the "world," or "civilization," to represent our life, where we are in it, and often what is just around some sharp curve in the road.

Saving the *Only* Life You Can Save

Saving the World

Ted, a depressed and disillusioned twenty-four-year-old, complained that he had lost control over his life. His fear of making wrong choices had paralyzed his ability to change his circumstances. Once idealistic and wanting to do something important in the world, even save it, he now felt completely powerless. Just as he was trying to decide whether or not to return to college and complete a degree in computer science, he had this dream:

> I'm on an island somewhere off the northern coast of Canada. I see Superman flying and carrying two nuclear warheads under his arms. He was worried and didn't know what to do with them. He drops one in the Atlantic ocean and the other off the coast of Canada. I hear a deep throbbing sound of nuclear fall-out. Canada is completely gone.

If you are *Superman*, "you're trying to save the world. You have gifts and it's your duty; you're an invincible force," Ted said. Thinking about his waking life, he realized that he had been trying to do just that: *save the world*. In Ted's dream, Superman, in spite of his powers, lets go of the nuclear warheads. He *drops* what Ted described as "weapons of destruction on a mass scale; the shock wave wrecks everything." Ted, with a jolt of realization, said, "Wow! I've been hit with that shock wave and it's the effect of dropping my personal mission to save the world!" Ted had assumed a Superman role, a role guaranteed to create a series of disappointments and failures.

I asked Ted what it would be like to *be* Canada? "You're very rich in natural resources but you're an *ignored* country," he replied. The "fall-out" from his role change wiped out Canada, a representation of Ted's own *natural resources*, which, in fact, he had been ignoring. Instead he was foundering in a sea of depression and had increasingly isolated himself (the "island" in his dream) from his natural abilities and talents, from his authentic nature, and from his friends. He realized the impossibility of the Superman role and felt tremendous relief when he actually let go of his "impossible mission." From his dream, Ted understood that first he needed to save himself, tap into the *natural* riches in his own psyche. Only then would he really be able to make a difference in the world.

Solving Problems with Symbolic Inquiry

You can dialogue with any dream figure in your waking life to solve problems and when you have difficult choices to make. Simply imagine being, while fully awake, your dream image. Imagine yourself thinking and feeling as though you *are* that dream figure. For example, Ted could imagine being *Canada*, the "ignored" land with all the resources. *As Canada*, he might explore how Canada feels about a new job he is considering.

Self-Exploration: Using Your Dynamic Imagination

Relax, close your eyes, and sit quietly where you will not be disturbed or distracted. Begin by imagining a blank screen in your mind's eye and place a recent dream image on the screen. Hold the image without manipulating it; let it have its own autonomy. Wait for the image to do something *on its own*. It will be apparent when this happens because the image will change or do something that is totally unexpected. Try this with different images and record your experience just as you would with a dream.

Next, pick out a dream image, figure, or creature that you feel represents an important part of your Authentic Self. This image might be a person, an animal, a city, a particular landscape, or an unusual tree. Place this image on your mental screen and ask any questions you like. Here are some possibilities:

- Who are you?
- What is your role in my life?
- Where have you come from?
- What do you need from me?
- Ask for help understanding what to do about a decision or problem you need help with.

After some practice and success with the above, try starting without any image at all. Instead *invite* anyone or anything from the inner world to come to you and begin a dialogue. It often takes patience and practice before you begin to get good results. Again, be sure to record your experience.

The soul thinks in images.
—Aristotle

CHAPTER 5

𝒟

Who You Are *Not*

No man for any considerable period, can wear one face to himself, and another to the multitude, without finally getting bewildered as to which may be the true.

—Nathaniel Hawthorne

Untying the Knot: Persona, Identity and Authenticity

The persona is that which in reality one is not, but which oneself as well as others think one is.

—Carl Jung[1]

James Joyce observed, "We walk through ourselves, meeting robbers, ghosts, giants, old men, young men, wives, widows, brothers-in-love."[2] Our dreams put tremendous energy into showing us who and what *does not* belong to us. Such dreams are like master sculptors, removing everything from the marble that is not the authentic individual. When we understand and work with this powerful dream dynamic, our authentic, original nature gradually emerges from the depths. Before we can leave the "ordinary world," we need to understand *who we are not*.

For our purposes, the "persona," originally meaning a *mask*, refers to the roles that we put ourselves in to interface with society and to survive in our collective world; chameleonlike, the persona is usually the costume that we *assume we should* display in public. This "public image" or persona enables us to adapt to our surrounding world, but this adaptation often entombs the Authentic Self. Granted, our survival and civilized social interaction require some degree of compromise. However, modern life and social pressure present a sad reality: Most people follow the collective herd, *never* realizing the immense treasure hidden in their own natures, never resurrecting the Authentic Self from its tomb of conformity and adaptation.

Roles We Play in Our Dreams

Little by little we were taught all these things. We grew into them.

—Adolph Eichmann

In actuality, most of us wear many masks—masks suitable for the occasion—but two stand out: our "in public," or collectively-inspired persona, and our "private" persona. Often our "private" persona becomes compensation for the forced, compromised public face, and thus we oscillate between these two extremes, *neither* of which expresses the Authentic Self.

Show Me the Money

Odette hated her work as a lingerie model but tolerated it for the money. "It's like being on display in the zoo—a bunch of animals drooling over you. I hate them and I hate myself." In her mid-twenties, Odette was a statuesque combination of femme fatale and natural innocence. She complained that her job was pushing her deeper into a pit of low self-esteem. She brought this dream which she called a nightmare, to one of our sessions:

> I'm talking to my boyfriend, arguing about a Rave party in
> Colorado where some girl had died. He says he'll call Michelle.
> I'm very upset.

Odette described her boyfriend, who owned a nightclub and organized Rave parties, as intelligent, passionate, and driven. When she imagined *being* a Rave party, she explained, "I'm a place where you can be yourself, go crazy."

As for Michelle, Odette thought she was "the coolest woman in the world. She knows how to ask for what she wants." In her dream she felt jealous of Michelle. Odette did not know who had died at the Colorado party.

Odette's dream gives us an example of the consequences of authenticity pushed underground when we put on a costume, put ourselves in a role or circumstance that prevents us from being authentic. Each day she put herself in a work environment that threw mud on her sense of self, making her irritable, angry, and depressed. As her self-degrading job piled more and more dirt on her essential nature, she felt increasingly attracted to Rave parties—places "where you can *be yourself*, go crazy."

But Odette knew her constant thirst for partying was not good for her, that it was even dangerous—the dead girl in her dream. She was caught in a web of dangerous *compensation* for her buried authentic life, which she unleashed at the Raves. Her authentic nature was coming out, but in a potentially destructive environment that could literally prove fatal. Her dream presents her with a solution: Her boyfriend, her intelligent, passionate side, must "call Michelle." She must connect with that part of herself she described as a person who "knows how to ask for what she wants"—those qualities of her essential nature that hold Excalibur, that hold her own power to be who she really is.

Odette began to create space in her life for her Authentic Self, space not involved with Raves, but instead creative space for her to *be herself*, to "go crazy" without any danger of harm to herself or others. She quit the job that had been cutting her self-worth to pieces. It did not take long for her to notice that her obsession with partying had fallen into the background and was no longer such a powerful influence in her life. And with welcome relief, the dark clouds of her depression began to lift.

Exploring the dream:

- When any addiction or obsession appears in your dreams, ask yourself what *it* does for you. Look for qualities that feel extreme, opposite, contrary to your "normal" behavior.
- Create space in your life to practice these qualities in a setting or circumstance that is creative, constructive, and healthy.
- If your dream has any implications for your day job, you need to consider changing your work to something that *supports* your innate nature. Allowing money to smother your essential nature in the wrong work is a death sentence to a meaningful life.
- In Odette's dream, the Rave party was an electric whirlwind of unleashed inhibitions that prevented her from connecting to her authentic nature in the rest of her life. The Rave party in her dream was *not* a part of Odette's Authentic Self. The Rave party represented a seductive self-medication—a dangerous consequence of repressing her essential nature.

Exploding the Family Tree

Our dreams, when we pay attention, affirm our progress, usually with images that impress upon us the real significance of what has happened. Carrie, an architecture student, had been struggling with low self-esteem. After considerable effort on her part to extricate herself from negative parental influences involving drug abuse and serious neglect she had this remarkable dream:

> I walk into my mother's bedroom and realize I'm in the house I grew up in. I look out the window and notice that the landscape has changed around. I can actually see Medford, the town I grew up in, in a close-in valley. It's dark outside and in the middle of the yard is a tall tree trunk with no branches or top, just a big knot near the top. Then I remember that I'd climbed up the tree a long time before and stuffed the knot full of fireworks and explosives. Just then, a green spark flies into the hole from somewhere! The whole thing explodes magnificently into a huge green fireball. All sorts of fireworks sparkle and pop around. Then a huge green stream, like a rocket, explodes out of the hole and heads down the hill for Medford—the tree is wiped out! I'm transfixed at the window, hoping for—I don't know what sort of destruction. The stream hits the mountainside, exploding houses and causing a huge mudslide to slide down violently into Medford! I could see it was going to wipe out the church too. It was phenomenal to see it! I thought, I don't think I'll tell anyone I put those there. But somehow it was exhilarating.

Carrie's dream, with stunning images, illustrates the awesome power and energy released when we free ourselves from negative family programming. Carrie realized she had "exploded" her family tree along with the gnarled knot of parental expectations and their negative, gloomy attitudes about life and about women. Carrie looks at this amazing scene *through* her mother's bedroom window. She described her mother as particularly demeaning of women with their primary purpose in life to be subservient to men, and to serve as sexual objects for men. Imagining being this branchless tree, Carrie explained, "I'm very big and very old—dead—nothing growing or green. I've been dead a long time and with no branches I can't support or shelter anyone anymore. I'm old and useless."

Survival Structures

Carrie's parents were Christian fundamentalists and this green, exploding force is going to also "wipe out the church." Her dream means that the restrictive, negative, religious ideas and absolutist rules that put down women are also ending. For Carrie, the "exploding houses" in her dream represented *survival structures* she had constructed in order to adapt and to survive in her family as a child. These structures would no longer "stand up." And Carrie would no longer live her life under the influence of those self-destructive ideas and attitudes.

This dream became a transformational marker in Carrie's life—a new beginning free of outside influences that were effectively preventing her from living her authentic life. She felt that she had many more choices, more potential, and that she now had the power to create a meaningful life. She had indeed pulled Excalibur from a massive boulder.

Exploring the dream:

- Identify the survival structures in your dreams—how you survived in your family and the roles you played in order to survive and adapt.
- Observe your thinking: those ideas and attitudes related to your survival structures. Compare them to what *you* really think and feel. Eliminate each and every idea and attitude that does not fit or feel right for *you*.
- Replace each of these outside, implanted attitudes and ideas with *your* own ideas, values, and feelings.
- When you explode one of your old survival structures that has become a barrier in your life, you will have newfound energy and power to move forward in your life.

Exploding the Family Van

Anne, a twenty-eight-year-old musician and songwriter, had been using her dreams for several years to extricate herself from the trauma of growing up in an abusive family, and to give her the confidence to follow her passions—music and psychology. Her father, a minister of a large church, had sexually abused Anne for years. After she left the church in her early twenties, her entire family, all members of her father's church, shunned her, refusing to have any contact with her. This dream affirmed her inner work and the courage to live her own life:

I am on a river in the white Dodge van with several others in-cluding my parents. I stand up towards the front and realize we are moving fast, too fast, so I walk back to my seat in the back and put my seat belt on. The seat belt was somewhat difficult to put on. Suddenly the van explodes, I land in a lake and I am left floating by myself on my seat with my seat belt still on. The water is warm and feels like a hot springs. I love the warmth.

As soon as Anne told me the white Dodge van was their main family car for years when she was a child, and her "seat in the back" was actu-ally where she used to sit, the dream's meaning became obvious. Anne's dreamwork and applying it in her waking life had "exploded" the fam-ily van. That family structure or vehicle was blown apart. She was no longer strapped into her families' belief system, ideas, expectations, and the church. She was now really on her own and in her authentic life's journey.

But her dream also says that even after the explosion, a remnant is left—the seat belt, which Anne felt represented "something to keep the little girl in me safe and secure." She would have to be aware of the de-sire for safety and security in making choices and taking the risks asso-ciated with her music career. And she would need to talk to that little girl, comfort and reassure her.

When the van explodes, she finds herself floating in warm water and she "loves the warmth." The dream comforts and supports her, floating and embracing her within the *natural* warmth from the river, a nurtur-ing, womblike experience. It's as if her dream portrays a rebirth in the natural world, which would be a new beginning in her natural life.

Exploring the dream:

- Once we have worked our way through and out of some destruc-tive, collective situation that does not belong to our authentic character, dreams inevitably confirm and affirm our accomplish-ment.
- In Anne's dream, the *Dodge van* and the *seat belt*—a *manufac-tured* (mass-produced) restraint—have nothing to do with her Authentic Self. Instead they represent familial containment, influ-ences, and restrictions. The river and the natural world represent aspects of Anne's essential nature and the womblike, emotional warmth and comfort she will experience from living her own life.
- Remember to explore the *natural* and the *unnatural* elements in your dream thoroughly. But be careful to keep your images in the

context of your life and your dream. Just because a man-made object is in your dream it does not automatically indicate it's an outside influence.

Discards: Not This, Not That

A good friend told me about a dream she had after working hard to extricate her Authentic Self from a swamp of negative attitudes and expectations from her family. Her dream also affirms her inner work and shows her that she is in the process of getting rid of old family baggage, *stuff*, "junk" that does not belong to her. This is her dream:

> I was with my parents and grandmother in a car in Los Angeles, driving down a road we used to take on family outings when I was a kid. My father was driving. I got out and walked home because there were many tasks to be done. When I got home there was much unpacking to be done. People I had worked with at *Head Start*, my good friends, were helping me. We were working in my bedroom and a front room. The objects being brought up were old, dilapidated, and dirty. I said to throw out most of the things. My father came home. But I was overwhelmed by all this old junk that we still had to get rid of.

Her dream helped her understand how much junk she had been dragging through her life. And it gave her wonderful encouragement, showing that she was indeed unburdening herself. She had been feeling freer, empowered, no longer contained in or hammering herself with her father's strictness and his "Do what you're told" mind-set.

Toothless

Most people have had dreams about losing their teeth or teeth falling out. Teeth definitely represent something authentic, unique, and natural. As with fingerprints, we can positively identify someone from their teeth, their dental records. A workshop participant reported this dream experience:

> I recently dreamed that all my teeth fell out, one at a time and usually at embarrassing moments. I was extremely relieved when I woke up and still had my teeth in my mouth.

Elias Canetti, author of *Crowds and Power*, talks about teeth as part of a natural process of "seizing and incorporating."[3] If we imagine *being* our teeth and we inquire of ourselves, "What is my job?" we, as teeth, might reply, "to bite through things, to break things down into digestible bits and pieces, to make something easy to swallow." This dreamer's teeth fell out at "embarrassing moments." Whenever the dreamer encounters a situation that causes her to feel *self-conscious*, her teeth fall out; she loses her natural ability to just be herself in any circumstance. Therefore, in many instances, problems with teeth in dreams relate to obstructions to our being authentic.

The dreamer realized that each time she feels self-conscious or uncomfortable with herself because of outside influences, she loses a part of her authenticity because she momentarily backs down from being confident and comfortable with who she is—and a tooth falls out.

Exploring the dream:

- In dreams about teeth, imagine *being* your teeth *exactly as portrayed in your dream*. In our example dream, a tooth's experience would be quite traumatic, uprooted, *falling* out, losing one's grip, dying, becoming useless, separated from where I (as a tooth) belong. With any body part or organ in a dream it's important to think about the *role* of that particular part: *Which* tooth fell out? A "wisdom" tooth?

- Teeth can also injure and destroy, tear things apart with force. And they often allude to our ability to use our muscle, as in: "This . . . puts real teeth in it."

- Stick to the experience of your dream images within the context of your dream. Don't *manufacture* meaning; don't put something on your dream that has nothing to do with the original dream.

- When you are imagining being a particular part or dream figure, especially an inanimate object like a tooth, remember to ask, "What is my job?"

- Then think about your waking life and see what circumstances, memories, situations, or what part of yourself—for example, a part that has very little self-confidence—brings up feelings that remind you of how your tooth felt in the dream.

- Think back and recall embarrassing moments in your life. What happened to create your feelings of embarrassment? What were you hiding, or what was exposed? How do these experiences relate to you being your natural self, at ease and authentic?

- Do you see any recurring patterns, particular circumstances that always cause you embarrassment?

- What about your public image and your private view of yourself? What happens when someone sees through your public image?

The Tomb in My Mother's Closet

A good friend in her mid-fifties, who felt directionless and confused, told me about a recurring nightmare she had as a child: Her mother would be tying her to a heat register and she would wake up screaming. She recently had this disturbing dream that she could not get out of her mind:

> I'm in my mom's house where I grew up. I discover a tomb under mom's closet, like a grave. It's filled with all kinds of shoes and I'm looking for my size. Mom was sitting there, in the closet, next to the wall. She says, "I can't feel my feet."

Working on the dream, it became clear to her that her dream wanted to shock her into realizing she was living someone else's life—her mother's to be exact, who had passed away four years ago. Her mother was a glamorous woman who spent her life putting on a show to impress others.

When she became the "shoes" *in* the "tomb under mom's closet," the *shoes* said, "I'm no longer needed; our life is over. We'll never fit *your* (the dreamer's) feet." The shoes represented her mother's life, like an archaeological record, a dig into the layers of *impressions*, all the different images and roles her mother would *slip into* to fit the occasion.

"Let the dead bury their dead"—good advice for my friend, who had spent her life struggling to meet her mother's expectations, to gain her mother's approval and love. To please her mother, she consistently violated her own values, which, if expressed at all, would always antagonize her mother. Her dream exposed the "closeted" mother image, a *body* of alien attitudes responsible for sending her down countless dead end roads in search of what she believed to be her own life. And the mother has "no feeling," in her feet—no *life*, no circulation, no *feeling* connection to all that the feet represent: freedom, movement, direction, support.

Imagine not being able to feel your feet. How would you balance, stand, or walk? It would be like a part of you dying. Maybe these patterns, these negative mother-roles *are* dying; maybe there is no more life in the dreamer trying to walk in her shoes. Maybe the dark side of the mother, a bad ghost, is dying. Maybe a haunting is ending. Maybe a second funeral is in order. We could say that when she tries on her mother's shoes, she is trying to fit into someone else's expectations and example, that when she puts herself into that closet she is slowly going numb, slowly killing herself.

Her dream reveals a *still-living* "mother" in the closet with all her shoes. So is this image a part of the dreamer's psyche; is it a visitation from her dead mother; is it her *inner mother*? Not necessarily. And we don't need to concern ourselves with these questions in order to understand this type of dream. We need only stick to the image, ask the right questions, and let it (the image) speak to us.

Her dream is certainly showing her a dramatic representation of exterior influences and their consequences in her life. In this dream, the mother in the closet is most certainly *not* a part of the dreamer's authentic nature. But there is no doubt that somewhere in her psyche a little girl is still trying to please her mom, trying to fit into someone else's shoes.

Exploring the dream:

- Remember that when you are *in* a structure in a dream, it usually means you are under the influence of a set of ideas and attitudes. In the dream above, a spider web of vanity, illusion, and superficiality had caught the dreamer.
- Be alert for dreams of childhood homes or a parent's current house. Dreams tell us over and over that parental influences—good, bad, and often tragic—do not die with the physical death of parents. These influences live on, inspiring and guiding but often misdirecting and blocking our creative potential.
- When your dreams reveal negative parental influences, it means those influences, ideas, and attitudes are impacting your life *right now*.

In Hot Water

Dreams are astounding in their ability to point out experiences in our life that we might later make light of. A dream comes along and says—usually with unsettling images—that the experience not only hurt us, it deeply affected us back then and it's still affecting us in the present.

Amy Tan, the best-selling author of *The Joy Luck Club*, had a dream when she was six years old that was so "frightening" she still remem-

bers it. "I was running away from my mother. I escaped, but then someone else caught me and held me under a faucet of hot water—until I
turned into a bunch of linked sausages."[4]

Here is a likely interpretation: Amy's dream, like a cruel witch,
catches her with its scary transformation. Her dream says that when she
was a child, her mother's anger—the *hot* water—effectively changed her
behavior, turning her into "link sausage," a *processed* meat (a finely
chopped, seasoned meat that is cooked or *cured*) and a "link" just like
(conformity) all the other sausage; she is placed under a spell where she
cannot be herself. And "someone else" catches her, meaning her mother
turns into someone else: a woman boiling with anger that turns her into
"chopped meat." Amy is indeed "in *hot water*." Amy survived her
mother's wrath by turning into "link sausage": something *processed
and cured* of being different.

Self-Exploration: Asking Your Dreams for Insight and Guidance

Asking your dreams for help in making choices and decisions is an excellent tool to help you through a particularly difficult time. The practice going back to ancient Greek and Roman times, is commonly known
as "incubating" dreams, or "a ritual invoking of dreams, usually for
medical purposes, by sleeping in the temple of a particular god or hero."[5]
In modern dreamwork, incubation means asking your psyche for help
on anything that concerns you: your health, a relationship, decisions,
your career, or help understanding a puzzling or recurring dream.

For example, if you need to make an important choice about ending
a relationship, give yourself time before you go to sleep to brainstorm
all the potential consequences of ending things, and the consequences of
continuing the status quo, doing nothing, which is also a choice. Then,
just before sleep, formulate a brief question that states the problem as
clearly as possible. As author, Phyllis Koch-Sheras explains: "Whenever
you concentrate intensively on a single issue or problem just before
going to bed, you are likely to set the dream incubation process in motion and continue to work on the issue in your dreams that night."[6]

How to Frame Your Questions—What to Expect

In our example about whether to end a relationship, you might ask:
"What are the consequences if I stay in my relationship with Mark?"

Keep repeating your statement until you fall asleep. If you have difficulty focusing or find your mind wandering, number your statements in sequence: "One—What are the consequences if I stay in my relationship with Mark?" "Two—What are the consequences if I stay in my relationship with Mark?," etc. Be patient and persistent with this process—no two people recall dreams alike. Don't feel anxious or pressured, but trust your own psyche. It may take several nights of repeating your question before you recall a dream.

When you do have a dream, your first impression of the dream when waking—nearly always a literal reaction—will likely be skepticism. You need to override any initial inclination to dismiss the dream because it seems to be unrelated to your question. More than likely, your dream *will* be related to your question and just needs interpretation and reflection. Metaphor and symbolism can at first appear to be utter nonsense to the literal, logical side of the brain.

Something to keep in mind when you ask your dreams anything is the fact that dreams come from a place that is essentially autonomous. That is to say, when we inquire about a certain problem, our dreams often respond with unexpected solutions or guidance. In this sense, dream incubation has valuable potential, but we are also opening a Pandora's box, frequently getting an answer but not the one our waking ego would like or have expected.

Avoid asking *closed* questions that require a *yes* or *no* answer. Dreams like to give us the *consequences* of making choices, of taking *that* highway, of selling everything and moving to Morocco. Our dreams normally (there are *always* exceptions to any rule or generalization about dreaming) do not make choices for us. An example of an exception to this dynamic would be an emergency or a crisis situation that results in a dream showing us consequences with images so disturbing they shock us into not setting foot on that path; the dream has indeed made our decision quite clear, and we go against such dream red lights at our own peril. Dreams of this latter type come under the category of warning dreams, which come, usually at the eleventh hour, to help us avoid stepping into some pit unnecessarily.

Questions can be crafted to explore a variety of personal issues, as well as societal and political problems—a largely unexplored area in contemporary dreamwork. Here are some examples:

- Show me how to understand and develop my creativity.
- Help me to understand my authentic path in life.
- When I awake I will remember my dreams clearly and completely.

- Show me anything that is preventing me from living my authentic life.
- Clarify the cause and meaning of my illness.
- What must I do to heal my illness?
- What is causing my depression?
- Where is this relationship taking me?
- How can I effectively contribute to creating a better world?
- What can be done to make my community a creative, vibrant community.

Hidden Parts

That Thirty-Thousand-Year-Old Inner Child

> There's a boy in you about three
> Years old who hasn't learned a thing for thirty
> Thousand years. Sometimes it's a girl.
>
> This child had to make up its mind
> How to save you from death. He said things like:
> "Stay home. Avoid elevators. Eat only elk."
>
> You live with this child, but you don't know it.
> You're in the office, yes, but live with this boy
> At night. He's uninformed, but he does want
>
> To save your life. And he has. Because of this boy
> You survived a lot. He's got six big ideas.
> Five don't work. Right now he's repeating them to you.
> —Robert Bly[7]

Dreams reveal a vast inner array of parts—known and unknown, children and infants of all ages, people about our age, older people, parents, friends, figures near death, people already dead. Even when we dream about people we know, they are often portrayed at an earlier age. Robert Bly's "thirty-thousand-year-old boy" (or girl) represents ancient, inherited, instinctual survival and adaptations necessary to the survival of the species. But allowing these "parts" of the psyche to have free rein in the unconscious, or entirely repressing the energies they represent, often leads to disastrous consequences. As long as these "parts" function incognito in our unconscious, we will have a difficult time living authentically and we will not be able to differentiate ourselves from societal impulses that are not a part of the unique individuality.

And herein we encounter a dilemma: Some of our inner parts *do not belong to us*. Instead they represent forces and influences that we need to separate ourselves from; when dragged along on our inner journey, these alien ideas and attitudes interfere with and prevent us from being ourselves.

When I first left the business world to study psychology, my "make money" self, who had been quite effectively absorbed in my business life, protested vehemently and thought I would be living on the street if my philosopher/psychologist self began directing the show. My *make-money* self has created a lot of fear in my life and I still have to negotiate between these two parts. This "make-money" part of my psyche also represents a lot of potent life style and economic influences regarding money and its uses in our contemporary world—some useful, others clearly self-destructive. When we encounter such inner conflicted parts, understanding our dreams will help us to clearly distinguish useful aspects from the destructive parts, facilitating a synthesis and integration so that we can get on with our real work and passion in life.

The Pleasure Trip

In our Radical Dreaming process, identification of "parts" of the psyche that have a negative collective orientation is a crucial element—not to bargain or negotiate with these parts, but instead to expose these implanted influences, boot them out of our inner world dynamics and identify how they have influenced our waking life, our attitudes, and the choices we have made.

This dream of a fifty-year-old artist who was working on a difficult relationship of long standing with her mother provides an excellent example of how parts affect one's psyche:

> Mom, Frank (an old friend) and I are on a pleasure trip in France. I am concerned because my mother and I do not speak French, which means Frank will have to be taking care of us. Sitting at a breakfast table, Frank is being superior, impatient and grudgingly translating for us. I realized that I do know the French words for some things such as "pain" means "bread." Mom is being her squeamishly negative self, criticizing, judging

whatever is different from her point of view. Later I am alone
with one of my current girlfriends and complaining about having to be on this trip with my mother, about how difficult she is.

Frank was the son of wealthy, aristocratic parents from France. The
dreamer said "Frank could be arrogant and make others feel stupid."
Her mother was being her usual self in the dream and she felt put down
by Frank and judged by her mother. She explored her associations to
France by imagining *being* the country of France, explaining, "I have a
lot of great art and beauty—it's intimidating. I have historical weight. I
feel like an elegant goddess, exquisite sculpted marble . . ." In essence,
she was describing an important aspect of her "Self," which sometimes
shows up in dreams as a particular city. And we need to remember that
it is the *dreaming ego* that feels intimidated by the beauty and elegance
of her French Self.

Her dream tells her that she is dragging "Mom" along, meaning her
mother's influence that makes her feel bad about herself. Internalized in
her psyche and operating in the unconscious, her mother's attitudes and
criticisms would torment her through her own negative self-talk. In fact,
these influences do not belong to her at all. In the dream, she at first feels
the need to rely on Frank, an arrogant and superior figure that comes
between (interprets) her and her own authenticity.

The reference to bread in her dream is the psyche's way of saying that
something in the unconscious needs to be eaten, taken in, digested—she
understands "some" things about what France represents. Her "bread
of life" is her connection to France and all that it implies about her real
identity. Her dilemma will center around distinguishing herself from
parental influences. The dream helped her to clarify and eliminate self-
defeating attitudes, judgments, and demeaning thoughts that she had
been inflicting on herself.

Dangerous Extremes

Caged Passion

When some experience has caused us to abort our normal emotional
and psychological development, our dreams often return to the precise
time of the event in order to show us the origin and cause of a current
problem. For example, Phil, an attorney in his mid-forties, brought this
dream to one of our sessions:

I had a young girl (in her early twenties) in captivity in a cage for sex. I was very afraid she'd recognize my car's license plate number. I was afraid I'd have to kill her. She was hungry. I gave her a sandwich. I was afraid of getting caught.

His mother—a strict, religious fundamentalist—had deeply shamed him as an adolescent when he became interested in sex. He had grown up under the perverse influence of his mother's religious attitudes, which looked at sex as something bad. As an adult he found that he tended to demean women but craved indiscriminate sex with women who would not require any real commitment from him. He associated his early college life, when he was "having a ball," with the young girl (*his* early twenties)and his first experiences with women.

After working on the dream, he felt that the young girl represented an aspect of his own creative side that his early experiences with his mother's attitudes about sexuality and women had trapped. He realized if "sex is bad and forbidden" then he must keep *her* in a cage; he must keep his "women are only good for sex" outlook locked up. The fear of getting caught again illustrates the waking ego's literal reaction to the dream's content. Yet she is "hungry," and he feeds her. The "caged" side, the imprisoned "twenty-something" part, as well as his attitudes and ideas about women and sexuality need his help, his attention. He is afraid he will have to kill her, perhaps referring to his waking ego's reaction, but also indicative of the collision between the dreaming ego and the dreamer's own creativity that is so tied up with his sexuality and views about women. His desire to have sex with her indicates his desire to connect with this aspect of his own nature.

In Phil's waking life he attempted to connect sexually through dominating women and keeping them inferior. Ironically, he had trapped his own feminine side and she is hungry, needs nourishment. "I'm trapped and I'm afraid," Phil explained when he imagined being the caged woman. All that she represents in the way of creativity, feelings, intuition, and life itself is "hungry."

Moreover, the dream tells him that he needs to address his twenty-something creative self, the part of himself that went underground when he chose the legal profession instead of following his passions: photography and writing. He realized that he had kept this caged young girl imprisoned for years, which had been wreaking havoc in his life, particularly in his relationships with women.

Such images tie up tremendous energy that when released into one's conscious life is deeply transformative. It is important to keep in mind that this dream was not in any way literal, it is highly symbolic of an inner dynamic for the dreamer who indeed felt creatively frustrated and regretted his career choices.

Phil went to work identifying and eliminating the attitudes and stereotypes that demean women and sexuality. And he began to write again.

Dreams About Work

Sleeping with the Enemy

Dreams strike like lightning when we are violating our essential nature by keeping ourselves in the wrong work. We cannot live a fully authentic life as long as we remain in the wrong career or work.

Let's return to Naomi. She had survived and repaired most of the damage from growing up with an alcoholic father and coping with a mother who ignored her feelings and treated her like a doll to dress up. Now she wanted to change her role of caretaker in her family. She knew it was time to start taking care of herself, to create the time and space for reading, reflection, and her creative interests. But that meant leaving a full-time position in a medical clinic—a very difficult proposition for someone used to pulling her weight, being practical and responsible. She felt guilty and selfish in spite of a supportive partner who made more than enough money for their needs and continually encouraged her to go ahead and quit the job. In the middle of this sand storm of guilt and feeling selfish she had a dream that shocked her out of that job.

> Dr. Edwards and I were sleeping in a double bed, each of us clearly on our own side. But in the night his arm came around me. This felt like a gross violation. I quickly got up and slept on the floor.

Naomi's dream reverberated through her life like thunder. It was an ear-splitting wake-up call! "Dr. Edwards is not ethical in his practice; he misleads patients," she explained. Dr. Edwards was her boss and owned the clinic where she worked. From her dream, she realized she was "sleeping with the enemy," violating her authentic nature, and unnecessarily limiting the time for her creative life. She quit shortly after the dream. Her creative life blossomed along with her love of nature, hiking, and marathon walking. She recently told me, "Life is good, very good!"

Finding Dave Brubeck

An unusual public figure in a dream can represent valuable, detailed insight into who we are. Dennis, a sales executive in his mid-forties, realized he could no longer maintain the status quo, a state of affairs that felt more like a prison sentence than a real life, an interminable passing of days that had disconnected him from his passion. He had this dream:

> I'm talking to my actual therapist (the author), who looks older in the dream and does not really look like my therapist. I'm telling him about a dream that had three words in it: "etude," "etudinal," and "Brubeck." Suddenly I notice that he looks like the jazz musician Dave Brubeck.

When a therapist appears in a client's dream, the therapist most likely represents a person's own inner counsel. Of course it becomes important to know what qualities and attitudes the therapist represents to the client, who may be projecting certain expectations on the therapist instead of relying on his/her own inner work.

Whenever unusual words show up in dreams, it always proves valuable to check out the root meaning of the words. So we looked up the word, "etude," which means "a piece composed for the development of a specific point of technique," like a preliminary "study."[8] Now the dream began to make sense for Dennis. Dennis realized his dream was showing him that he was in the "preliminary study" phase, a preparation for his major composition, his masterpiece, which he felt meant making his life a "masterpiece." In this sense, his authentic life is the "work," his *opus*. Although we could not find "etudinal" in the dictionary, he connected this word to "attitude"—the attitude he should apply to his present life.

The therapist looks like "Dave Brubeck," who he said was one of his favorite musicians, known for his jazz compositions incorporating unusual meters. Here his dream gets more specific about what his *attitudinal* approach ought to be like: Dennis said that Brubeck represented "innovation, improvisation, constant experimenting, breaking the established rules for jazz." Dennis also told me that in Brubeck's innovative album *Time Out* (1957), he abandoned the 4/4 meter of earlier jazz compositions to experiment with a different time signature for each piece on the album. His dream inspired him to try out new rhythms in his life, to slow down, to experiment, improvise, explore different possibilities, and take a closer look at the "rules" he was *unconsciously* following in his life.

Following Gandhi

This dream, like an old friend carrying a mysterious gift, came knocking one evening at the door of a forty-seven-year-old woman I will refer to as Natalie. Natalie found herself mired in a life of empty routine, chained to a series of onerous jobs in retailing that relentlessly chewed up her time, leaving her exhausted and drained at the end of the day:

> I'm taking a bath, feeling very exposed. My husband says "I have a wonderful surprise." It's some man who has written a book about how dreams heal. The only thing the man is afraid of is that after his illness there won't be a driving force big enough to propel him onward. Then I notice the book, a small one, six-by-six inches, has a picture of Gandhi on the front. I think, It has taken me forty-seven years to find out what the dream of Gandhi meant that I had years ago when he said to "follow" him.

In her mid-twenties, Natalie had a powerful dream of Gandhi, the Indian political leader and social activist whose nonviolent protests eventually forced the British to leave, enabling India once again to govern itself. She had always admired Gandhi's rebellious nature and his refusal to accept subservience and humiliation under British domination.

Now Natalie's second dream about Gandhi's enigmatic suggestion, "Follow me," slid under her life like molten magma, like a second chance to do something meaningful with her life. For her, Gandhi represented a deeply significant part of her authentic nature, a fiery, rebellious spirit, that she had locked up in the basement, pushed out of her life and her awareness for over twenty years. No wonder Natalie now complained of "inflammatory" problems with her health—*heat* in her joints, repressed anger, fire burning deep in her psyche that screamed for expression, for an outlet.

And just *who* was Gandhi? An important question, and you can be assured that her dream chose Gandhi for a specific reason. Gandhi advocated "home rule" and self-sufficiency for the Indian people. Now "Gandhi" finally made sense. Her dream wants her to throw off the iron yoke of foreign tyranny; it wants her to expel those self-restrictive ideas and self-imposed rules that had invaded her life, erected barricades and guard stations everywhere. The dream wants *her* to be the ruler of her kingdom, and it wants her to live through her Authentic Self.

Natalie realized that she now had to find a way to express this vital aspect of her authentic nature. She began to explore creative ways to give her inner Gandhi outer expression. She began to use her long dormant artistic ability to create fabric art with a social message for women, to address through art her anger about how women are treated around the world. She began to release her creative fire into her life and her "inflammatory" condition mysteriously slipped into remission. Her doctor commented, "You're very lucky." Natalie had pulled her Excalibur from the fiery core of her unique nature. Her dream had given her a priceless gift.

For Natalie, Gandhi symbolized the reawakening of an indispensable aspect of her essential nature, and her dreams, like a wise old woman, told her she must make room for her Gandhi nature in her waking life—she must "follow" this priceless aspect of her Authentic Self. And this all happened just in time, for the dream contained a warning: " . . . the man is afraid . . . that after his illness there won't be a driving force big enough to propel him onward." Our dreams tell us that we are in a state of "illness" when we are living someone else's life, following the herd, conforming to the soul-killing dark side of society's "shoulds" and "should nots."

Exploring the dream:

- When a dream presents you with a current or historical hero/heroine who is empowering and inspiring, imagine being that person and ask: "What is my life like?" "What is my job?"
- Find out all you can about that person. Read a biography or autobiography about that individual.
- Search your waking life and your own psyche for attitudes, ideas, and characteristics that fit the dream character.
- Eliminate those ideas and attitudes representing self-defeating, outside influences, particularly those ideas and rules, like the British Empire in Natalie's dream, that attempt to destroy the heroine.
- Develop a plan to create space in your life for the qualities the person represents.
- Find a way to place these qualities in the world. *Start now*!

Where Do We Belong?

Charlotte, a soft-spoken, forty-four-year-old single mother with a six-year-old daughter, was struggling to extricate herself from a harried life she said was perpetual motion. She told me once, "John, I feel like I'm caught in this huge machine that never stops." She was working as a counselor in a mental health clinic when this dream definitely threw a monkey wrench into that machinery.

> I'm in a public restroom with a row of stalls. There's a clear glass cylinder, like a large vase sticking up about six inches from the center of the toilet. It's partially filled with water. I tell someone it's dangerous. If someone sits on it they are going to be really hurt, cut badly.

"I'm serving a larger group of people; I'm sort of bleak and stark," Charlotte said with a tinge of hopelessness in her voice as she described what it was like to imagine *being* the restroom in her dream. "Actually that place (the restroom) reminds me of the one at work," she added. Becoming the glass vase, she explained, "I've been put in the wrong place. People can't see me in here. I'm afraid I'm going to be sat on, broken. I'm meant to contain something—flowers!

"You know," Charlotte continued, "if someone sat on that vase it would cut them up pretty badly in certain areas: the sexual area, etc.,—the creative parts . . ." "That restroom; I've been taking care of other people's shit!" she said, with a voice like a sword, filled with passion, power, and a bright anger that could have shattered concrete.

Working with the dream, Charlotte realized she had put herself in the wrong place: her current work environment was restrictive, boring, and unfulfilling, particularly to her creative side. A talented artist, she had given up her artwork years ago, buried her natural genius. From her dream she realized that she was endangering her true passion: her love of art and her artistic talent. She had been wanting to get out of her job for several years. Her dream gave her the encouragement she needed to sell her home, move to a much smaller town, change her work, and create a life that would enable her to integrate her artistic side.

The vase that needed flowers—a representation of her creative, authentic nature—was in the wrong place. That dream vase not only was in the wrong place; something was missing—flowers. Flowers are natural, each blossom unique, each arrangement a one-and-only creation. Such images are often powerful metaphors for a unique life. This part of the dream resonated powerfully for Charlotte, who had felt for a long time that something was missing in her life.

One month later Charlotte quit her job and moved to a village nestled high in the Colorado Rockies, where she is now recreating her life, doing her best to live authentically.

Exploring the dream:

- Look for what is *missing* in your dream, like the flowers in Charlotte's dream.
- Something obviously missing in a dream needs to be explored and often is an important key to understanding a dream.
- Be alert for something, like Charlotte's vase, that is out of place or in the wrong environment.
  - For example, a workshop participant had a dream image of a polar bear in a train on its way to a large city. If you are that polar bear, you are definitely in the wrong place, out of your natural, authentic environment; something is *happening* to you. Something wild and natural is entering the "city," the "civilized," planned, controlled places in the dreamer's psyche—maybe just what is needed in her life?
- Charlotte's dream is an example of the power of dream images to speak to us, to complete stories, to transform the *unnatural* into the authentic, natural, essential nature.
- The restroom in her dream represented the outside world, a collective situation she had put herself in, a dynamic that had imprisoned her authentic life. That "restroom" was *not* a part of Charlotte. It was a public image her dream chose to warn her about a self-destructive collective circumstance where she "took care of other people's shit."
- In her waking life, Charlotte had to be careful to avoid "taking care of other people's shit" in any manner that would again put her in a situation that blocked her creativity or prevented her from living her own life.
- Charlotte also found a vase that looked like the one in her dream and kept it filled with flowers to remind her of the importance of caring for her natural, genuine, creative life.

Life Taking Shape

A few days after leaving her job, just as she was launching her adventure into a new life, Charlotte had this dream:

I'm in an art class and I'm shaping a round object out of clay, like a mandala shape. I keep getting more clay from the seashore where I notice some small sea creatures have died and washed

up on the shore. Next I put a cylindrical, clear piece of glass art
in the center of the clay piece.

"That glass art piece feels like the glass vase in the restroom dream,
but it's changed, more artsy and swirled on top," Charlotte observed.
After working on this dream, she realized the mandala-shaped clay piece
she was shaping *was* her new life, a unique work of art "taking shape."
And *she* was the artist and the designer. Now the glass vase had moved
into the center of a "mandala," into the center of her new life, no longer
out of place *in* the restroom. "Mandala" comes from the Sanskrit,
meaning "circle," and refers to a variety of ritualistic geometric designs
symbolizing the universe, a sacred space, or sacred enclosure.[9] She was
moving her life into a sacred space, space for her to be herself.

She obtains her clay from the seashore, a natural, fine-grained earthy
material produced by weathering of granite-type rocks. In other words,
her dream uses material that the storms, the elements—*life*—have *worn
down*, as the raw material to create a new life. Moreover, this clay comes
from the seashore, where two worlds meet, land and sea. Charlotte felt
the "washed up," dead sea creatures were her old life and also her attitudes about being too old to start over, feeding herself with the poisonous
idea: "I'm all washed up."

Once we step across a threshold into a more authentic life, our
dreams will inevitably reinforce and affirm our decision, usually impressing upon us the true significance and consequences of our choices.

Dreams and Creativity

Seduction: The Hidden Meaning of Sexual Dreams

Most sexual dreams are not literally about sex. Instead sexual dreams
are more often exploring creative dilemmas: the process of creating new
life, connecting to our passion and creative potential. For example, a
good friend who had been trying to restart her art career dreamt that
she was trying to make love with her ex husband but could not quite do
it because he couldn't maintain an erection. Their marriage had ended
long ago and they did not have any interest in getting back together. So
my friend's dream did not have any literal connection to her waking life
at all *except* on a symbolic level. She told me that her former husband
was in fact an artist. Her dream used sex, the act of creating new life, to

show her that she was unable to get back into her creative life because she could not maintain *her passion*—the "erection."

Men Without Hats

Making Love to the Poet

Julie, in her early thirties, was the office manager for a law firm, a job she put up with to "pay the bills," a job she described as "stressful and anxiety-producing." She had graduated with a degree in English literature, planning to be a writer and possibly a poet. That dream seemed long lost and forgotten. When I first met Julie, she was discouraged and depressed; she had lost any hope of ever returning to her passion for writing. We began working with her dreams, which quickly focused on obstacles to her creative life. Here's one example:

> I'm in front of my college, the Student Union (we called it the
> "Hub"). It's winter and I'm barefoot, going to a poetry reading.
> I had to walk through broken glass. The poet was sixty-ish with
> a beard. I had sex with the poet in the Hub. A woman tells me,
> "He's serious!" But I dismiss it.

Julie's dream made sense to her almost immediately. Her college represented the time in her life when her excitement and determination to be a writer were like a rising sun—"one of the best times in my life," she explained. Walking through the "broken glass" to get to the poetry reading was like "going through something nasty, mean, dangerous, a barrier," she said. "If I imagine being that broken glass," she continued, "someone's been careless, dropped something—my writing?"

I asked Julie *who* dropped it. Recalling her cavalier dismissal in her dream, she said, "The part of me that doesn't take poetry seriously." Julie's dream had shown her an enormous boulder blocking her writing, an attitude about poetry that she knew came from her parents and a society that did not value poets or poetry as serious life's work. She realized that she had to banish those ideas and attitudes if she was to follow her passion and live her own life.

This dream and others gave her the courage to restart her writing. Julie recently published her first book of poetry and is well on her way toward her "golden city."

Exploring the dream:

- In Julie's dream, having sex with the poet meant connecting to her own creative spirit. Her spirit is "serious," but her *dreaming ego* dismisses it.
- An outside attitude, like a parasite, had attached itself to her psyche. Without active effort in her waking life to rid herself of this view about poets, she would never even be able to start.
- *Starting*, taking one small step, even if only a few minutes each day, moving her hand with the pen, became her first priority. Julie carved out serious space and time for her writing, establishing her own creative space in her home, and she began to write each day. Her dreams and that small step changed her life.

Incest or Lost Potential?

This dream illustrates the dangers with looking at dreams in a literal sense. It also shows how the dreamer can then entirely miss the transformative potential in the dream. The dreamer was a middle-aged executive with asthma and had this dream soon after becoming aware of his daughter's pubescence:

> I am with my daughter . . . she wants to have sex . . . we walk around the block trying to find a secluded place . . . everywhere is too public . . . finally we hide in a clump of bushes and have sexual intercourse there.[10]

His dream was actually interpreted as "unsymbolized incestuous wishes."[11] By a psychologist. But what if this dream intends to reconnect the dreamer with his own lost potential, his soul life, his creative spirit that perhaps was abandoned long ago when *he* was his daughter's age?

Getting It Just Right

Our dreams seem to say that gender orientation is unique for each person; that each of us has a distinctive blend of masculine and feminine characteristics. Of course it helps to understand just *who* we really are as we work to understand this exploration of our creativity. Consider the following example from a depressed young man who told me that he felt his life was totally off course, that he did not even have a real sense of his own identity.

Matthew, a lanky twenty-nine-year-old art teacher, felt self-conscious and confused about his sexual orientation and his lack of traditional macho qualities. Sensitive and introverted, people often mistakenly thought he was gay. After considerable work with his dreams and shedding a lot of ideas and values that were *not* a part of his authentic nature, he had a remarkable dream:

> I'm on a beach by the ocean. I notice two attractive women swimming, so I swim out to join them. As I reach them I see the end of this wooden pole sticking up out of the water. Then the three of us are under the water and we are each grabbing the pole with both hands in three different positions. Suddenly the pole seems to slip into place deep below us, as though it has connected to the very core of the earth. I feel a tremendous sense of rightness, satisfaction, of everything being just right.

This dream was the master key opening the door to Matthew's authentic sense of Self. Everything fell into place. He felt like he had come home at last. He felt solid, grounded, connected to his Authentic Self. He realized that he had a *unique blend* of masculine and feminine qualities: "Two parts feminine and one part masculine," he said with a knowing smile that radiated confidence, self-acceptance, and contentment. Matthew's dreams, like treasure maps, had led him right to his essential nature. He had indeed found *himself*.

The "pole" in Matthew's dream, like a column or the Tree of Life, depicts a powerful, stabilizing force, the "pole of the earth," the "world axis."[12] Of course, these images symbolize Matthew's "world," his psyche, the *axis* of his essential nature around which the starry firmament of his life turns. He now has a firm grasp on his own inherent character and on his world.

Like Matthew's dream of the pole and the two women, dreams make a compelling case for a multi-faceted Self with gender and sexual orientation more like an elaborate mosaic, not just a simple either-or, gay or straight dualism.

Working with dreams like Matthew's reminds me of the extraordinary capacity of our dreams to reconnect us to ourselves, to weave their "delicate magic" into our night world and our day world. And from whence does such magic come? I like the 15th-century Indian poet Kabir's explanation:

There is a Secret One inside us;
The planets in all the galaxies
Pass through his hands like beads.[13]

Lightning Bolts: Using Poetry to Stay Connected to Your Dreams

Start reading poetry you like on a regular basis. Good poetry incorporates powerful images that enhance and inspire our imaginative faculties. Reading poetry tends to help dream recall, and it helps us better understand metaphors and symbols.

PART 3

THE ADVENTURE

Midway on our life's journey, I found myself in a dark woods, the right road lost.

—Dante, *The Divine Comedy*

CHAPTER 6

✍

Someone Is Stealing Your Life

To live fully we need both, the contractive comforts of the known, the expansive adventure of the unknown.
—Thomas McKnight, *Windows on Paradise*

Leaving the Ordinary World

We cannot live in a world that is interpreted for us by others. An interpreted world is not a home. Part of the terror is to take back our own listening, to use our own voice, to see our own light.

—Hildegard von Bingen

In this stage of our inner quest for the Authentic Self, we experience a loosening and a falling apart of our old life. The earth begins to tremble under our feet and, like a snake shedding its skin, we leave behind our former, familiar ways of relating to the world.

As the Authentic Self awakens, breaking through the ice-layered ego and emerging into our conscious awareness, it begins to push aside all the junk we have piled on from the outside world. It begins to transform our identity and sense of Self. We then find ourselves smack in the middle of nowhere, in exile, without a map, our old life a crumbling ruin receding into the night, our new life nowhere in sight. This passage from our old life to our new life is a disconcerting but essential part of our inward journey, for we must let the old habits and patterns that have held us prisoner die a natural death so that we can enter the golden city of our own authentic life.

From the perspective of our Authentic Self, our exile from the world of conformity and adaptation to social pressures is the first step in the quest to find and live an authentic life that actually will make a difference in the world. In my life, I left the ordinary world when I joined the spiritual group—a difficult ordeal but the beginning of the search for a life that had purpose and meaning beyond just survival and adaptation.

Something Is Trying to Steal Your Life

Just as we are leaving our old, *ordered* world, thieves seem to materialize out of nowhere, trying to steal our resolve, our insight, and our inspiration. Dreams portray burglars, robbers, authority figures, priests, police, military officers, dark figures breaking into our house, stealing things. Doubts, self-criticisms, self-judgments, the wrong work, fears— other people's opinions and expectations—these are the thieves that try to steal our newfound determination to live an authentic, creative life.

Your thief may be a friend who tells you that you're crazy to try that in this world. Or, a parent who asks, How will you support yourself doing that? Or, even more deadly, your own fear of the unknown sends a bullet right through your heart. We all have *natural* anxiety and fear that accompany us when we venture into creative space. Leaving the status quo, leaving something known and comfortable in spite of its soul-numbing routine, can feel like a terrifying leap, in the darkest night, off a high cliff into the unknown. We fear going back and we fear not knowing what lies ahead.

Kidnapped

Jack, an outgoing thirty-five-year-old with three master's degrees, complained of being alone and angry. The possibility of doing anything meaningful that would make a difference in society or help prevent the inexorable environmental deterioration seemed overwhelming, like fighting an impossible battle. He found himself in a dark storm of helpless frustration, growing anger, and cynicism when he dreamt that "his girl-friend was kidnapped by a group of militants."

Jack realized that the "militants" represented *his* militant side, his anger and passion about social injustice and damage to the environment. He had no outlet for his passion. Instead he spent his evenings bartending, and he had long ago given up trying to do anything with his education in environmental science and geography. As a result, his anger had become like a flame thrower out of control; anyone could and often would get burned. "I'm in everybody's face," Jack explained. "I'm way too direct. I will get up during a movie, go right over to someone and tell them to stop talking during the show." He described his girlfriend as a very creative, passionate person, someone he had grown to love and respect. His dream was telling him that his dammed-up anger and passion had turned him into a militant who was *stealing* (kidnapping) *his creative life* (his girlfriend).

His dream shocked and inspired him to refocus his anger and his creative energy on his passion: to start doing something now about social injustice and the environment. He began to write articles and explore ways he could contribute and make a difference. The flame thrower was becoming a finely tuned blowtorch—anger and passion redirected into meaningful work. Jack had stepped back into his life. His indiscriminate anger and militancy toward others, including his girlfriend, softened. He no longer felt the need to be "in everyone's face." And his relationship improved dramatically.

The Clock

A search for perfection or a state of ultimate enlightenment is a railroad to nowhere, a ghost train filled with grandiosity and egotism. Author Marc Barasch gave this example in his book *Healing Dreams*: Maureen had been a dedicated member of a spiritual group for several years. "I was trying tremendously hard to follow all the tenets, which said that I was an unawakened person, just a collection of jumbled parts that might someday, if I did everything right, become enlightened." She finally had a compelling dream that convinced her to leave the group.

> One of my teachers appeared in the form of a majestic clock so enormous it stretched all the way up into the heavens. But when I asked to see myself in the dream, to my disgust, I was shown a steaming turd! This did *not* help my sense of worthiness.[1]

A few months passed before Maureen eventually came up with a possible meaning to her dream: "I realized the dream was saying my teacher was entirely mechanical, while I had within me the beginnings of organic life."

Her interpretation seems to fit, but let's take a look at some additional possibilities. If we imagine being a spiritual teacher in the form of a "majestic clock," we *are* an "enormous" authority figure, a master of *time*—*time* is everything. From my (the clock's) perspective the dreamer is just a *pile of shit* at my feet far below—insignificant and worthless. As this *clock teacher*, I've overwhelmed the dreamer; I'm consuming her life from the heavens to the earth—taking up an "enormous" chunk of her world, the space in her life, devouring all of her time and all of her life.

Now, let's imagine *being* that "*steaming* turd." As the turd, I'm *steaming*, fresh, I've just been ejected—squeezed out. And I definitely feel insignificant, a real *pile of crap*! Going a little further into this "shit," we need to ask (as the turd), How did I come to be in this form? How did I end up like this? Well, I *am* excrement, I am waste, what the body does not need for nourishment. I'm what's left after everything life sustaining has been extracted, processed out of me. Perhaps her dream is showing her what it will be like when she is *ejected* from the towering, clock teacher; that deriving a sense of worth from following an outside group's ideology reduces the follower to a state of utter worthlessness. That steaming turd is fertilizer, on the ground, going into the earth. Maybe some humility is in order for a new beginning, new growth. Now the images in her dream are really speaking to us. The impact of sitting at the feet of her teachers' wisdom—the group's belief system— has reduced her to a worthless pile of excrement. The more she tries "tremendously hard to follow all the tenets," the more worthless and inauthentic she becomes. The gigantic ego of the teacher requires a devalued, needy, willing-to-be-saved, follower. She definitely needed to escape the group, get her *head* out of that dragon's jaws.

Losing My Teeth

When we have put something on ourselves, something that is supposed to change who we are or our appearance, we can count on a reaction from our dreams. A five-year, passionate search for fame and stardom had fallen apart for Jeff, an inspiring actor, twenty-eight years old and drop-dead handsome, when this dream slammed into his mouth. He had been using his dreams to get out of the self-imposed pattern of "being what other people expect me to be." Jeff wanted desperately to just be himself, to be authentic without that "weight on my head," that self-inflicted pressure to always be putting on an act. Here's his dream:

> My teeth were falling out. My back molar caps were undoing. I saw the metal stick out from my teeth. I want to grab it to try to bend it back but my molar fell out. Then another molar fell out and it was all mostly happening on my left side. Then some of my front teeth, except my two teeth in the very front, fell out

and I began to swallow them but I didn't want to. I stuck my finger in my mouth to relax my tongue and allow the teeth to come out. I tried to get them with my finger. It worked. Then I noticed I had a metal retainer down my throat and it was coming up. I slowly pulled that out. I remember losing most of my back teeth.

Jeff's mouth appears to be the scene of a real disaster. Let's go through the steps and interpret this dream:

1. *Walking Through the Dream—Direct Observations:* Jeff explained that they were his actual teeth in the dream but he did not really have any metal caps on his molars. He did wear a retainer—braces used to hold teeth in place and correct irregularities—as a child. His dream is using a reference to his childhood because it is relevant to his life now.

2. *Awakening the Dream—Dream Alchemy:* You recall that in Step Two, we imagine *being* each dream element exactly as in the dream. "I'm losing my grip. I feel out of control. It's kind of like a death," Jeff said when I asked him to describe what he experienced when he imagined *being* one of his molars falling out.

   Then I asked him, "What is your job as a molar?" "I help break things down into bite-sized pieces," he replied. When I asked him what it would be like to imagine being his mouth with his teeth falling out, he said, "It feels like the old teeth are falling out to make way for new teeth. I can feel new teeth ready to come in." Here his dream tells him that he is in a transition: the old falling away to make room for "new teeth."

   It's important to understand exactly what molars are—teeth we use to *grind* food, to break food into small pieces so that it can be swallowed and digested. So we could say that Jeff's dream is saying that his old way of taking in nourishment is dying, falling apart.

   As the "retainer," which he almost swallowed, he said, "I keep things in place so everything looks just right. I'm trying to shape you—it's vanity!" Jeff "pulled that (the retainer) out" of his throat—he pulled out the *outer*, unnatural influences that were controlling his speech and behavior and preventing him from being authentic.

3. *Linking Dream Images and Symbol:* Remember to begin this step by asking yourself this question: In my waking life, what circumstance, situation, person, experience, or part of myself,

past or present, feels like or reminds me of my experience as the image in my dream? In linking your experience, notice your choice of words, the language and phrases your experience of *being* the image evoke. They often open obvious connections to circumstances in your waking life.

Jeff linked his feelings of being "out of control" and "losing his grip" to his recent dangerous, out of control behavior with drinking and sex, another way he could fit in and be part of the group. This old way of relating to others was falling apart. And his self-destructive behavior was an understandable opposite reaction to his extreme concern and control of his appearance. When we repress a part of who we really are, there are consequences. We are likely to find ourselves acting out the exact opposite of what we are trying to be.

He connected "death" to letting go of his chameleon persona that changed his behavior according to what he thought others expected him to be. "I'm afraid to let go of the old Jeff," he remarked. Similarly, he linked the "retainer" to his obsession with looking perfect, keeping his appearance "just right"—something he could no longer "swallow." And he also explained how he would modify his speech and his choice of words in order to fit a particular social environment. One of Jeff's chief dilemmas had been the struggle to be himself instead of always putting on an act to impress others. Trying to be something for others was draining and exhausting—a millstone around his neck.

4. *Freeing the Authentic Self—Pulling the Sword From the Stone:* Jeff's dream has now given him specific information he needs to separate his Authentic Self from his false self, to remove the mask so the real Jeff can be seen and heard. The retainer is *metal*, an *unnatural*, implanted, manufactured device, as were the metal caps on his molars. Jeff realized he had to get the "metal" out of his mouth; he had to get rid of the collective, societal notion that he needed to adapt and conform to outside expectations about what he did for work, how he looked, and how he acted.

5. *Summarizing the Dream:* Jeff called his dream "Falling Teeth." New teeth were on their way, teeth free of implanted controls, free of *unnatural* influences that were not a part of his Authentic Self. Jeff would now be free to speak *his own* mind, to

"relax" his tongue, to get a new grip on his authentic life, to be nourished from the inside out, not from the outside-in. Not an easy task by any means, but his dreams would be helping him every step of the way. He would now be more in control of his life and his destiny.

6. *Integration:* To integrate this dream into his waking life, Jeff began to watch and reflect on his thoughts, his attitudes, and his speech—the specific words he chose for different situations. He began to differentiate between what were outside expectations and influences and what were his own ideas and his own natural way of interacting with others. He also began to explore changes in his appearance, letting go of his obsession to look just right to please others and experimenting with different, more casual attire that felt more connected to his real identity and to his Authentic Self.

The Catalyst (The Call to Adventure)

Living on the Shell

Dreams are remarkable in that they not only warn us about approaching illness, they also explain what we have been doing to ourselves that has contributed to if not caused a health problem. Marc Barasch, in his book *Healing Dreams*, explains how his dreams helped him survive a serious encounter with cancer. "One evening before falling asleep, I scribbled, in some desperation, a formal request in the dream notebook I'd started to keep: *What is the direction of a cure?*" That same night he had this dream:

> Under the ground a white, snake-like worm is turning in upon itself in a perfect spiral. When its head reaches the center, blinding rays of light shoot out, and a voice solemnly intones: "You have been living on the outer shell of your being—the way out is the way in!"[2]

Barasch's remarkable dream tells him that he has been living on the *surface* of his life. His dream wants him to turn his attention to the *inner* realm. According to his dream, the healing he seeks will be found within. We might look at the "outer shell" as referring to an aspect of the waking ego, the hard, *protective* covering, the persona, or interface between the individual and the outside world. Indeed "shell" literally means "the usually hard outer covering that encases certain organisms."[3]

Work Tremors

> *It seems an odd way to structure a free society: most*
> *people have little or no authority over what they do*
> *five days a week for forty-five years. Doesn't sound*
> *much like "life, liberty and the pursuit of happiness."*
> *Sounds like a nation of drones.*
>
> —Michael Ventura[4]

Another Anxiety Dream About Work

Most people completely dismiss a common, silent scream from the Authentic Self: anxiety-ridden dreams about our job, our work environment, or our chosen career. We dream about waiting tables and there are too many people to be served; we can't find the food. Or we're back working at the job we left years ago but the building is dark and empty. These scary dreams are another type of catalyst, a powerful knocking on a door shut and locked by our need to create the illusion of security, comfort, and safety within a particular job or career.

It's still dark early in the morning when Jack, a young man in his late twenties, awakens with a jolt. Feelings of panic slowly subside as he realizes that the impossible predicament at work that seemed so utterly real a few seconds ago was just a dream after all. "Another anxiety dream about work," he assures himself, noticing that his heart is still pounding from the experience.

Most of us have at one time or another had dreams like Jack's "anxiety"-ridden dream about "work." In fact such work-related anxiety dreams are extremely common and are nearly always dismissed as just stress, or we say we are working too hard. In reflecting back on my life and reviewing my dream journals, I discovered that I too had numerous work-related anxiety dreams during the times I was in the wrong work. What really struck me was the fact that after I changed professions from business to psychology and writing, I did not have any more anxiety dreams about my work.

What if, on a deeper level, such dreams are desperately trying to tell us something about our *authentic* life's "work," our unlived life and our *real work*—the vocation that would free our unique potential and passion. What if such dreams are silent screams from an Authentic Self that has been overwhelmed by expectations from family and from society. Suppose there is indeed something terribly wrong with how we are spending our life energies. Suppose our anxiety is a result of the threat of non-being, of the tragedy of living someone else's life—suppose your authentic life *is* stuck fast, embedded in the anvil and stone of collective demands and expectations. In dreams, *our life* is the project our dreams are working on.

Cutting Prices

Sometimes an apparently mundane dream about work contains the key to removing immense boulders blocking our path. Larry, a jovial, forty-something "Master Mason," had recently moved to the U.S. from London. He had been trained in and specialized in fine tile work, mosaics, sculpture, and custom designed floors. Larry's work was definitely creative and he believed that his work gave him a sufficient outlet for his creativity. Always rushed and feeling behind schedule, he would arrive at our sessions looking like he just climbed out of a construction site. He told me about a work-related dream that had been bothering him:

> One of competitors was cutting his prices to get business. I was really upset and wondered how he could afford to work at such cheap rates.

Larry explained that the person in the dream was actually a competitor who did tend to bid jobs too cheaply. Meanwhile, Larry had more work than he could keep up with, mostly from referrals. When we explored how Larry's "work" as a master craftsman in stone, tile, mosaic, and sculpture would feel about "cheap rates," the dream's meaning began to emerge. His *work*, which often involved a lot of creativity and original design ideas, said, "You don't appreciate my value, my creativity—I'm being undervalued."

I asked Larry to tell me more about his creativity. "My work is very creative, which I love," he explained, "but I also have been wanting to get back to my paintings for a long time."

"What paintings?" I asked, surprised and curious.

"Well, I've had this idea for a series of paintings about the environment, paintings that would make a statement, wake people up to what's happening to the planet, the forests," he said. He went on to explain that he felt he was a "pretty good artist," but right now his work was the only outlet for his creative side. From his dream, he realized he had been devaluing his creative side, "cheapening his authentic life and his creative spirit with the classic societal group-think that art, particularly for a 'man,' is impractical, unrealistic, not a 'real job.'" Now his dream inspired him to begin working on painting, and here's what really matters: *now* Larry's life will begin to take on deeper meaning and purpose as he uses his unique creativity to fully release his own potential, which *will* impact our world. Larry's "mundane" dream about his work had pointed him right to a major obstacle to his creative life that he was entirely unaware of.

Larry left our session inspired. He had removed a big chunk of his authentic life from the barbed wire of self-defeating *outside* influences—all from another one of those "work" dreams.

Identifying Warnings and Self-Destructive Symbolism in Dreams

Here's a warning about warning dreams: Because it's in the nature of these dreams to use images some dream workers like to label as "archetypal" (or they will say the dream is about this or that mythic story), we need to be careful to rely on the dream's images to understand what they mean without attaching any preconceived labels or theories. Here's an example of Jungian psychology's "archetypal amplification" of a dream, giving it a mythic parallel as part of the interpretation:

> *A dreamer was warned by an electrician that he might accidentally be executed by a high tension wire if he did not stop fooling around.* His dream was interpreted as his symbolic encounter with the transpersonal lord of the thunderbolt and ruler of the energies, Zeus.[5]

Putting a dream image in a mythic specimen jar has the effect of abruptly halting any further inquiry into the potential meaning of the image. In our example, we would want to explore the "high tension" wire, an image loaded with important implications for the dreamer. We need to look up "high tension" wiring and find out what it is and how it works. We would certainly want to create a dialogue with this *high "tension"* wire, this dangerous *current* of high voltage, super-charged energy:

- Where is it going?
- Where has it come from? The power company?
- What is it, precisely?
- What is its job?
- How did it become a "high tension" wire?
- What is life like as the high tension wire?
- How would it "execute" the dreamer?
- Why?

Then we would want to link the results of our questions to the dreamer's life, and you can rest assured that something serious is threatening the dreamer which renders Zeus and his thunderbolts irrelevant and unnecessary. This is why dream dictionaries, which have set meanings for dream symbols, never get to any real meaning in a dream.

Under Attack

A woman in her mid-forties had finally managed to extricate herself from years of an all-consuming corporate career. She had this dream just as she was considering returning to the corporate world for what she thought was economic necessity.

> I am working with Julie (a co-worker from my corporate days who worked incredibly long hours). We are reviewing some business charts. I feel really bored. We go outside and I realize we are under attack. Missiles are coming in from another country—seems like China. It's very scary because we can't see who's doing it. I'm surprised that other people nearby are not concerned about the attack.

She associated her location in the dream with Taiwan, and when asked to imagine *being* the country of Taiwan, she explained that she felt threatened by China because, as Taiwan, she had *just recently won her freedom* from mainland China and they wanted Taiwan back. This dream illustrates how the psyche warns us when some situation tempts us to return to a collective trap. China represents a powerful authoritarian system in the world, and in particular, China, at present, symbolizes a classic dynamic for any individual who manages to escape from a one-sided, group-dictated life: That "you should"-saturated world wants us back. Indeed, it will most assuredly come after us, luring us back with some promise of paradise, some monetary Edenic ideal—a Faustian bargain with dire consequences for the individual soul.

Does this mean that no one should work in the corporate world? Not at all. But for this dreamer, her psyche did not want her to return to that life because her corporate persona had became bigger, more important than her individuality and had prevented her from connecting with what she needed to be doing in her life. It turned out that she was an excellent writer and a natural teacher, new vocations that she was now able to explore.

The upside of this dilemma is that once we have managed to begin living more of our own lives, the psyche becomes very protective. When we are about to step back into some soul-killing pit, it will warn us in our dreams. The dark side of our collective world does not want us to step *outside* its borders, its rules and authority. In this sense, humanity's greatest threat is not from actual warfare, but rather from group-centered ideologies that prevent individuals from living authentic lives—mass-minded expectations that completely thwart individual human potential and creativity. The dreamer is "under attack" by her former role in the corporate world. For her, returning to that workaholic world would be at the expense of losing her soul.

Prostituting Ourselves

A woman in her late forties dreamt that she became a prostitute to overcome her financial problems. She had the dream immediately following her decision to abandon a creative project in order to make more money. She was selling herself, selling her passion in life, for money. Money and security became thieves stealing her authentic life.

Condemned

Nothing is more dangerous to living an authentic life than involvement in a destructive group or organization, which includes any group that makes its mission or agenda more important than the individual. At the height of my commitment to my spiritual group, I had this dream:

> I found myself in medieval France, at night, standing on a narrow cobblestone street outside a vast complex of church buildings. I knew that Joan of Arc had just been condemned to death by the church. I felt the awful horror of what had happened, that an innocent life was about to be extinguished by ecclesiastical authority. Even worse, I was somehow a participant in this drama, part of the official priesthood. Rain began pouring down.

Some dream interpreters would refer to a figure like Joan of Arc as an *archetypal* figure representing a universal heroine, a feminine version of the *hero* archetype. In a dream she might represent nobility, sacrifice, and courage, human contact with the archetypal kingdom, the gods, the divine powers. Other popular interpretations would suggest that the dreamer needs to get in touch with his/her inner heroine. Some metaphysical or New Age dream interpretations might suggest that Joan of Arc represents a past life memory of the dreamer—what I actually thought for a long time, but I could never see any relevance to my current life. Other methods would re-enter the dream and manipulate Joan out of her predicament. While reassuring, interesting, and valuable processes up to a point, these approaches, by prematurely labeling, manipulating, or interpreting the dream, miss the real value and tremendous significance of such a dream as to one's *current* role and potential in the world and also as portraying a quite real *collective* threat to one's freedom and passion, and one's authentic life.

Using the Radical Dreaming process, we would not be concerned with defining Joan of Arc as an archetype, a goddess, or a past life memory; instead we would look at Joan of Arc and all other elements in the dream from a realistic, experiential perspective as a courageous, creative, passionate individual who committed herself to saving France—at that time a church-dominated, inquisitorial, collective monster that ultimately swallowed up her passion and uniqueness.

Through applying the Radical Dreaming process I was able to explore each dream element, differentiate those aspects that were not a part of my Authentic Self, and identify the collective influences in the dream. As a result, I realized that this dream was showing me that "ecclesiastical authority" had executed an aspect of my nature that Joan of Arc represented. For me, she represents that highly idealistic, often naive part of myself that sincerely wanted to make a difference in the world. She was a true heroine who *tragically placed her passion in collective hands*. She also represented a soul figure, an image representing life itself as well as our creative potential.

The religious group to which I was sincerely committed had killed an immense, significant part of who I really was. "I," my "dreaming ego," was complicit in this tragedy, meaning my conscious ego had *internalized* an outer authoritarian system (the complex of church buildings) that was dictating how I should live my life, what books I should read, where I should live, what I should do for work, how I should spend what scraps of time were left at the end of each day. In fact I had allowed the church to control my life utterly, inside and out. Church activities consumed so much time that, when added to my day job, nothing was left for my creative life.

The Death of a Brother

When we are about to make any decision that would significantly alter who we are, warning dreams inevitably appear to protect our authentic nature. This person had not been aware of any doubts about an imminent sex change operation when he dreamt that "he saw the death of a brother, and this saddened and depressed him." He did not actually have a brother, and quickly realized that the "brother" in the dream was the penis that he was about to lose.[6] Again, we see that the waking ego has its agenda but the dreaming Self often has other plans, and those plans include protecting our essential character.

Rape in Dreams

Lost Virginity

A young woman who was very upset about losing her virginity dreamt: "A stone had broken my windshield. I was now open to the storm and rain. Tears came to my eyes. Could I ever reach my destination in this car?"[7] Here we encounter a dream that has significance on different levels. This dream, again, illustrates how the psyche uses our waking life experiences as raw material for dream images. She felt the dream was symbolic of her lost virginity, which equated to her actual experience. But lost virginity also refers to the loss of one's virginal, untouched state, one's original, authentic nature.

Particularly for women, dreams of being raped or sexually violated often mean that collective, patriarchal, authoritarian ideas and concepts have invaded the psyche, which always triggers dreams that alert us to some immediate danger to our integrity as a unique individual. Her concern about reaching her "destination" in that car could refer to her journey and her life's *destiny*. Again, we see how the dream uses our waking life experiences as its raw material. And this dream once more exemplifies the need to be careful not to automatically assume that a literal, objective interpretation is *all* that the dream means.

Collective Invasions

The Nazis Break In

Lynne, a family therapist in her mid-forties, had serious concern written all over her face when she brought this recurring dream—she called it a nightmare—to a workshop. It was one of her first memories as a child and she had the dream over and over beginning when she was about four years old and mysteriously ending when she was seven. Its meaning had eluded her all these years and, like some dark creature chained in the basement, the dream still haunted her memories.

> The Nazis broke into our home and took everyone in my family. They didn't find me because I was small and hid behind the family safe in my parents' closet.

"We represent a greater good so our evil actions are justified," Lynne observed as she imagined being one of the Nazis in her dream. "We are superior, the pure race," she continued. Hearing her own words describing the Nazis hit Lynne like a bolt of lightning. "It's the Church, the Catholic Church!" she exclaimed with a shocked but knowing look.

In her dream she hid "behind the family safe" in her parents' closet, a place where she said her parents kept their "valuables." She wanted to feel valued, valuable to her parents, but their neglect and how they spent their time made Lynne feel devalued and *worth-less*. Lynne explained that her parents were totally involved with the church. When they were not at their jobs, they were at the church either for services or as volunteers. Her family moved to a different part of the country when she was seven years old, coinciding with the ending of her recurring dream. After they moved, her parents never became so caught up in any other church and she remembered feeling that she had her parents back. Lynne's dream of the Nazis coming into her home shows how an ideology can invade our life (come into our home) with disastrous consequences.

For those four years, Lynne's dreams tried to warn her about the gravity of her loss, that an insidious outside influence had broken into, *arrested*—damaged—a nurturing relationship with her parents. And she had lost this priceless connection with her parents during some of her most formative years. Finally understanding this childhood dream helped her realize that she still had a hurt, neglected, lost little girl in her psyche, a part of herself that needed her attention and her empathy. When we pay attention it becomes obvious that our dreams are intent on protecting our essential nature, the Authentic Self, from destructive influences.

Exploring the dream:

- When you have any group image or symbol in your dream—religious, political, military, or other—imagine being a dedicated member of that group. Ask yourself:
    - "What is my belief system?"
    - "How do I *feel* and *think* as a member of this group?"
    - "What are the rules in my group?"
    - "What does the group belief system forbid?"
    - "What do I believe about those who are not *in* my group?"
- Think about your waking life and look for connections: situations, circumstances, a part of yourself, memories—anything that fits and resonates with your experience of being a member of the group.
- *Eliminate* any negative, judgmental, or self-limiting ideas belonging to the group ideology—they do not belong to you and are *not* a part of your Authentic Self.
- *Replace the ideas* you eliminate with *your* thoughts, feelings, and ideas.
- *Create your own ritual* funeral for what the group represented in your life. For example, you could find an old coat you no longer want and perhaps using small scraps of paper attach the group's sayings, ideas, judgments, and self-defeating thinking to the coat. Find an appropriate place and burn it or bury it.

A Fire in the Basement

Ten years after leaving a well-known New Age spiritual group, a forty-year-old doctor discovered information on the internet, posted by former members of the group, that shocked him, drastically deflated a lot of the group's ideology, and exposed many cult-like characteristics. That night, he had this dream:

> I find myself in the white-walled, furnished basement of a house where I am the guest at some social event. There is a fire in the basement. I hide in a nearby closet as flames engulf the house. After the fire, I emerge safely from the fire and the rescue team is surprised.

This dream illustrates how the structures and buildings we encounter in our dreams often symbolize different aspects of the waking ego structure. His encounter with reality about the group ignited the "fire in the basement," which had been painted "white," another representation of a one-sided spirituality devoid of color. He realized that he had, through incorporating the group's one-sided theology, "white-walled" his persona, attempting to be "pure," enlightened in a dangerously restricted sense. His increased *awareness* about his beliefs became his way out of a collective prison. He had held on to certain beliefs about the group "in the basement," or just *below* his normal waking consciousness. This fire—his real, reality-based awareness about the group—soon engulfed the entire house, meaning that the fire utterly destroyed the group's implanted, alien ideology that *was* influencing his life. He survives, but now without the false ego structure created by this particular collective entity.

As we find in many mythologies, that which survives fire usually relates to the soul, to the Authentic Self, to qualities that are imperishable and lasting. From the ashes of this fire, he will be free to build a more authentic life devoid of alien, outside influences. And indeed he began to feel more connected and more authentic, more accepting and at ease with himself.

When an old structure falls apart we are usually left with some sort of an identity crisis. As our old belief systems burn down and fall away, we often encounter an uncomfortable feeling that we really don't know ourselves as well as we have imagined. In our dream example, the fire of awareness of reality—the truth—set the dreamer free from *implanted* beliefs, old ideas that he did not realize were still there, hanging out in the basement, ideas that were anti-Self and in fact did not belong to him. Identification and differentiation from these influences is critical in one's process of becoming completely unique, with integrity and character.

Home Invasion

Dreams often fill various rooms in houses with odd furnishings to indicate mind-stuff, ideas, and attitudes we carry around in our head. Or we encounter certain people, animals, creatures that have gotten *in* to our house—into our psyche. We dream that people we don't like have gotten into our house, or of a dead tree in the living room, or of corrupt priests running around upstairs.

Tricia surprised everyone in the dream group when she explained that she had spent the last two decades of her life in a cult. She described how, one day, after twenty years as a member of a large Buddhist sect in

California, she got up in the middle of a service, walked out, and never returned. She was totally burned out. The group had been consuming more and more of her time and energy and she had been mired in a swamp of depression and hopelessness for a long time. Her involvement in the group had also extinguished her creativity and love of art many years ago. She finally decided she had to get her life back. She brought this dream, which she had about a year after leaving the church, to one of our group sessions:

> We get to a hotel and I go to Carol's room, which turns out to be her house. (I have now had two dreams about Carol's house within the past month.) On her counter top is a picture of a living room with lots of oak furniture. As we wind through her house to go outside, we pass through her recreation room and it looks exactly like the picture. I turn around to take in the whole room and notice an odd looking "altar." It is purple, very artsy/craftsy, and is set inside what appears to be an old wood-stove. I am astonished to see such a thing in Carol's house. I can't decide if it is indeed a work of art or a Buddhist altar.

Tricia described Carol as a real zealot, a long-term member of the group. For Tricia, Carol represented the group's belief system. She lived her life strictly following the rules and practices as set down by the group's view of Buddhism. Working through the dream, Tricia realized that the actual *oak altar* she had in her home, which had been made to the group's exact specifications, was the same color as the "oak furniture" in her dream. Carol's "house," with lots of oak furniture, represented the group's rules, ideas, and philosophy that still were in her head; her thinking had too much *Buddhist oak* in it.

Her dream helped her to identify and remove the last pieces of oak furniture from her psyche—clearing her mind of a belief system, of alien stuff, of group-based attitudes and ideas that were preventing her from following her passion to be an artist.

Within a few months after she left, she returned to college to complete her degree in fine arts, which explained the "odd looking altar" that she "can't decide if it is indeed a *work of art* or a Buddhist altar." Her dream shows her that she is in the midst of a transition into *her* authentic life: worshiping at the altar of an organized religion, transforming it into an altar that felt to Tricia a lot like the kind of art she wanted to do. She is moving from an *outside-in* orientation to an *inside-out* approach to her life as a changing "work of art."

Playing with Her Head

A thirty-eight-year-old woman who found herself in the middle of a painful separation had this dream immediately following a gestalt group therapy session in which the facilitator was particularly forceful, aggressive, and judgmental:

> I was in [the] house where I grew up, standing near the washer and dryer. There was something wrong with the plumbing and water was gushing out, flooding the room. I am thinking that I have to tell my mom. Then, shocked, I see the severed head of an infant on a small table. I am desperately trying to help this baby, holding its head—it's still alive. My older brother is now there also. He's helping me, showing me how to help the baby.

The dreamer complained that the group facilitator had "played" with her head," giving her advice and judging her marriage without actually knowing her situation, causing her to feel confused and to not trust her own feelings. In working with this dream, she felt that the baby symbolized new hope for her marriage, a new beginning that was just forming for her. Her group experience severed the head of this newfound hope and plunged her into a new state of hopelessness and despair. She associated her brother with qualities of tenderness, empathy, and intelligence, describing him as "a very wonderful and unique person."

Good Girl / Bad Girl

An intelligent woman in her late twenties found herself without direction or meaning in her life, working at a job that was far beneath her abilities and socializing with people who were not intellectually stimulating or challenging. She had this dream:

> It's semi-dark and gray around me. I'm standing at the foot of a tall Maypole or flagpole of some sort. Jesus or God is at the top and is giving me a secret formula. It's a hair product. My hair is long, waist-length, with big loopy curls, luxuriant, wild, in anarchy. This formula will put my hair in order. As I add it, it seems sticky—I'm not doing it right? My hair is becoming gummy and stringy.

The Maypole is a tree stripped of its folliage, becoming the *axis mundi* around which the universe revolves. For the dreamer, the dances around the Maypole represented renewed life, sexual union, and the coming of spring. Ordinarily the pole represents the phallic or masculine nature and the discus at the top of the pole represents the feminine. But instead of the discus, the dreamer's Maypole had a Christian deity at the top. She felt this deity represented a rigid set of rules and expectations, of "thou shalts" and "thou shalt nots," absolutes, either-or, "good girl/bad girl." She realized that she was subjecting her "universe," her life, to outer, religious, male-dominated attitudes. And she thought the "secret formula" to put her hair "in order" was gumming up her natural, feminine, wild woman—her Authentic Self. An outside organization was threatened by her "anarchic" hair.

Hair often has to do with power, vitality and *ideas*, things that grow out of our head. And her "luxuriant, loopy curls," which the "sticky" religious dogma turned "gummy and stringy," represented a vital part of her authenticity. When she imagined *being* that gummy and stringy hair, she felt like something bad had been put on her, something that made it difficult (for her hair) to be loose, individual, and free—something that definitely did not belong there.

In order to follow a hierarchical religious attitude, she had to put herself down, at the base, debasing and demeaning her real personality. No wonder she kept surrounding herself with people who reflected her poor self-image. That is why it is so important to avoid people who put down our ideas and inspirations. But even more significantly, we need to differentiate ourselves from ideas and judgments that don't belong to us, ones that will "gum up the works." Inquisitional religious attitudes and judgments are still rampant, but for the most part they now reside within the individual psyche, where it is difficult to distinguish our own thoughts and ideas from those that have their origin in some group.

Ideological Substance Abuse

> It is terrible to destroy a person's picture of himself in
> the interests of truth or some other abstraction.
> —Doris Lessing[8]

Lets' return to Tricia, who spent twenty-plus years in a Buddhist, cult-like group. Four years after she left the church, several months of serious depression hit seemingly out of nowhere. She decided to ask for a dream to help her understand the cause of her depression: "I repeated many times, 'I would like to have a dream that will offer me insight as to my current depression.'" Here's her dream:

I am downtown with my dog, walking in the park blocks across
the street from the old court building. I look behind me and notice an odd looking, androgynous woman with very short hair
walking close behind me. She is wearing black jeans and a tight,
white, singlet T-shirt. Because I am bending over to hold my
dog's choke chain, I feel very afraid and vulnerable, and in the
next instant the woman grabs me, and then I realize she has in-
jected me with something. This frightens me so much I immediately wake up from the dream. I feel as though I have a foreign
substance coursing through my veins.

Tricia's dream proved to be a powerful wake-up call from her psyche.
She said the area she was walking through in the dream was the actual site
of a huge Buddhist rally that she attended over twenty years ago. "She
represents Buddhism," Tricia said, "that oriental woman in the dream."
A little sheepishly, Tricia admitted she had still been doing her Buddhist
meditations and prayers even though she was no longer in the group.

Suddenly everything made sense in the dream: Her dogmatic, strict
"spiritual practices" were a "foreign substance coursing through [her]
veins." Her dream had graphically portrayed the effect of daily *injecting*
herself with an alien belief system that had completely stopped her from
living her own life and pursuing her art career. Ironically, her "spiritual
practices" were keeping her in the group mind set. It was a life-changing
realization for Tricia. She stopped all her practices and rituals related to
the group and her depression lifted.

Crossing the Desert

No matter what we experience in our lives, it seems we each have
some patient old inner Alchemist waiting to turn our disasters into gold.
In December of 1975, I discovered a church in Glendale, California, led
by Ann Ree Colton, an intelligent, well-read, charismatic woman in her
early seventies. I was immediately drawn to her teachings, which blended
Eastern philosophy with Christianity and New Age metaphysics.* Without hesitation, I joined Ann Ree's organization, sincerely believing that I
had found my true spiritual path at last, and my spiritual teacher as
well. By August of 1976, I was intently and completely immersing myself in Ann Ree's spiritual philosophy and her many books when I had
this dream:

---

*See my book *Under the Influence: The Destructive Effects of Group Dynamics* for details of
this experience.

I saw Ann Ree, who was going back to California. I was going there also and decided to drive my car across the desert and follow her. I asked Ann Ree how far it was across the desert and she replied, "Two hundred and fifty miles." I noticed that Ann Ree had one eye that looked very dark, as if that eye could look into eternity and see beyond. She then picked up a small sparrow and it perched on her finger. Then she pointed out a black crow and told me to "watch it. It has a lot of milk." I looked around for my car but it was missing. Ann Ree told me I would love it there and she described many things to see, ending with the "white house."

This significant dream occurred just as I was becoming seriously involved in a group that would utterly consume the next fifteen years of my life. In trying to understand this dream, it's important to remember that by this time I had projected aspects of my inner Self onto Ann Ree as a contemporary guru, so that her appearance in my dream represented an aspect of my own inner teacher or Self. Ann Ree had become an outer world representation of an inner, spiritual dynamic. She had quite effectively "hooked" me in what can most aptly be thought of as a spell. And indeed I was *spellbound* in her presence.

When I was in the group, I thought the dream was a "confirming," that it was telling me Ann Ree was my true spiritual teacher. But years later, after leaving the group and re-examining this dream, I realized it had a very different meaning. So what exactly did this dream mean? First, it foretold a *long* journey, "250 miles" across the "desert," a barren dry place, a wasteland. I was at the beginning of a fifteen-year journey that effectively stopped me from following my own path in life, a *desert* experience where nothing could grow. I became a "follower" on someone else's path—a choice with tragic consequences for my authentic nature.

Jung once commented that there is a child in each adult that longs to return to paradise, to the womb state. Religious groups in particular constellate the *infant*, a regression to child-like states. In my example, I allowed this inner infant to assume control of my life, a very dangerous step!

For me, the *"white* house" symbolized the goal of the New Age church I was joining: purification, perfection and enlightenment, an *all white* teaching without any darkness or depth. The *white* house meant I was choosing a one-sided approach to the inner life, a fragmenting, splitting group dynamic that always ends up destroying the creative potential in the individual. Moreover, I could not find *my car*, which for me meant I had lost the ability to travel under my own volition. I still am not sure about the 250 mile distance. I am inclined to look at this particular 250 miles as symbolic of the time and effort my involvement in Ann Ree's church would exact from my life.

The "black crow" may hold the dream's most important meaning. If I imagine being a crow, I am an opportunist and I will use anything to survive. In essence, I am a survivor and I will somehow find food in this place. Maybe it's the crow in me that managed to survive the church experience and use it to better understand how dreams work. Without my experience in a religious cult, combined with recording and observing my own and others' dreams during the whole process, I would not have been able to understand the real potential of dreams and how they react to our choices when those choices mean we are killing some part of our essential identity. This book would not have existed. Guess I owe that black crow!

Withdrawing Our Projections: Getting Real

> *It comes over me that I had then a strange alter ego*
> *deep down somewhere inside me, as the full-blown*
> *flower is in the small tight bud, and I just took the*
> *course, I just transferred him to the climate, that*
> *blighted him once and for ever.*
>
> —Henry James[9]

Henry James describes a classic dilemma common to the human species: projection of an unknown or unacknowledged part of the Self onto something or someone in the outside world. We *objectify* a part of ourselves, which enables us to create distance between ourselves and the most dynamic and creative parts of ourselves. Our new car with its gold trim package feels so elegant, we feel valuable, luxurious. We soak in satisfaction, like a warm bubble bath, temporarily whole again. An object designed to be psychologically and emotionally appealing has *hooked*, tricked a part of our Authentic Self; that sexy black Jaguar is now far more than just a new car. It has trapped part of our inner nature in its shiny black jaws. Powerful, fast, nimble, mysterious, beautiful—it has us under its spell. We have a new relationship. And we have also taken yet another detour, a pleasure cruise around our own authentic life.

Unfortunately this dynamic also prevents us from living out of our own authenticity. In fact, as long as our projections hold, we cannot know ourselves—our real capabilities and potential. So in order to live authentically, letting go of our projections on others and on objects, becomes a crucial step. Fortunately our dreams are experts at showing us the real nature of our diversions. With ceaseless resolve, dreams will steer our life away from illusion and unreality and toward our real passions and purpose in life.

Deciphering Recurring Dreams

A recurring dream is like that familiar pothole in the road we keep trying to avoid but always seem to keep hitting. Recurring dreams want our attention, poking their hands through the neat fences surrounding our life, persistent reminders that we need to listen to a voice from somewhere in the depths of our being.

Driving Underwater

Sue, a gifted therapist and a good friend, once told me about an unsettling dream that had been recurring for several years. She would be driving on a lonely, unknown road in the middle of nowhere and suddenly come to a lake, a river, or the ocean covering the road. She would then find herself driving right into and under the water, sometimes remaining on the road and every so often falling off the road into even deeper water. She would wake up feeling panicked.

After working with the images in her dream, a light bulb went off. With a sigh of relief, Sue realized that the dream was speaking to her about her work as a therapist: how her process actually worked, her way and style of psychotherapy. The unknown landscapes represented her clients and the lonely road was her journey *into* the unknown territory of her clients' psyches. Her natural empathy and therapeutic skills were taking her underwater, into the depths of her clients' feelings and emotions. Sue explained that now she understood why she had been feeling strangely anxious with certain clients. She would be sitting in a session when all of a sudden a strange mood of discomfort and apprehension would come over her without any apparent reason.

Sue's dream once again illustrates how dreams support and guide our lives once we are in our right work. Her dream gave her the confidence to accompany her clients into their emotional depths, *dropping down* into the unconscious, into their dreams. Her dream became an encouragement, a talisman she could use during therapy sessions when she began to feel that apprehension: "Here we go again, into the water." Her dream enabled her to appreciate the natural anxiety and fear produced by going into unknown areas of the psyche; as a result her empathy and respect for her clients increased. A dream that had been unsettling was now a wise counselor reassuring her about her work. And *that* recurring dream has never returned.

Exploring the dream:

- It's important to thoroughly explore landscapes, geography, the setting of a dream. An unknown landscape is often just that: an *unknown* area of psyche, an aspect of the Self we are unfamiliar with.
- In Sue's dream, exploring the landscape would also include the different types of water in her dreams—to imagine being a lake and becoming aware of what it's like to be that body of water exactly as the dream portrays. For example:
  - What's it like to have someone drive into you? Now you contain something new.
  - How would you describe yourself to someone who did not know what a lake was?
  - How did you become who you are as the lake?
  - How did you get there, covering the road?
  - What's it like to be in that environment?
- Sue's dream contains obvious information about outside influences—the different "bodies" of water—that she goes into as a therapist, representing the psyches of her clients, *not* parts of herself.

Consider the case of Jerome Cardan, the 16th century Italian scholar whose recurring dream prompted him to write his most famous work, the *Ars magna,* or *"Great Art,"* which was a significant contribution in the development of algebra.[10] While he worked on his book, he continued to have the same recurring dream. When his writing slowed down, his dream occurred even more often. Once the book was published, his dream stopped and never returned.[11] Cardan's recurring dream illustrates a significant feature of such dreams: When understood or resolved, recurring dreams either change or stop altogether. Perhaps he never understood the meaning of his dream. Maybe that dream wanted to have a voice in his writing and was satisfied once the work was completed. Or possibly that recurring dream was the prodding and encouragement from his *daimon* whose task was to inspire Cardan to finish his project.

Tying Herself Down

A common type of recurring dream often comes after a relationship has ended. For example, Maureen and her husband divorced ten years ago. She felt that she had long ago resolved all the emotions surrounding the ending of their seventeen-year marriage. So why did she continue to dream of Rob, her ex-husband? She described Rob as a traditional "country boy" who loved ranching and farming and his horses, all seven of them. He also worked for the Forest Service and had to travel a lot, sometimes for weeks at a time. When Rob was out of town she had to take care of the farm. Morning and evening, every day, rain or shine, if Rob was out of town, Maureen would be slogging through the fields, opening the gates, closing the gates, feeding and taking care of the horses. A lot of the time Maureen felt more like a hard-working hired hand than Rob's wife. She felt tied down and restricted. "I gave up my freedom for that relationship," she told me. "He refused to even look at any possibilities other than life on his farm. He was sure stuck," she said.

I asked Maureen to think about any ways she might be doing that to herself: restricting herself, placing limits on her life, "tying herself down."

"That's it," she said. "Oh my God, I've been trying to get free to travel and write again ever since Rob and I broke up. I keep getting myself stuck in situations and bad relationships that keep me tied down."

Her dreams were using Rob to warn her that she was still tying herself down, keeping her authentic life imprisoned. For Maureen, the Rob in her dreams did not just represent a masculine side of her nature. Instead, Rob represented "Rob," a person with qualities her dreams want her to look at because her experience with Rob put her in a tied-down situation. Her dreams want her to stop doing something to herself that prevents her from living her own life.

Maureen's recurring dreams ended. The last time we met she was downsizing, simplifying her life, selling her large home and arranging her affairs so that she could start living the life she had put on hold for so many years. Now, if Rob ever showed up in a future dream, she would be able to stop and check herself out: How might she be restricting or limiting herself? What was she just thinking about doing that would mean less freedom for her?

Maureen wanted to work with social service agencies that helped people living in abject poverty. But she first had to free her own authentic life in order to leave her "ordinary world" and create space in her life for her own potential to make a difference in society.

Exploring the dream:

- In any dream where a former partner appears, begin with thinking what your life was like when you were together, both positive and negative aspects.
- Then describe your former partner's personality, what he/she was like, good and bad points.
- Next imagine being that person exactly as portrayed in your dream and record your experience, your feelings, and thoughts.
- Think about your present, waking life and ask yourself what circumstance, event, choice, part of yourself, or area of your life evokes feelings similar to the experience above of working with your dream.
- Once you understand the meaning of your dream, determine to change your waking life to integrate the dream's guidance. In Maureen's example, her dream threw a spotlight on a self-destructive pattern that kept trapping her in a spider web of circumstances that prevented her from living *her* life.

When dreams take you into past events in your life, they are saying that something about *that* experience back then is relevant to your life right now. Usually recurring, relationship dreams are trying to get us to look at something we keep unconsciously doing to ourselves. Sometimes this dynamic is a slippery one to get a hold on. The dream is *not* saying we are just like that old partner. It is saying that we are probably doing something *like that* to ourselves. We then must stop doing *that* to ourselves.

Again, once understood, the dream provides the needed information about ourselves so that we can loosen the Authentic Self a little more—free up more of our authentic life and feel a stronger grasp on that magical sword.

Shadow: Opening "The Long Bag We Drag Behind Us"

*We need a shadow. The shadow keeps us down to
earth, reminds us of our incompleteness, and provides
us with complimentary traits. We would be very
poor indeed if we were only what we imagined
ourselves to be.*

—Marie-Louise von Franz[12]

The Dark Man in Women's Dreams

Sometimes a threatening stranger turns out to be a powerful part of
the Authentic Self. I met Barbara in a Dream Therapy Group. In her
mid-forties and recently divorced, Barbara was getting an uneasy feeling
about her new boyfriend. His behavior was beginning to remind her of
her ex husband's when this dream slipped through the back door:

> I'm in the living room relaxing on the couch. Suddenly I sense a
> large, tall black man behind me who must have come in the back
> door. He walks out of the kitchen and into the living room and
> comes up in front of me. He's a really huge, black African and he
> has two weapons that could harm me. I see a pair of large scis-
> sors in his hair. I feel very threatened. I'm paralyzed and say a
> prayer for protection. He disappears and I wake up, still feeling
> really threatened.

Who is this imposing black man? Is he evil—about to kill Barbara?
Or might he be something else altogether? "I don't know who he is. He
wanted something from me. He's armed and dangerous, after something—very determined and very assertive. He was dressed all in black,"
Barbara said.

When I asked her to imagine being this man in her dream and tell me
what his life is like, things got interesting. Barbara explained: "I'm a mi-
nority. I don't have equal rights. I have to fight for everything I want,
sometimes I take advantage of others to get what I want." A light went
off: "That's been my whole life. I'm kind of a women's lib person. I've
never had equal rights. That was the problem with my marriage and this
new relationship too," she said excitedly. "You know, he wasn't really
trying to hurt me. I think he just wanted my attention. Maybe he was
even trying to help. Guess my prayer stopped everything. Now I'll never

know," she added. She also began to think about her *automatic* prayer reaction in the dream. She felt this was the result of programming from her Christian upbringing that labeled anything "black" as evil and anything "white" as good and pure. She got the feeling that the scissors "in his hair" probably represented the ability to separate things, cut through stuff, especially thoughts and thinking, head stuff.

Barbara's powerful black man turned out to be a valuable part of her Authentic Self that came in through the *back door*, a part that struck fear and terror into her dreaming ego, relaxing comfortably on the couch. It's as though this man's qualities reach into her ego's safe, ordinary world, on the ground floor, on the level of everyday life.

Working with this dream, she also realized that all her struggles and suffering with unequal roles between men and women over many years had created this strong presence, an armed black man with all black clothing. "I think," said Barbara, "black is elegant and dressy." Now she could feel his power, his assertiveness, and his determination. And now she knew she could hold her ground in any relationship and not compromise her sense of fairness and equality. When needed, she could call on her inner "armed and dangerous" Self to confront inequality and injustice with *elegance, determination*, and scissors ready.

Exploring the dream:

- Barbara's dream again illustrates an important dynamic: What at first appears evil or bad to the dreaming ego often turns out to be the exact opposite.
- This dream also shows the importance of looking at the dreaming ego as yet another dream image, a dream character that needs to be explored.
- Her prayer actually short circuits the dream, ending it prematurely—a reaction that blocks the dream. A good opportunity to re-enter the dream in active imagination and ask the black man what he wants.

Rattling Skeletons

The Living Dead

For many years, Cheryl, a nurse and mother of three teenagers, held onto regrets and resentments about her divorce. Painful past events, old ghosts were haunting her life. As a result, she found herself feeling more and more angry and depressed. "I'm way too mad lately," she said, adding, "Resentments—I've got a list! I'm tired of fighting." She had this dream:

> People are trying to kill me but they're zombies They're dead but they look real. One gets inside. I have to kill it but it comes back to life. We try to escape—run for it. I kill one, a woman. We run out to the car and end up on an unfamiliar road. I still don't know what to do.

For Cheryl, the zombies represented something that "looks human but they're not. They don't feel; they're empty, dull, robotic, soulless— the living dead." A zombie, according to voodoo beliefs, is created by a supernatural power or spell that enters into and reanimates a corpse. While working through the steps to understand this dream, Cheryl saw that she was keeping herself under a spell, reanimating dead history with her thinking process. The past was stealing her life, preventing her from moving forward and living in the present. She began to change her thinking; she eliminated obsessive, repetitious thoughts about the past that were poking old skeletons. She replaced those thoughts and attitudes with new, constructive thinking about reanimating her authentic life. Her "I'm way too mad" storm clouds began to dissipate along with the zombies. The dead were returning to their natural state: dead and staying buried.

It's Bulletproof

It is apparent that the psyche loves to use our closest relationships to show us about ourselves, particularly self-destructive behavior. This means that most people have a lot of dreams about relationships, past and present. But these dreams also reveal ways we adapt to society as well as to other individuals. For example, a man in his mid-forties who was in a serious mid-life crisis had this dream:

> I'm making a telescope to see something and it's made of a new material that I created. It's revolutionary, like plastic was, but would revolutionize the world. The substance would behave by adapting itself to any situation—bulletproof, bendable—it could be anything. I think I should patent this and I'd be wealthy.

After working on this dream, what finally resonated for the dreamer was the *adaptable* nature of the substance. He realized that he had spent his life ignoring his feelings and intuition, adapting to all situations so that he never expressed any strong feelings, which "helped me be calm, cool, and collected, the opposite of my mother's behavior." Unfortunately, his bulletproof adaptability extended to his relationship to the world around him, particularly to his career, which he hated but stayed in, continually *adapting* to new, more difficult circumstances. The *dream ego* thinks this impenetrable substance is great, and in fact it has served as a protector, armor, but it also became the chief obstacle to his own reality and true Self. He had created, developed, and refined this miracle material over many years. This dream proved to be a *breakthrough* experience for him. He began to connect many disastrous side-effects of his adaptability including staying in the wrong profession, anger, and an "acid tongue" that until now had felt out of control. The dream also serves as a reminder that we need to be suspicious of the dreaming ego's reactions to the dream, that what may appear to be great may actually be a dysfunctional way of adapting to our world.

A Stolen Smile

When we have little or no sense of who we are, adaptation and the desire to please others can lead to rapid self-destruction; we begin to lose valuable parts of our authentic nature. This dream of a woman in her early twenties painted a disturbing image of loss:

> I'm very upset because my two front, upper teeth have fallen out. When I woke up, it was a relief to feel them, they were still there.

I asked her to tell me what those two teeth did for her, what was their job? "They help me smile," she replied without hesitation. "I don't smile," she added, clenching her jaw and obviously trying not to smile.

"What happened to prompt you to decide not to smile?" I asked, surprised and curious about such a tragic loss.

"My boyfriend told me I don't look good when I smile."

I recall that my mouth dropped open in disbelief at that point. I was appalled! She had allowed a valuable part of her Authentic Self to be stolen from her: her "smile." And what is a smile? It is a *natural*, authentic response to life, an expression of our unique humor, our ability to laugh at life, a form of self-nourishment. She was allowing an *outside influence*, her boyfriend's criticism, to silence an important part of her authenticity.

Exploring the dream:

- With dreams about your teeth, always imagine *being* the specific tooth or teeth and ask yourself, "What is my job? What do I do for this person?"
- Next, imagine *being* the teeth in your dream and experience what it is like to be falling out, coming loose, losing your grip—exactly as events happened in your dream. You might experience what one person described as feeling "no longer useful."
- Remember to also imagine *being your jaw, your mouth, your tongue*, and explore what it would be like to lose those particular teeth. Pay close attention to what you say as you imagine being the different dream elements. For example, in the dream above, from the tongue's perspective, losing those two teeth would make speech difficult; the dreamer is also losing a part of her *voice*, her ability to speak for herself and express herself.
- Think about your waking life and see what circumstance or situation fits your experience of role-playing the various parts of your dream.

The Lime Green Dress

Here's another example of the psyche's use of former relationships to prevent us from repeating old dysfunctional patterns. A thirty-nine-year-old writer had this dream about her ex-husband many years after their divorce:

> I am in the laundry room of my present home with my son. My ex-husband walks in dressed in a lime green silk skirt and a bright pink frilly blouse. We begin arguing. I realize my son is hearing everything and he's really embarrassed. We both leave.

This dream follows a common pattern of showing the dreamer, in a shocking manner, that she is somehow replicating a dynamic that is like some part of her former marriage. She explained that her ex-husband was indeed a cross-dresser and that they argued about it for years. They both kept it a dark family secret, never told anyone, and she struggled for years to accommodate her husband's cross-dressing in their relationship, while feeling very alone and suffering in silence. Her then husband was terribly ashamed and never "came out." Ultimately, the marriage failed and they divorced.

In working on this dream, she described the laundry room as a place that "allows all the dirty stuff to come in and get cleaned up." She also felt claustrophobic in the laundry room and expressed the need for more "space." Dirty clothing in this dream represented the feeling of being soiled, contaminated from the "dirty family secret." We wear clothing to interface with the world around us as a statement about who we are. It is as though the shame and secretiveness have soiled the dreamer's persona and now the cleanup work must begin. But cleanup work on what? The circumstance no longer exists. Here we have an example once more of the psyche's methodology: It does not waste time on anything irrelevant to the dreamer's present and future life circumstances.

With this type of dream, interpretation must focus on how the dreamer might be doing something *like* or similar to what the dream illustrates. Further work with the dream and role-playing her former husband in the dream reminded her of a comment he once made about his cross-dressing: "The degree to which I hold it in is the degree to which it takes over my life." At this point the meaning resonated for her. She had been holding in memories of serious abuse and neglect from her mother, suffering in silence for her entire life as well as never confronting her mother. She had never "come out." She was indeed doing something to herself *like* her ex-husband had done to himself. Her "secret" needed "space." In fact, her actual claustrophobia may have a lot to do with keeping secrets confined to small spaces in her psyche. Understanding this dream made it clear to her that she had to begin telling her story and letting her family know about the abuse she had experienced. She had to put this "dirt" into hot water, go into her feelings about her mother. Alchemically, the dirt needs to undergo *solutio*—cleansing through a solvent, water. In her dream the soil needs *hot* water; it needs intense feeling and emotion.

The fact that the dream takes place in her current home shows that her secretiveness about her mother was adversely affecting her new family and her son. She often found herself obsessing about her experience with her mother, feeling depressed and angry but unable to talk about it. It was "taking over her life."

Role playing was an important part of exploring this dream—becoming each person *as they are in the dream* and also becoming other major symbols such as the laundry room. For example, you would ask yourself, What is it like to be this laundry room? As a laundry room, what is my job, my purpose? What is it like to be wearing the lime green silk skirt and pink blouse? Imagining herself as the skirt and blouse, she said that the skirt and blouse screamed "Notice me!" When we find particularly graphic or startling imagery in dreams it means that our psyche wants our attention; it wants us to attend to something *now*. A laundry room is a container, a place where we clean up soiled garments— shadow work of sorts in the sense that the garments we put on represent a compromise between who we really are and the world around us. The soil does not actually belong to us but clings to our garments. In dreams, soiled clothing often refers to ideas and attitudes that have been *pro-jected*, put on us, or an experience that has corrupted our true nature. Edward Edinger explained, "Psychologically, the dirt or sin that is washed away . . . can be understood as unconsciousness, shadow quali-ties of which one is unaware. When one is psychologically clean, one will not contaminate one's environment with shadow projections."[14] Applied to our example dream, this means that as long as the "dirt" re-mains in the unconscious, it is likely to be projected onto others. Thus we find ourselves seeing our dirt in the other, a dynamic that creates tremendous difficulties in relationships. Additionally, the "dirt" may not really belong to us. Instead we may be taking on outside attitudes that are true psychological and emotional contaminates. We have to sort out our own dirt from collective dirt that has been put on us. This involves a lot of inner reflection and self-honesty. It means *knowing* ourselves in-side and out. Dreamwork provides one of the best tools to aid our inner research and understanding ourselves.

> *You already have the precious mixture*
> *that will make you well. Use it.*
> —Rumi

CHAPTER 7

Turning Back–Refusing the Adventure

Social pressure is the enemy. How in heaven's name are you going to find your own track if you are always doing what society tells you to do?

—Joseph Campbell[1]

The Consequences of Doing Nothing

It will not come closer—
the one inside moves back,
and the hands touch nothing, and
are safe.
. . . The toe of the shoe pivots
in the dust . . .
And the man in the black coat turns,
and goes back down the hill.

—Robert Bly[2]

Suppose we choose not to work on our life, not to struggle trying to understand our dreams? What if we give up trying to find our passion and our authentic life? Such a *refusal* has immense consequences for both individuals and for society. Quenching the spirit, refusing to attend to one's essential nature, deforms life into an outside-in, backwards orientation. The conscious ego and persona reign supreme, arrogant in their walled-in temples and monuments of pseudo-reality, soul-shoved-into-the-dungeon empires. In spite of apparently great accomplishments and hard work, refusal means a ticket to nowhere: a defective life stumbles into a wasteland, a limited, dead world devoid of depth, significance, and meaning.

Dead Meat

Our dreams roll out the heavy artillery when we turn our backs on living our own lives. In fact, they will unerringly point out exactly what we are doing to ourselves, often using images designed to shock the ego out of its deadly complacency. Here's an account of just such a dilemma beginning with a dream:

> I am sitting at a dinner table eating meat. Suddenly I notice that
> it is the dead body of a man that I eat.

The dreamer lives on the money his deceased father left. In spite of all the advantages this kind of life offers to him he is unhappy because he wants to prove to himself and to his family that he is a useful member of society and is able to make his own living. In the dream, he literally lives off his dead father.[3]

His dream shows him the chief obstacle to living his own life is his economic dependence on his deceased father, which keeps him locked in a gilded cage, a comfortable prison. He has become a cannibal.

In turning our back to inner exploration, we also lose our individual power of affirmative action in the world; we lose our opportunity to make a difference. And the collective world loses the value created from living a distinct and utterly original life. Life turns into a state of entombed waiting for approaching disintegration and death. As this biblical passage warns, describing what life becomes as a result of a refusal to engage one's unlived life: "Because I have called and ye refused . . . I also will laugh at your calamity; I will mock when your fear cometh; when your fear cometh as desolation, and your destruction cometh as a whirlwind; when distress and anguish cometh upon you."[4] Similarly, this much misinterpreted (literally) Latin saying that has probably converted millions to Christianity: "Dread the passage of Jesus, for he does not return." The gods then become our demons, our tormentors, and as Joseph Campbell points out, "obviously, if one is oneself one's god, then God himself, the will of God, the power that would destroy one's egocentric system, becomes a monster."[5] Thus we have dreams with all manner of wrathful entities, scary images, serpents, poisons, monsters wanting to devour us—all intent on doing us in. And we have unsettling dreams of loss, dreams of wanting some valuable object but being unwilling to pay the price.

Refusing the adventure severs our connections to our inner nature, in a way dividing the psyche into two species, like H. G. Wells's saga

The Time Machine. In a world hundreds of thousands of years in the future, the human race has split in two: the Eloi, a naive, peaceful society, live on the surface while the Morlok, a race of brutish mutants, have evolved in underground communities. The Morlok harvest the Eloi, taking them into their shadow world and eating them. Remarkably, the Eloi put up with this cannibalism. Similarly, when we turn our backs on our true potential, we are *choosing* to sacrifice our authentic lives, to allow self-destructive, societal influences to cannibalize the soul, devour our creative ideas, rip our authenticity to shreds.

The Porpoise and the Mandolin

I first met Laura in a weekly dream group. In her early sixties, her exuberant personality gave no hint of her profession as an accountant. She had recently ended an agonizing thirty-three year marriage. On one hot July night, she brought a dream that ripped up the tracks her life was sliding down:

> I'm at a big attraction, like a Sea World. The crowds are huge. A large porpoise is the main attraction; it's swimming in a deep concrete canal. Everything around is lush and rich. Then I'm in a very cluttered gift shop and I see this exquisite mandolin for sale. I offer to buy it if it's less than $1,000 but the clerk says it's $2,222. I ask why it's so much but there's no answer. I notice the back of it is slightly crumpled.

For Laura, the "big attraction" was a place "designed to make money by amusing and entertaining people." And the crowds "are huge," indicating she is likely in a social situation in her dream. As part of the crowd, she has come to see a wild creature, to see it up close, perhaps to feel a particle of what it would be like to be such a creature. But the concrete canal imprisons this porpoise, separating it from its natural environment. Laura described the porpoise as "playful, but confined—a big fish in a small pool." When she imagined being the porpoise, she said, "I have all this capacity but I'm not using it; I'm in the wrong place," her voice breaking with sudden emotion. "It's my work," she said. "I'm in the wrong place."

But the mandolin's meaning unearthed a deep regret and heartache. Laura explained that in her twenties she had loved music and that she had especially loved the mandolin and had learned to play it. "I'm hand-made, unique. I feel rejected and damaged, unappreciated, left on the shelf to collect dust. Where is my home? People don't see me but I can help make music," Laura said, letting the mandolin in her dream speak to her. Hesitating, tears welling up, she added, "It's the musical, creative part of myself."

Laura will buy it if it's less than $1,000 but her dream presents her with a dilemma: the mandolin will cost her $2,222—a curious series of "twos." She realized that her dream was telling her that a rejected, damaged, musical part of herself has a price tag beyond what she is willing to pay. She must make a profound choice: to once again reject a valuable part of herself or resolve to pay $2,222 for the mandolin. In fact, Laura realized that she had been feeling rejected, and because of her age was also feeling old, ready to be "put away on the shelf."

When something in a dream has a price, our willingness or unwillingness to pay the price often means that we are deciding whether or not to put our energy into something. Laura's dream ends with her decision left hanging, unresolved. She would like to get the mandolin at a far lower price—with much less effort. Her desire to reconnect with her inner musician—a straightforward reference to a valuable aspect of her Authentic Self—might not happen; it's her choice. She might *refuse* the adventure, turn back, put a valuable part of her genuine nature "back on the shelf," spend her remaining years with another unsettling spiritual abortion gnawing away at the fabric of her life.

Numbers in dreams can take time and effort to decipher. Let's do some dream mathematics. Laura must make a $2,222 effort. I'm reminded of the words from an old Sonny and Cher song: "It takes two, babe." And in her dream it would take "two" to create music: the mandolin *and* the musician. *One*, $1,000 or less, will not do it. Three zeros follow the number one. A zero means the absence of something; there's *nothing* there. In the Taoist philosophy, a zero symbolizes the void, nonbeing. Perhaps her dream suggests that with just the ego she is alone, "one," in a state of non-being.

Might the mandolin be an instrument of the Self—the music, the unique melody of an authentic life? Plato thought that the number "two" was a digit without meaning, since it implied a relationship, which then introduced a third factor.[6] Perhaps her dream *demands* a relationship between the mandolin and the musician, creating a third thing: music. Without such a relationship, this connection to the mandolin, her music will never be heard. Of course her dream does not necessarily mean she needs to start playing the mandolin; that would be a literal interpretation. But she could play the mandolin as a way to ritualize her dream's meaning, to serve as a reminder of the dream's message for her life.

Her dream prompted her to think seriously about leaving a job she said was exhausting her. And she began to explore ways to reconnect with her creativity and her love of music—to create time and space for these valuable aspects of her essential nature. Laura knew she would have to overcome the part of herself that was resisting putting the necessary energy into her efforts.

Exploring the dream:

- When numbers show up in your dreams in the form of a price or cost of something, first explore *being* the object with the price tag. For example, if you were to imagine being the mandolin in Laura's dream, you would feel unappreciated and undervalued by Laura, who is only willing to pay "less than $1,000."
- Be alert for wild creatures, like Laura's porpoise, that are *out of place*, removed from their natural environment. The porpoise is in a theme park, a public place, a social situation. And because the porpoise is contained in a man-made structure—the concrete canal—her dream suggests that exterior influences are impeding and restricting the natural abilities and real potential of the porpoise. In such a situation, the porpoise cannot be fully *authentic*; it can only move within certain limits and it must *perform* to survive. Of course, the porpoise symbolizes a powerful, playful, natural part of Laura's authentic nature that she has confined.
- Remember to ask *what your life is like* when you imagine being an animal in your dream. It's important to imagine being *in* the exact situation your dream presents. And don't forget that dream images of the Authentic Self can strike terror into the dreaming ego, and usually do.

A Formula for Self-Defeat

Sometimes, turning our backs to our own potential happens by default; old programming takes over and our ideas and inspirations self-destruct before they ever see the light of day. Remember Margaret, who felt called to explore a new approach to teaching dance and movement? She had this dream in the midst of her struggle to get rid of self-defeating, negative self-talk:

> I'm in a science classroom. The teacher hands back exams. I got
> mine and it was a "D," or an "E." I had studied for the test and
> knew all the answers. I wanted to take it over again.

"I'm about *formulas*; my job is to subject people to certain sets of information—defined sets of rules. The stuff comes in and I apply the rules," she said, describing herself as the class. Then I asked Margaret how those formulas would work in her waking life. "It's doubt—that's a big one. Somewhere in my head there's this dark cloud of gloom that immediately labels my ideas as pointless; I constantly question whether something is reasonable or unreasonable," she explained, adding, "No creative idea gets past the test, the formula—it squelches everything!"

Margaret's dream has zeroed in like a laser on a self-destructive pattern, a way of thinking that methodically smothers each creative idea, almost like a serial killer. Moreover, her dream explains that the "formula" originates in a "science classroom," a structure that represents a specific approach to life. The word, "science" derives from the present participle of *scire*, meaning *to know*.[7] Margaret's scientific *formula* approach to her creative life was based on the need "to know" in advance the outcomes and the consequences of her ideas, to make her creative life into an exact science.

She applied her new insight in her waking life to change the old formula and develop a new way to support her creativity and intuition. As she removed herself from that science classroom with its *pass-or-fail* exams, she suddenly had more options; more ideas and possibilities began to blossom. Margaret could feel the passion welling up, the excitement of being free to go with her ideas, join her own creative process instead of mentally poisoning everything.

This dreamwork reminded her of yet another recent dream:

> I'm in a big abandoned house; it's trashed. I'm holding my niece
> Jody on my hip. Then she's gone, kidnapped by a guy. We're all
> sitting around waiting to hear about her.

Margaret explained that her niece was about two years old in the dream but she is actually five years old. I asked her if she had any memories of what her life was like when she herself was about two years old. "I was left at my grandmother's house when I was two. I remember feeling helpless and scared—a sense of being *irrelevant*," she said, looking surprised and angry. "That's why I don't think anything I do is important or matters," she added. An important part of Margaret's inner work would be to reconnect to that little girl and begin healing the part of her self-image that feels abandoned and unimportant.

Missing the Train

Researchers studying the relationship between dream content and the onset of disease have discovered a particular type of recurring dream that often comes long before cancer becomes apparent. Their research suggests that "Cancer can be seen as a 'growth' process that lives wholly in the body; the impetus for growth has existed in the psyche but has been impeded, or deflected . . . taking place incorrectly in the body rather than in the whole being[.] There is evidence that prior to the onset of cancer, development has been hindered for some time. There is, for example, . . . the frequency of recurrent dreams among cancer patients. . . . Such dreams mean that a core issue has needed attention for some time. The recurrent dreams we have heard of are of one particular type: they allude to the dreamer's being stuck in his or her 'journey of life,' for example, being on a train and not getting anywhere, or having their motor car go continually off the road: in sum, being stuck in a hopeless and helpless position."[8] In one instance, a cancer patient reported having this recurrent dream for up to ten years prior to finding out he had cancer:

> I am trying to arrive at a destination—usually a city—to keep an appointment. I never get there and I agonize over long periods of time. The modes of conveyance—usually trains like the New York City subway—turn out to be going in the wrong direction, or I have taken the wrong train, or connections are missed, or mysteriously I am not on the train on which I started, etc. The dream exhausts me![9]

He understood the dream to mean that he was unable to get his life moving in the right direction—an extreme example but one that illustrates the potential consequences of not following our own path in life.

In another example, Robin Royston, M.D., a doctor in East Sussex, England, reported a patient who told him about a terrifying dream of a black panther attacking him, sinking its claws into his back "between my shoulder blades just to the left of my spine."[10] Royston's patient eventually developed cancer, a melanoma (*melanos* means "black") in the exact place on his back where the panther had attacked him.[11] The obvious connection to his actual cancer does not diminish the dream's underlying intent. We can imagine that *black panther* representing wild, natural, instinctive energy that was after the dreamer. And what if the dreamer had ignored that wild, natural side for many years? Maybe his cancer was the end result of repressing an important part of his natural instincts.

Curiously, a *black* panther is a leopard born in an ordinary litter but without spots. When it happens that they are completely black they are known as *black panthers*.[12] Perhaps the dreamer was born different, not like his siblings or his parents. Perhaps he tried to fit in to the family, adapt and change his behavior so that he would be accepted. The "black panther" would have to live in exile, banished into the unconscious, into the night shadows—growing angrier, more hostile, finally attacking the ego-self that had turned its back to a valuable part of the dreamer's real identity.

Killing Our Dreams

"How do I disarm, kill my dreams?" Vera asked, after realizing the meaning of a recent nightmare:

> I was holding a newborn baby and I'm supposed to cut it up. I proceed to cut its arms off. I wake up, horrified!

Vera had spent a lifetime killing her dreams and suffocating new ideas—her babies. She did it with poisonous, negative self-judgments that efficiently dispatched each and every attempt to live her own authentic life.

So who was this inner viper? As it turned out, there was no "inner" viper. But there *were* several "outer" vipers. Vera had been struggling for years to escape her mother's stinging, negative comments about her intelligence and abilities. A failed marriage and divorce from an equally judgmental partner poured salt in these old wounds, adding to her already in-the-pit self-esteem. Finally, society had thrown a dark burka of conformity over her life, selling her on the necessity to be subservient to men, to be a "good housewife."

Vera's dream intended to *shock* her into self-transformation—a wake-up scream. Such dreams, while terrifying and disturbing, come to save us, to extricate us from some collective swamp we have wandered into.

Exploring the dream:

- Many apparent nightmares are saviors in disguise.
- Dreams of mutilation can be blood-stained metaphors urging us

to look at how we are crippling our potential and our ability to live a meaningful, authentic life.

- In such dreams, be sure to explore any weapons by *becoming the weapon* and asking:
  - In Vera's dream, for example, ask: "How do I (as this knife) do what I do, cut off the baby's arms?" The knife might answer: "I can do this easily because of my *sharpened edge*, my *hardness*; I'm metal, cold, very strong. The baby doesn't have a chance."
  - The knife *depends* on the dreaming ego's participation, it needs the dreamer to *hold* the knife, to *accept* the idea, the thought. Without the ego's participation, the knife is *powerless*. And you recall that the dreaming ego and the waking ego are two sides of the same coin.
- In Vera's dream, the knife is *not* a part of her authentic nature. Instead the knife represents a cluster of potent, implanted, outside influences she has internalized to keep her separated from her *Self*.
- The symbolism of the knife fits: the blade like a sharp mental "tongue lashing," each critical thought like a deadly thrust slashing a creative, new idea (the baby) to pieces.
- We need to pay close attention to what happens to a baby or infant in a dream, as it often represents vital new life, creative inspiration, a *vulnerable* beginning, a fresh start—something brand new, just born.

Vera began working to eliminate these outside influences; she observed and recorded her repetitive mental self-criticisms and began to snap these "implanted" poison arrows in two, replacing them with her own ideas and her innate knowing of her own real identity and value.

Falling Apart

Not long after her nightmare dream Vera had another dream about her mother, who had recently died after a long illness:

> My mother was in the hospital and her insides were coming out from beneath her rib cage. The nurse was trying to put everything back behind her neck.

"She's falling apart," Vera commented, imagining what it would be like to be her mother in the dream. "The nurse doesn't have a clue what to do with the stuff that's coming out," she added. Because of Vera's efforts to become psychologically and emotionally free of her mother's critical nature, her dream creates a gory scene affirming that all her mother's stuff, which Vera had taken in and *internalized,* is indeed "falling apart" and "coming out"—a healing psychological death, an ending, a final curtain.

For Vera, the nurse represented the role she assumed in taking care of her mother. Her dream shows her that this caretaker (the nurse) does not know how to handle the "falling apart" process. Vera's "nurse" is also a collective figure: the medical establishment's way to fix a problem, what's acceptable, how things "should" be done. The nurse puts everything "back behind her neck," an action Vera said felt like hiding something in the wrong place. In this transition, Vera will have to deal with a powerful *caretaker impulse* that does not know how to *handle all the stuff coming out.* Moreover, it is her caretaker inclinations that will probably attempt to make her regress to living in the old patterns with the old ideas that, while known and comfortable, proved to be lethal assassins of her authentic life.

Exploring the dream:

- A dream figure like Vera's nurse can be a role *and* also represent important aspects of the dreamer's nature. The nurse would then represent a caring, nurturing part of Vera's nature, but a part that outside ideas, stereotypes—both good and bad—also influence.

For individuals who turn their backs on their inner life, dreams seem to fade out, to withdraw. Such individuals rarely remember dreams other than anxiety-filled or nightmarish, monster-filled ones. The soul seems to retreat from one's conscious life, leaving one under the tyranny of the waking ego structure, which then becomes our teacher. That Latin saying epitomizes this dynamic: "Dread the passage of Jesus, for he does not return."[13] We have the example of Lot's wife, who became a pillar of salt when she looked back after being called out of her city by Jehovah. And a Persian city that was once "enstoned to stone"king and queen, soldiers, inhabitants, one and all—because its people refused the call of Allah.[14] Poet Langston Hughes asks, "What happens to a dream deferred?":

> *Does it dry up*
> *like a raisin in the sun?*
>
> *Or fester like a sore—*
> *And then run?*

Does it stink like rotten meat?
Or crust and sugar over—
like a syrupy sweet?

Maybe it just sags
like a heavy load.

Or does it explode?

—Langston Hughes[15]

Recurring Humiliation

Sometimes social pressure to tolerate and accommodate evil becomes a tidal wave, overwhelming a person's sense of right and wrong. In the late 1930s, future victims of Hitler's Nazism were having disturbing, foreboding dreams—dreams intending to prevent a social disaster and also intending to awaken individuals to the impending firestorm: the approaching lethal, ideological plague. Nearly everyone chose to disregard those dreams, to keep them secret, their "silent screams" of horror—a collective *turning back*, a retreat from inner truth and authenticity and a leap into the jaws of the "many-headed beast."

In 1933, "Three days after Hitler seized power in Germany," writes the German journalist, Charlotte Beradt, "a certain Herr S., a man of about sixty and the owner of a middle sized factory, dreamt he had been crushed . . ."[16]

> Goebbels was visiting my factory. He had all the workers line up in two rows facing each other. I had to stand in the middle and raise my arm in the Nazi salute. It took me half an hour to get my arm up, inch by inch. Goebbels showed neither approval nor disapproval as he watched my struggle, as if it were a play. When I finally managed to get my arm up, he said just five words—"I don't want your salute"—then turned and went to the door. There I stood in my own factory, arm raised, pilloried right in the midst of my own people. I was only able to keep from collapsing by staring at his clubfoot as he limped out.[17]

At first glance, this dream's meaning seems to be obvious, but the dream's real significance rests in the figure of Goebbels, who represents Hitler's Nazism *coming into* Herr S.'s factory, meaning he has allowed all that Hitler represents to get into his head: his thinking, his ideas, his rationalizing of evil. Herr S., as the *dreaming ego*, finally gives in after tremendous resistance, raising his arm in the Nazi salute. A stark lesson about the propensity of the *dreaming ego / waking ego* to survive at any cost, even when that means sacrificing the individual's authentic life and essential character. Once the outside influence has been accepted, the *implant* is in place, we are hooked up, wired, a manufactured tooth on a gear turned by the massive machinery of some collective aberration.

In his dream, the figure of Goebbels has *nothing* to do with Herr S.'s authentic nature. In fact, Goebbels can leave because Herr S. will now do his own brainwashing; he will do Goebbels's work for him. The dream shows uncanny precision in picking out Goebbels, the Nazi *propaganda* minister (1933–45) who exploited the German radio, press, cinema, and theater to launch propaganda against the Jews and other groups. He was intensely loyal to Hitler. After Germany's defeat he murdered his family and killed himself.[18]

Herr S. will live his life wearing the bloodstained uniform of a totalitarian system. Had it occurred to Herr S. to take his dream seriously and refuse to give in to the pressure to conform, refuse to go along with the crowd, and refuse to *put up with* Hitler's regime, he would have had a completely different impact in his world. This dream haunted Herr S. and recurred many times, each time creating ever more intense feelings of humiliation and alienation. In each dream, he told Beradt, "The effort of lifting my arm was so great that sweat poured down my face like tears, as if I were crying in front of Goebbels."[19] In one dream, "while struggling to lift his arm, his back—his backbone—breaks."[20]

"Herr S. was upright and self-confident," writes Beradt. "His factory, where he had employed many an old fellow Social Democrat for as long as twenty years, meant everything to him." Baradt observed that Herr S.'s torturous dreams combined with his passive acceptance of Hitler left him feeling "alienated not only from all that [was] real in his life but also from his own character, which had lost its authenticity."[21]

We need to ask ourselves what we might be accepting, putting up with in our lives: working at a job that drains our energy and kills our spirit, dragging around a ball and chain of family expectations, caught in the swift current of social pressure to play a particular role in life, an economic merry-go-round of consumerism that trains us to endlessly play someone else's game?

As we cross the threshold into the 21st century, our dreams paint a grim picture: that we are indeed putting up with soul-killing influences and forces that do not belong to us: from anxiety-ridden dreams about work to ones about nuclear devastation and horrific wounding, our dreams continue to focus relentlessly on any dynamic that threatens our ability to live authentically with integrity and freedom.

Teeth Knocked Out

I discovered a disturbing parallel with dreams about losing teeth. In Beradt's collection of Germans' dreams during the Third Reich, she found numerous examples of a common recurring theme that typically went like this: "I awoke bathed in sweat. As had happened many nights before, I had been shot at, martyred, and scalped—had run for my life with blood streaming and *teeth knocked out*, Storm Troopers constantly on my heels."[22]

Problems with teeth continue to be a common image for many dreamers. It seems that dreams use *teeth* to represent the loss of something vital to life. Might such images be saying that we are subjecting ourselves to some self-destructive *group-think* that has crept into our life? Without our teeth, a lot of things become problematic if not impossible: We cannot adequately chew food, making it difficult to take in nourishment; we lose our ability to speak coherently; we cannot "bite" through things; we suddenly have a lot in common with an infant— helpless and needing "baby" food—relying on others, outside authorities to tell us how to live our lives.

In our era, police and military images have replaced the Germans' "storm troopers." Now people dream of being *arrested*, jailed by the police, which usually refers to internalized societal rules and expectations blocking our path and preventing us from being authentic.

Trapped on the Twenty-fifth Floor

Doing *nothing* seals us into the status quo. Doing nothing pushes us into a victim role, blaming others for our predicament: the environment, our parents. Doing nothing is a life-numbing choice, often with tragic consequences for ourselves and for society. When we choose to keep our dreams out of our waking life, we are choosing to "refuse our magnificent adventure."

A successful, apparently content New Yorker, married with three children, who worked in a Manhattan office building, had this dream:

> The automatic elevator stops with a jolt. The doors slide open, but instead of the accustomed exit the passenger faces only a blank wall. His fingers stab at buttons; nothing happens. Finally, he presses the alarm signal and a starter's gruff voice inquires

from below: "What's the matter?" The passenger explains that he wants to get off on the 25th floor. "There is no 25th floor in this building," comes the voice over the loudspeaker. "Easy," the passenger tells himself. "They are just trying to frighten me." But time passes and nothing changes. In that endless moment, the variously pleading and angry exchanges over the loudspeaker are the passenger's only communication with the outside world. Finally, even that ceases; the man below says that he cannot waste any more time. "Wait! Please!" cries the passenger in panic. "Keep on talking to me!" But the loudspeaker clicks into silence. Hours, days, or ages go by. The passenger cowers in a corner of his steel box, staring at the shining metal grille through which the voice once spoke. The grille must be worshipped; perhaps the voice will be heard again.

Most often such a refusal happens because we refuse to let go of what our waking ego believes to be our own interests. Without input from dreams and one's inner exploration, these " ego interests" tend to reflect stagnant, collective ideals, goals, and images into which individuals invest tremendous energy. As our life progresses, we wake up one day and realize that all the structures the ego has built are eerily empty, void of meaning and purpose. And we have the haunting feeling that we have been an actor in someone else's life, that we have missed something profound and *that* something has been lost deep in the shadowy past, buried by the years of neglect spent pursuing what?

Demons in the Night

Nightmares

Murder, monsters, beasts, rapists, predators, clawing fear, mutilation, decapitation—nightmares sink their teeth into our night world, plunging us into a black sea of fear. What could be the purpose or intent of such throbbing dream dramas?

In my experience, nightmares fall into two major categories that I refer to as *Type one* and *Type two*:

Type one nightmares include those that *intend* to shock us in order to get our attention—*shock therapy* from our psyche. For instance, I once had a dream of a tiger stalking me, intent on killing and eating me; that was a *Type one* nightmare. Such a dream alludes to a *wild* cat, something instinctive, natural, powerful, and completely authentic wants to get me—perhaps my dreaming ego? A nightmare in this category *intentionally* drags us into its dark den in order to wake us up, get our attention. The dream creates *valuable* terror, terror the Authentic Self often uses as a last resort, trying to save our genuine life.

Type two: In contrast, these nightmares result from serious trauma in our waking life. These dreams are usually quite literal and detailed, replicating an actual event we have experienced in our waking life. For example, I recently met a young woman who was in an apartment building two blocks away from the World Trade Center buildings when the terrorists attacked. She watched in horror from her apartment window as the buildings collapsed. She saw people jumping from windows, others hurled out from the explosions and fire. She began having recurring nightmares of being trapped in the wreckage of one of the planes that had hit the towers.

Her dream was showing her that she was caught in the "trauma," the "wreckage" of the event. Her "normal" life had crashed; the event had wrecked her emotionally; she was indeed an "emotional wreck." It is therapeutic to interpret all nightmares regardless of their origin. In many cases, just understanding the nightmare takes the sting out of it; it loses some of its intensity.

In circumstances of severe trauma: accidents, witnessing death, earthquakes, natural disasters, it is still appropriate to interpret these dreams and, if recurring, to intervene. One method that has proved to be effective is what one researcher calls "Imagery Rehearsal Therapy."[23] Dr. Barry Krakow, medical director of the Sleep and Human Health Institute in Albuquerque, New Mexico, has developed a technique to change the images in nightmares. "Our dreams," he explains, "start out as replays of traumas after a traumatic event." But, according to Krakow, when nightmares continue over a long period of time, they become destructive. "The nightmares somehow take on a life of their own. They become a broken record, a habit, a learned behavior," says Krakow.[24] Over time the nightmares actually retraumatize individuals.

Krakow's method involves rewriting the nightmare, replacing disturbing images with comforting images. The rescripted dream is then rehearsed over and over throughout the day and before sleep. Research indicates that about 90 percent of the time *Imagery Rehearsal* will either end the nightmare or modify it dramatically.

Dreamwork over many years has convinced me of the validity of one of Gestalt's underlying assumptions: "You never overcome *anything* by resisting it. You only can overcome anything by going deeper into it. If you are pursued by an ogre in a dream, and you *become* the ogre [when you work with the dream], the nightmare disappears. You re-own the energy that is invested in the demon."[25] You also go "into it" by exploring the dream and trying to understand its meaning. A correct interpretation will often stop or mitigate a recurring nightmare.

It is never too late to begin the quest for our authentic life. In each of us there resides a golden treasure, a secret garden, a special world. We can always choose to turn around and face the rising sun of our essential spirit—a spirit that wants to sing its song, write its story on the landscape of our life. For we are indeed, as Shakespeare observed, "such stuff as dreams are made on."

CHAPTER 8

✺

Invisible Guests

When all the souls had chosen their lives, they went before Lachesis. And she sent with each, as the guardian of his life, and the fulfiller of his choice, the daimon that he had chosen.

—Plato, *Republic*, Book X

Attendant Spirits

You don't grasp the fact that what is most alive of all is inside your own house.

—Kabir[1]

Chances are your dreams have already introduced you to what the Greeks called a daimon, an "attendant spirit," Latin for *genius*. One often appears in animal form and sometimes *cloaked* in the appearance of a deity, god or goddess, or a mythological figure. Occasionally, an attendant spirit appears as a wise old woman or man, a wizard, a teacher, a guru, an animal, or just an unusual, unknown figure. It's not uncommon to have several daimons or inner mentors who materialize as you work seriously with your dreams.

Our dreams and our imagination inevitably present us with such figures, remarkable autonomous images that become a source of unique, life-changing insights about who we are and what we must do with our life. We will now explore some of these fascinating *characters*, these "invisible guests," who appear in our dreams.

A Ravishing Bird

When he was eight years old, writer Allan Gurganus had a remarkable dream he described as "so real you're sure that it's happening." Here's his dream:

> I was in my knotty pine bedroom . . . with the bed quilts pulled up over me. I heard a sound in a black walnut tree right outside my window. That was strange. It was a kind of shuddering, tinsley, rustling sound. I leaned out of my bed and looked and I saw the tail of an enormous beautiful bird. We're talking about a bird that was probably forty feet long from head to toe. It had a kind of peacock tail and the feathers were as big across as palm bows. It was the most ravishing thing I'd ever seen. It was all the colors. All those rich blues and greens and purples and reds that you see in a peacock, but it was a huge, seemingly mythological bird that had somehow come to rest in the tree outside my room. . . . This extraordinary creature was preening itself.[2]

Gurganus certainly met a unique daimon, one that was "outside," not *in* the house—something the house cannot contain. That "ravishing" bird was *outside* the influence of family; it was "enormous," free, colorful, a fantastic creature captured for a timeless instant in the magic bell jar of his dream. Perhaps his mythic bird represented his waiting, enormous creativity, his potential greatness, his gift for writing that would carry him right into his authentic life.

Taking the Lid off the Sun

Many of these "attendant spirits appear *outside*; it's as though what they represent, their world, cannot be contained within any ego-related house or structure. A participant in a dream group brought this dream to one of our sessions.

> A short dream this a.m.: I heard a creaking sound. It was a large black tree with one long branch creaking and swaying back and forth. It was between some power lines above a railroad track. I looked up and the long part swung toward me—now the neck and face of an ancient, black brontosaurus.* I was afraid, but I stayed put. It asked my name. I said "Alaysa." It said that with his "people" Alaysa meant "taking the lid off the sun." He had

---

*From the Greek: *brontê*, thunder, and *sauros*, lizard —"thunder lizard."

a friendly, wise face. He asked if that meaning felt true to me and said, "I must take the lid off the sun."

This powerful dream marked a turning point in the dreamer's life. The dreamer explained that she had been "hiding her light," not allowing herself to "shine," keeping a lid on her Authentic Self.

Meeting the Elephant King

You can use the technique of active imagination to find and connect to your own inner attendant spirits by imagining a descent into an inner world. A descent does not necessarily infer going down as much as it provides a metaphor for our inward journey, going *within* and into the world of the unconscious.

After a lot of trial and error with my own attempts at active imagination, I had an experience that deeply affected me and has been a source of inspiration and support ever since: I met what I know to be one of my own inner mentors, an image living *outside* the range of my ego's world. It represents an important part of who I am, a figure I have come to call the "Elephant King." I began by imagining an entry place for my descent. This is a description of my experience late one evening while lying on my living room floor with the lights out. I began by imagining an entry place somewhere in a beautiful national park high in the mountains of Colorado, a place I used to visit to refresh and recharge my spirit:

> I had to move a thick covering of vines from the cave entrance. Cautiously stepping inside, I found myself standing on an uneven, rocky floor that disappeared into darkness just ahead. Moving slowly forward, I suddenly realized that the cave floor had become a covering of thin branches. Now my feet are sinking into this floor as if there's nothing supporting it. I stop at what appears to be the end of the cave floor. An ominous-looking completely black hole in the floor now blocks my path. Reassuring myself that this is a dream, I step into this blackness and fall through a vertical stone tunnel in what feels more like a gradual, floating descent than an actual fall. I sense that I'm going down a great distance.
>
> Finally, I come out of the blackness high above a moonlit landscape. Once more, I'm slowly floating downward, as though returning from having been ejected into the night sky. Eventually

I land on a winding, ascending pathway with massive stone walls on both sides. The path leads to a gigantic structure on the mountain top that at first glance looks like a medieval castle. I can't quite make out all the details in the darkness, but I am impressed by the size and complex, unusual architecture; it's like nothing I have ever seen before.

Suddenly, I notice a woman standing beside me wearing a smoky-blue robe with a hood. I realize she will escort me to the building. We proceed up the path, eventually reaching an immense arched entrance with massive double doors. My guide opens the doors, taking me into a vast entry area with ornate, painted ceilings several stories high. I'm supposed to wait while she announces my visit to whoever lives here. She disappears through another oversize door into another room. Returning, she motions me into a colossal, circular domed room. In between arches sweeping skyward, the dome opened to the night sky and a breathtaking panorama of stars. At the far side of this astonishing space, seated on an ornate gold throne, was a remarkable being in a red and gold robe. Similar to the Indian deity Ganesha, he had the head of an elephant and the body of a man, but with thick, elephant-like legs and arms. This being, whom I have come to call the *Elephant King*, then stood up, walked toward me, and began to dance and whirl around the room, wanting me to join him. I was reluctant, not knowing what to do, so I just watched in stunned silence.

Thus began what would become regular visits to the Elephant King. He became my inner mentor. I realized that, for the first time, I had applied a blend of Shamanism and my imagination to reach a symbolic, inner place of wisdom and insight—insight that would prove to be far superior to my conscious ego's knowledge and often disturbingly at odds with my waking ideas and attitudes.

Many of my clients and friends have been able to access similar beings through active imagination: one of a *Spider Woman* with a diamond-studded jacket, a *white cobra* with a golden crown, *Dionysus*, a *polar bear*, a *black panther*, a wise old woman or man, the *Tree Cutter*. Such images eventually enable us to access the unconscious anywhere, anytime, and mine the priceless wisdom available to all of us. They become our doorways to the inner worlds and we do not have to follow any outside group, religious authority, or any other *expert*.

Shamanism and Dreamwork

Exploring dream animals is certainly a form of do-it-yourself Shamanism. In fact, I have come to the conclusion that each of us can, through our own dreamwork, become our own Shaman. I no longer trust someone else to tell me who or what I am. How can anyone assume such arrogance and power over another individual? When we access and explore animal images in our dreams, we can be sure we are connecting with exactly what is needed for our life right now. Our own dreams save us from the dilemma of an outside authority, a Shaman or any other individual, telling us who or what creatures we should be working with.

I like the way of looking at animal images, whether in night dreams or in waking dreams, that author James Hillman describes. He suggests that we try to integrate dream animals into our waking life, even when we are repelled by them. He writes:

> Animals wake up the imagination. . . . Let's say you have a quick and clever side to your personality. You sometimes lie, you tend to shoplift, fires excite you, you're hard to track and hard to trap. You have such a sharp nose that people are shy of doing business with you for fear of being outfoxed. Then you dream of a fox! Now that fox isn't merely an image of your "shadow problem," your propensity to stealth. That fox also gives an archetypal backing to your behavior traits, placing them more deeply in the nature of things. The fox comes into your dream as a kind of teacher, a doctor animal, who knows lots more than you do about these traits of yours. . . . Instead of a symptom or a character disorder, you now have a fox to live with, and you need to keep an eye on each other.[3]

Wild animals in dreams more often than not represent *natural, undomesticated* and *uncivilized* characteristics—important attributes that can help us to see in the dark, give us claws, instinct, natural wisdom, and power when we need them most. A particular animal that keeps appearing in our dreams is a likely candidate for a dream daimon, a potential source of guidance and wisdom from a deeply authentic part of who we are.

Authenticity is a wild creature's most valuable attribute. It can be an immense help in understanding ourselves. In their natural state, animals live their lives *outside* the rules, pressures, and laws of society. Dreams usually set loose animal images when we are in dire need of their help. Dreams also are quick to show us how we are hurting the animal side of our psyches.

The Sleeping Elephant

When I first began to dream of elephants, I was totally enmeshed in a church group. In my dreams, there was always a problem, usually with baby elephants, injured elephants, elephants bumping into me under a dinner table in the church. Whatever these elephants represented, I was having a continuing variety of problems with them. After I left the church, my elephant dreams went through a transformation. One dream in particular stands out as a powerful catalyst that helped me to connect to the elephant as a dream daimon and symbolic mentor:

> It was a clear night and I was flying high above the African continent. I began dropping slowly toward the earth and eventually landed on my feet in front of a strange scene: A colossal, black, African bull elephant lay sleeping about ten feet in front of me. On either side of the elephant's head stood a dark native warrior with a spear, like guardians of the elephant. One began to pull on one of the enormous tusks and I thought, Uh-oh, they're going to wake him up! He did wake up, and then stood up, a tremendous, striking figure silhouetted against the night sky. The next thing I know, I'm riding on this elephant and we're moving across the continent in giant, effortless, bounding strides. I feel a tremendous connection and exhilaration—we are finally on our way! This creature *knows* where he is going.

Now I had an elephant "to live with," and I knew that somehow this great animal, who had been sleeping while I was busy "saving the world," slogging through a religious swamp, was now awake and would be a powerful part of my destiny and my attempts to live authentically.

Wolves in Sheep's Clothing

A word of caution is in order about this dream dynamic: Some dream images of gurus, ministers, and other spiritual authority figures represent belief systems, quicksand, dangerous ideological wastelands. Dreams usually expose these charlatans with what I call a "contradicting" dream. As an example, His Holiness the Dalai Lama once dreamt that his spiritual teacher came to him: "My guru came to me dressed in a business suit."[4] His dream seems to contradict his guru's role as a spiritual mentor by clothing him in a "business suit," the commercial world's uniform of conformity to the world of buying and selling—selling religion?

The dream image becomes the *antidote*, perhaps for the Dalai Lama, to wake him up to what the organization he heads is really doing and the group role he has adopted. His dream may mean to free him of the "business" of selling Buddhism, to enable him to become more authentic by showing him another side to his guru, "just another businessman." I have not spoken with the Dalai Lama about his dream. I wanted to give you an example of how you can use the Radical Dreaming process to explore potential meaning in others' dreams as well as your own, on a fundamental level.

In a similar example, a good friend of mine told me that just as he was becoming extremely interested in the teachings of Sai Baba, a popular East Indian guru, he dreamt that he was in an old, run down movie theater and Sai Baba came in and walked down one of the aisles dressed in a frumpy gray business suit. My friend said he was shocked to see this renowned spiritual teacher looking like that. I told him, "Your dream just yanked you out of that pit." His dream did not want him to waste his time and his life following someone else's path. He soon dropped his plans to follow Sai Baba's teaching. This is not to say that Sai Baba is bad, just not my friend's path. This example shows, once more, how our dreams protect our authenticity.

Finding a daimon (an inner mentor) in your dreams, or a mentor in the waking world, is completely different than *following* a guru or any ideological system, which requires childlike conformity and adaptation. The word, "mentor" goes back through Latin to a Greek name meaning a "wise counselor." A dream mentor or daimon connects you to your own inner *wise counsel*.

The Tree Cutter

Most helpers, teachers, and mentors in dreams appear as unique figures or creatures. Connecting with these personifications of inner wisdom carries the potential to ignite transformation and change in our waking lives—*if* we apply the dream's wisdom and help.

Justin, a bright, forty-year-old engineer, was frustrated and bored with his nine-to-five corporate job and desperately wanted to find meaningful work, something that would provide an outlet for his passion about social problems and the environment. He had this dream just as he was struggling to find a way to carve out more creative time for his real interests:

> I'm watching a tree cutter cutting down pine trees. He left the oak tree alone that I was standing in. I was standing on a long, slim branch with a tuft of leaves on it—an old branch. I was holding another branch for support. We talked. It looked better when the trees were cut away. We talked about how a garden could be grown now.

Justin said the "Tree Cutter" was a "regular working guy," a bearded outdoor type but not anyone he knew. "Pine trees grow in groups and crowd out the light," he said, adding, "They're all the same. The oak tree," Justin explained, "is more unique and special." When he imagined himself as the oak tree, he said that it "felt freeing, like I have breathing room, space around me."

The pine trees in Justin's dream, while natural, symbolized crowding, a group of similar trees, a *stand*. In his book *Crowds and Power*, Elias Canetti suggests that a forest has what he calls "multiple immovability." He explains: "Every single trunk is rooted in the ground and no menace from outside can move it. Its resistance is absolute; it does not give an inch. It can be felled, but not shifted. And thus the forest has become the symbol of the *army*, an army which has taken up a position. . . ."[5]

Justin felt his dream was showing him that he needs the Tree Cutter's help to clear space, to get rid of some conformist ideas and attitudes—social pressure and expectations to be just another pine tree disappearing in the crowd. He needed to clear ground in his psyche so that he could plant a garden where his authentic life can grow, blossom, and support his unique "oak tree."

Working with the dream:

- The "Tree Cutter" knows how to *clear space* in Justin's life. He knows what to eliminate in order to create "breathing room."
- Justin began to eliminate his "pine trees," unnecessary activities that were repetitive and time consuming—activities he described as "having a good time, but not really accomplishing anything."
- He used his new "free" time as creative space to brainstorm ideas and interests, to read, and to reflect on his life. This creative space became his *secret garden*, fertile earth in which the seeds of his creative potential can take root.

A Menacing Lioness

Diana was struggling with complex family problems while working long hours in a demanding, exhausting job. She felt stuck, trapped economically in what seemed to be a labyrinth of impossible circumstances. Just when things were blackest, she had a scary dream, one she called a nightmare:

> I am in a foreign country, probably Turkey. We (my husband was with me and several others on an outing) go to a huge, deep lake and begin swimming. Two boulders provide the only underwater footing, yet even if I stand on one of them the water is up to my chin. Also they are some distance apart, maybe forty feet, and I'm not a strong swimmer. I become aware that a lioness is swimming nearby. She is gradually becoming more and more menacing. The others are some distance away and seem to be having a good time, but I am beginning to panic.

Many dreams that at first feel like nightmares unravel, often turning out to contain real treasure. Again, it's that old dreaming ego, the "me" in the dream reacting literally to the dream drama; this is the situation in Diana's dream. At one point, as we were working with her dream's images, she said, "That's it—my life feels like I'm just keeping my head above water." She added, "It's scary. It (the lioness) might make me have to move off that boulder."

I asked her to describe a lioness to me, assuming I had no idea what such a creature was. She explained, "It's a large mammal. It can be ferocious. It's powerful, impressive, protective, wild, unpredictable." I asked her if she saw or felt any of those qualities in herself. She hesitated, "Not much anymore, except for my 'ferocious' anger about society and world problems."

Diana's "lioness" turned out to be a valuable part of her authentic nature, a powerful, capable, instinctual creature that *was* after Diana's "just keeping my head above water" ego structure. She began to feel her lioness nature and she began to act and "move" off the immovable boulders of her circumstances. She now knew, as the lioness, she could swim through and out of that "deep" water. When I last saw Diana, she was well on her way to changing her life and her circumstances—her inner lioness nature was *moving* her off the boulder, transforming her life—all from a dream!

Exploring the dream:

- Diana imagined the two boulders being her job and her family problems; ironically, the qualities that the lioness represents are just what's needed to "... make [her] have to *move* off that boulder."
- She described the lake as a "passive force." We can glean a lot more information from the image by looking at how such a "huge, deep lake" would form with a likely scenario going something like this: A deep, *depressed* area gradually fills with water, probably from rain, from melting snow, or from some inlet, a stream or runoff emptying into the depressed land.
- As the lake, there's a feeling of just *passively* taking it, the water, all in, accepting without protest whatever you're given; as the lake you are inactive, dependent on the weather, the elements. You are not proactive and nothing at all like the lioness. Watch out!

The *Uninvited* Guest

Dreams have a habit of introducing astonishing characters into our lives at just the right moment. Sometimes a character drops in, an *uninvited* guest who turns out to be the exact medicine we need to get ourselves out of some dilemma.

A Celebrity Guest

Pamela, a forty-six-year-old fiery redhead, was feeling depressed, helpless, and anxious about her daughter and her grandchildren, who were embroiled in a stormy family crisis. She had a dream that helped to lift her from a murky swamp of depression that was slowly pulling her under.

> I had just arrived at my home and when I went to put my key in the door, a man in his fifties with a large dog on a long, brown rope leash walked up to the door. I felt threatened and tried to keep them out but the dog got into the house before I could stop her and then I'm panicked the man would have to come in to get the dog out. He got into the house. I felt threatened by him; was he going to attack me? Then the dog peed on the entry floor. I'm appalled! I'm watching the man and suddenly realize it's Jerry

Seinfeld, the comedian. Then he unzips his pants, takes out his penis and starts spraying pee all over my living room. Some of it gets on me too. I'm grossed out, watching in disbelief! I just couldn't believe what he was doing. Meanwhile he thinks it's hilarious; he's laughing, having fun. I still feel a little anxious and confused and the dream ends.

Pamela's panic and fear in her dream once more illustrates a typical reaction of the dreaming ego, which reacts literally to the dream.

"The dog's leash was so long that the dog could pretty much go wherever he wanted. He had a lot of freedom," Pamela said. The "dog" gets "into" her house first. In other words the qualities that the dog represents get *into* her awareness, *into* her psyche and into her life. The strange man follows, but once he's in the house, he *transforms* into the sitcom star, Jerry Seinfeld. "When I realized it was Jerry Seinfeld, the dog was not on the leash anymore," Pamela explained.

Her dream shows her a potential transformation, a metamorphosis. Jerry Seinfeld traits, qualities she described as "quitting while you're ahead, good common sense, looking at life with a sense of humor"— these *qualities* unleash the dog. Becoming Jerry Seinfeld frees the dog, removing the rope from around her *neck*. Her dream connects her to a powerful part of her authentic nature, a part that can look at life with a sense of humor, a part that has the power to heal her depression.

"My marriage feels like that long leash," Pamela said, wincing. She had been experiencing chronic neck pain for several years. She complained, "My husband stays in control of everything, especially the money. But he wants me to have my own interests." Her dream says that the "Seinfeld" part of her psyche also carries a key to her freedom from a controlling husband. A dog, in contrast to a cat, knows how to *adapt* to our world. Pamela's dream illustrates how individuals *adapt* to circumstances that *depress* their ability to live authentically.

"Jerry's penis is having a great time—it's totally natural," Pamela said, smiling. Peeing *is* a natural process, a release, a relief. It's as if everything Jerry Seinfeld represents marks his territory and the dreamer cannot escape this golden shower ("Some of it gets on me too."); the dream's effect, its blatant sexuality, its message and meaning *get on her*, transforming her conscious attitude and her outlook. The penis also discharges the seeds of new life. It is a creative instrument.

Pamela's dream comedian exploded her depression with perfectly timed humor, with a lightened-up approach to her life. She focused on balancing her tendency to look at life too seriously with her newfound

Seinfeld humor. She now had a transformative sense of humor, a gleaming new sword to slay the dragon of depression and cut the rope around her neck. She realized that to be controlled she had to continue to agree with the status quo.

Exploring the dream:

- When a celebrity shows up in your dream, find out all you can about that particular person.
- Imagine being that individual and ask yourself: "As this person, what is my life like?"
- Be alert for *uninvited* guests in your dreams. They often represent important aspects of your Authentic Self that want "in" to your life.
- Once you determine that a dream figure is important and does represent a part of your essential nature, create space in your waking life for the qualities that dream image represents.
- Look for any physical symptoms that relate to your dream images, like the leash around the dog's neck in Pamela's dream. Physical symptoms are often part of the long-term consequences of self-imposed exile from the Authentic Self.
- When any image of control or restraint shows up in your dream, explore how you might be doing this to yourself. Look for ways you adapt, how you survive: in your relationships, at work, with your family, in society.
- When sexual organs appear in dreams, look at your creativity: Where is it? How does it function in your life?

Butchering Creativity

For example, a depressed computer programmer who had kept the lid on his creativity for years finally dreamt that he had cut off his penis with a butcher knife. In his waking life, he realized that he was "butchering" his creativity with negative judgments and criticisms of his creative ideas. It turned out that these particular negative criticisms had their origin in his family dynamic and in society.

Going Back for the Ruby

Sometimes a dream offers us multiple choices as though we are being tested—we are choosing among potential lives, or we arrive at an intersection where suddenly three directions open like ancient doors into three different kingdoms.

An intense thirty-five-year-old journalist, Kay had recently escaped from what she called a "religious cult," the Jehovah's Witnesses. She told me about a remarkable dream she had after she left the Church, and said, "Now I feel it's time to go back for that ruby." Here's her dream:

> A Spirit (seemed like a "he" but not personified) offered me treasures. One was a pile of academic books—they're growing. I say "No." The books evaporate. Then he offers me another gift. It's an Assyrian bas relief of a Mayan pyramid with a door that somehow has uncanny power. As I'm looking at it a poison mist drifts out. I say "No," again. Finally, he offers me, in his hand, a magnificent, massive, rectangular ruby, which I decide I want for my "art." I put it on and a laser light comes out of the ruby and burns a trench in the earth. I'm afraid it's more power than I can control so I ask for a seed-garnet necklace. It refracts, but nothing like the ruby. Then I see an amethyst in a plain setting with a silver filigree and I say "Yes," that's what I really want. It's the right choice.

When she had the dream, her initial reaction, as the dreaming ego, was to reject the "ruby" because she was "afraid it's more power than I can control." The ruby with all its power and focused laser light is too scary for her *dreaming ego*, which again provides an excellent example of the frightening aspect of the ego's encounter with an aspect of the Self; in our waking life we settle for something less, something beneath our potential. In Kay's dream, her dreaming ego wants the "amethyst in a *plain* setting."

A powerful dream, it stuck with her. She could not forget that image of the ruby and its awesome, focused red light, burning a trench in the earth, digging and unearthing, what? Needless to say, Kay did focus on her creative life and has transformed her world using the power and magic in her "ruby."

Exploring the dream:

- Kay's dream illustrates the importance of treating, for most dreams, the *dreaming ego* as yet another dream element, one schooled in survival techniques in our waking life. Her dream shows how terrified we can all be, at times, of our own potential.
- The "ruby," image, while representing redness, blood, vitality, directed passion, light, and fire, is a unique and authentic, precious

stone. It has the ability to emit a *laser beam* of light, a dream image that we can also look at quite objectively. A laser beam is what scientists call "*coherent*" light, an "esthetically consistent relation of parts," what physicists refer to as "having waves with similar direction and amplitude."[6] Here, the ruby gives us a wonderful metaphor for the Authentic Self, a unique integration, a set of relationships with "direction and amplitude."

- Also interesting is the fact that *agitation* begins the process of producing a laser beam: electrons are first excited to a higher energy state by an energy source, a process called "stimulated emission."[7] It's as if Kay's dream portrays a life process: the Self as a creation of time, heat, pressure, agitation—bumps in the road, unexpected upsets, occasional earthquakes—the jarring events in life, as well as the beauty, the intensity and passion, the red flame of creation burning trenches in the quiet landscape of our ordinary world.

Lucid Dreaming: Benefits and Drawbacks for Your Journey

Lucid dreams are just that—dreams that seems so real we have difficulty distinguishing them from "real" experiences in our waking life. Most of us have experienced lucid dreams or lucid moments in dreams. Usually, in a lucid dream we become *aware* at some point that we are dreaming.

Given their own development and *autonomy*, lucid dreams can be interpreted like any other dream. However, the popular practice of manipulating and controlling the dream, treating it like a video game, can quickly short circuit the dream's real meaning and purpose. The disturbing, almost cult-like mind-set of lucid dreaming as psychic entertainment degrades the dream world, turning it into an adult Disneyland—an often *addictive* amusement park for individuals who don't want to grow up. The authentic adult fantasy world means imagining and creating a meaningful life that will impact society.

Mental Play-Doh

We have to ask ourselves, *Who is it that wants to manipulate the dream?* Of course it's the *waking ego* editing the dream drama before even having a clue about what the story intends or means. Author and dream researcher Marc Barasch provides one example of how playful dream manipulation can create scary consequences. He writes:

One lucid dreamer told me how he had become adept at manipulating his dreamworld, conjuring up at will rooms full of beautiful, compliant women. But once, when he was amusing himself by "flying over Detroit, knocking over the hats off men," one of his made-up people reached up and grabbed his foot, unnerving him so much he awoke. He began to wonder: "I'm no longer so sure my dream characters are just mental Play-Doh."[8]

In certain circumstances, lucid dreaming does have therapeutic potential to help individuals overcome and confront fears, particularly from some past experience or trauma that has adversely impacted their life. In this respect, lucid dreaming can be therapeutic, similar to hypnosis, which has proved to be effective in treating post traumatic stress.

Some lucid dreamers report interpreting their dreams while in the dream state. Of course the immediate question arises regarding *who* is doing the interpreting.

While attending an Association for the Study of Dreams conference in Ottawa, Jane-Lewis White, a dream researcher and Jungian analyst, overheard a woman describing a nightmare:

> I was sitting in the cafeteria and overheard a woman, a "lucid" dreamer, describing a troubling nightmare to a friend. In her upsetting dream, *she had been caught in a swimming pool filled with garbage.* She boasted that, thanks to lucid dreaming techniques, *she had been able to clean up the garbage and change the image of the dream.* She was pleased and proud of her success, but I . . . was startled. Why would she want to do that—change or throw away the image of the dream and, at the same time, throw out the possibility of understanding its meaning.
>
> . . . I was amazed to discover that there were people in the world who attended to their dreams and clearly valued them, but who did not trust the unconscious to speak/reveal truth in its own way. To violate a dream by altering the text or image seemed not only irresponsible but psychologically dangerous.[9]

Tibetan "dream yoga" has evolved into another rather ominous way of looking at dreams that can separate individuals from a dream's deep, life-changing intent. This viewpoint, which is another "group's" theory about dreaming, suggests that we look at the dream world *and* the waking world all as a dream. Thus practitioners of Tibetan dream yoga work to become lucid in their dreams so that they can change the dream and "dispel illusions," changing any dream image that is fearful or un-comfortable. On one level this is a technique to *escape* from the dream's real intent and also escape from the challenge to create meaning in life.

Many dreams present us with frightening images that are *intended* to shock us into taking action about serious health issues. Other dreams that at first feel nightmarish turn out to be priceless ingredients in the creation of an authentic life. In our dreams, what at first terrorizes us more often than not, ends up saving us. What if we kept changing these images into something pleasant and fun? We would effectively abort the remarkable flow of wisdom and guidance from our own inner nature.

While dream yoga's ideas may contain elements of truth—many physicists theorize that solid matter and consciousness do appear to be interconnected on a quantum level—this view of life tends to depreciate a person's responsibility to do something with his/her life. Instead, if life *is* "just a dream," not *real,* why bother about it and why worry about society or the environment? Turning our dreams into amusement rides for the ego, we can languish in paradise, comfortably asleep for years like Odysseus under the sirens' spell, forgetting to *live our life.*

> *Most do violence to their natural aptitude,*
> *and thus attain superiority in nothing.*
> —Baltasar Gracian

CHAPTER 9

Dreams at the Edge of the Forest

Setting Out: The Quest

You must find your own path. Go your own way,
which is both terrifying and exhilarating. No one can
tell you any longer the way, because there is no longer
one prescribed way, but only a way—your way, which
is as valid as any other as long as you live it honestly.

—Robert Johnson[1]

King Arthur's knights had all taken their seats for the evening dinner, but Arthur would not let the meal begin until an adventure had been decided upon. The knights decided to go in pursuit of the Holy Grail, but "They thought it would be a disgrace to go forth in a group. Each entered the forest that 'he' had chosen where there was no path and where it was the darkest."[2] We enter the forest of the unconscious where it is the "darkest," or unknown to our waking consciousness, by taking our dreams and imagination seriously.

Dreams now begin to provide direction and encouragement, launching the ship of our unique destiny into uncharted waters. Without making decisions for us, they point us in the right direction, like navigators. We become explorers into our own future potential, into our essential natures, and our adventure begins in earnest.

We have dreams about cliffs: hanging on to a cliff, standing on the

233

edge of a precipice, a road on the edge of a cliff collapses, falling off a cliff, driving off the edge of a cliff and plunging into the water below. And people dream of entering unknown places, leaving childhood homes, or being arrested by the police.

Threshold Dreams: Treasure Maps from the Unconscious

"I stood before a dark cave, wanting to go in," was the dream of a man just beginning therapy; "and I shuddered at the thought that I might not be able to find my way back."[3] At any beginning in life, for that matter, at the start of any new endeavor, the psyche often presents us with a particular type of dream that magically opens a door to a new world. These dreams typically symbolize the current central issue or dilemma in our life. Additionally these *threshold* dreams often provide a wealth of insight into the present and future course of our inner journey. It's as though the inner world, the soul, responds to our intent to change and to work on our life with a symbolic representation of what lies ahead.

Brain Damage

Dreams sometimes present threshold experiences as a journey. Kim, raised in a strict Catholic family and now in her early forties, said she was "very aware now of a mid-life crisis." One rainy winter night, Kim brought a dream to a group session that had frustrated many attempts at interpretation. She wondered, "Could this be a menopause dream?"

> I am about to go on a journey with three middle-aged people, a man and woman I don't know and another man I know slightly (not in real life). The occasion is solemn and the day is gray. We are on a steep, rocky, snow-covered mountainside. The three people are wearing plain, grayish robes and their heads are shaved. At some time in the past, for some unknown reason, they pounded long, construction-type nails into their heads in decorative patterns. One man has a very dense nail design of tight concentric circles that cover the entire top of his head. The other man and woman have much smaller nail patterns.
>
> We all know that they will die at the end of our journey because the nails have damaged their brains. Even though the nails were pounded in some time ago, they are only now causing a numbness which signifies impending death. Death will come

soon to all of them, but first to Circle-head. I am concerned about him, but he is a stoic and resigned to his fate, as is the woman.

Kim's dream felt big. She said it seemed "like a matter of considerable importance, spiritual or life-changing." Her dream also has a feeling of a self-inflicted crucifixion: " . . . they pounded long, construction-type nails into their heads." Kim described the nails as "sharp, hard, cold," and they could "kill soft, vulnerable living tissue." Kim realized that each nail represented a rule, an absolute, a law that she had put up with, that she had "pounded" into her head. Nails are manmade, *manufactured*, and mass-produced. If we imagine *being* "construction-type" nails, we are *rigid*, inflexible, and our primary job is to hold a structure together. For Kim, the nails represented the destructive influences from her Catholic upbringing, which her parents, particularly her father, reinforced and followed. Nails in decorative patterns reminded her of the necessity to "look good," to be "moral" according to the church's views about good and evil, to think "good thoughts," to police her own imagination.

Kim's dream told her that she was beginning a journey involving death and transformation; the ending of three aspects of her personality, the removal of Catholicism's iron nails from her head, the ending of outside, mind-*numbing*, influences that have nothing to do with her authentic life and the ending of an *unknown* third thing. Kim was on a journey *into* her life.

Planned Development Meets the Forest

The Second-Growth Forest

At his first psychotherapy session, a very depressed and suicidal architect in his early thirties, whom I will call Ross, described this initial dream:

> I am walking down a long alley. On my right behind tall fences are rows of banal apartments. On my left are the scrap remains of a second-growth forest being developed for housing. There are no roads or trails connecting the apartments to the woods, only the alley between. I make *my own trail* into the woods and surprisingly find a beautiful river. I walk upstream looking for its source.

After working with this dream, he realized that it begins with a warning: "a second-growth forest being developed for housing," meaning he is in danger of settling for the world's—others' ideas about his life and his work—encroachment ("housing") on the Self, the "forest." And it is "planned" development from the outside world, the opposite of individual creativity, which by definition is *unplanned*. We could also look at the waking ego as the *planner* of the development. Even so, the dream brims with symbology of his planned, ordered life, compartmentalized in the rows of "*banal* apartments," dreary commonality where each unit conforms, fitting into the whole structure. But when he makes his "own trail" into the forest, he encounters a "beautiful river." His dream presents him with two worlds, one of banality that is ending and a journey just beginning, perhaps to find the source of the "beautiful river."

The Award

After a solid year of serious dreamwork, Ross was able to articulate a completely different approach to architecture that began to attract considerable interest and attention from his colleagues and a local university that wanted him to develop classes on his ideas. Finally he had a remarkable dream:

> I am presented, by an older man, a special award similar to a grant. It is a lifetime stipend to insure that I keep doing what I am doing. My nomination is by others without my knowledge (Here is that mysterious "we" in dreams again). I read one of the nominating letters written by a former mentor who supported my idiosyncrasies and peculiarities. His assessment of my efforts is absolutely beautiful! Unbelievably happy, I start to cry.

Here, Ross's dream assures him that he will have the psychological and spiritual resources needed to support his passion, his unique, creative path, and his authentic life.

Shelved and Leashed

A woman in her early thirties had decided to extricate herself from a twenty-year dependency upon social services and the mental health system. She had this dream the night before her first psychotherapy session:

> I dreamt of going to see a social worker for housing and income help. And I witnessed a male social worker holding a strong rope

like a leather leash or harness tied to a human being who was in a cage up on a shelf. This poor person was acting like an animal, shitting on itself and digging in garbage. I felt so bad for her bondage but I felt powerless to help her.

Her dream is pretty straightforward and uses stark images to impress upon her the *real* nature of her "bondage" to the system, which has imprisoned her and kept her life "on a shelf," of no use to her and of no use to society. Once more we see the typical pattern of beginning the real work of reclaiming one's life and *that* beginning effort coming face-to-face with some obstacle. She realized that she had to face the "powerless" part of herself as well as an authoritarian, controlling aspect—"holding the leash"—a role she had put herself in that kept her leashed and caged. The system's ideas and attitudes do not belong to her but have been implanted; they are social intrusions from society and her environment. She had allowed the system to prevent her from living her own life. Her dream marked the beginning of the journey back to her life and her escape from a disempowering system of aid that had turned her into a prisoner "digging in garbage," other people's worthless waste.

The Spider and the Ballroom

Carol, a woman in her early twenties was struggling to find and live her own life and extricate herself from extremely negative parental influences, particularly from her mother. After about a year of intense dreamwork she had this dream:

> I'm in a room like a foyer in a huge mansion or building. A big, black spider about the size of a dinner plate is trying to get me, preventing me from getting to a door. I try to go around it and somehow end up crushing it by accident with my back—pieces of the spider are scattered on the floor. At that instant the door opens to a grand ballroom and I enter what had been a secret room; it is magnificent, ornate, beautiful, with thick plush carpet. There are male and female dancers there and suddenly I notice a frightened little girl is with me. I run and dance and leap with great joy.

After working with the dream images she felt the spider represented her mother's influence and especially her mother's negative stereotyping of women, especially her belief that women just need to please men sexually, that this was their purpose. The beautiful "secret room" opens the instant she "accidentally" kills the spider with her "back." Her dream correlated to her increasing awareness of ideas and attitudes that belonged to her mother and were *not* a part of who she was. She had a completely different view of sexuality.

She described the dancer as the "artist," the inspired, free part of her *Self*. Carol felt that the little girl, "about eleven or twelve years old," represented her experience during an especially difficult time when she was deeply traumatized by her mother's powerful, derogatory admonitions and warnings about being a "woman." This "little girl" was frightened at the prospect of leaving her mother's influence, negative as it may have been. When she imagined herself as the *grand ballroom*, she felt the immensity and magnificence of her own real nature; she felt a powerful new aspect of her real identity that gave her renewed courage to strike out on her own path—and with "room" to have a "ball"!

The spider begs further exploration. Her dream presents her with a *big* (the size of a dinner plate) spider, in effect saying this is a huge issue, "bigger" than she realizes. She kills the spider by turning her back to it, by putting it behind her, out of sight; the dream says that what the spider represents surprisingly falls apart when she turns around, looking forward. Now the spider—her mother's negative influences—no longer holds together; Carol, through her own discrimination (identifying the difference between her mother's influences and her own ideas), has taken the spider apart, which opens the door to the "secret room," an important image of her unique individuality.

Wildness

One of the great paradoxes of trying to find our authentic life is that we are almost certain to encounter terrifying parts of our authentic nature, parts of our unique character that our adapted life has forced out of the "civilized" places in our ego-nature. Folk tales and stories have told us for centuries that all sorts of demons and tricksters dwell in areas outside the familiar village boundaries. In other words, once we leave the comfort and protection of the village—our familiar but ordinary world— we encounter dangerous presences. And the more we live highly adapted, conformist lives, the more dangerous *our* "wilderness" becomes.

The Hottentots describe an ogre that lives outside the village among the scrubs and dunes. This creature, said to travel in packs, hunts humans, tearing them to shreds with cruel teeth as long as fingers.[4] In many parts of the earth we encounter a treacherous one-legged, one-armed, one-sided creature—the half-man—invisible if seen from the off side. This one-sided character (called *Chiruwi*, "a mysterious thing"), according to Central African folklore, says to the individual who encounters him: "Since you have met with me, let us fight together." If thrown, he will argue: "Do not kill me. I will show you lots of medicines"; and then the fortunate person becomes a physician. But if this half-man wins the battle, his victim dies.[5] So these ogres start to sound a lot like angry, exiled parts of ourselves, a mysterious wildness that has the potential to turn a person into a physician, but only after we engage it in battle.

In many cases, the actual beasts and dragons that modern individuals must slay are society's imperatives that dictate the boundaries of human existence and creativity. We are sure to encounter formidable adversaries the instant we begin to move through and into the wild places in our own nature. It is then that all the forces—commonality and mediocrity—attack, seeking to bring us back into the comfortable prison of a *normal* life. Additionally, we are taught while very young that wildness is *not* acceptable. And as children, most of us quickly learn to repress our wild side, at least while our parents are around.

Navigation: Crossings and Boundaries in Dreams

Death Drives down This Road

Our dreams love to show us "choice" points: times in life that we are faced with life and death decisions, when the choice we make often means the difference between living our own life and stepping onto a dead end road that eats our years like some asphalt beast. Kay, an exuberant thirty-five-year-old, was in the rapture of rediscovering her creative side, which included a serious talent for writing and a love of fine art and glass sculpture. She was also recovering from her lifelong involvement in a large church that she said was "like a cult." She had left the church four years ago. She brought this dream to one of our first sessions:

I'm standing, with my back to it, on the edge of a vast wheat field. There is a high mountain off in the distance. A wind comes

and blows the wheat back from me. A black asphalt road is right
in front of me. I want to step onto the road, but I can't because I
will be betraying something if I step onto it.

Kay's dream powerfully reinforced her decision to focus on developing her creative life, doing what she loved and felt passionate about.
When I asked her about that asphalt road, she said, "That's the road
down which death drives. I can no longer live by logic and reason, but
only by my dreams." Having just freed her life from an ideological
prison camp, Kay was smack in the middle of a potent life-transition:
leaving a life directed and shaped by religious doctrine and stepping *into*
her own authentic life.

When I asked Kay about the wheat field, she said, "It's thousands of
voices. It reminds me of my ex-husband and our life in Kansas, all the
wheat fields—and the church—always doing what I'm 'supposed' to
do."

Exploring the dream:

- Here again, we can rely on our dreams' uncanny ability to assem-
  ble the perfect cast of characters and images. The "black asphalt"
  road is manmade. That road's job is to direct and control traffic,
  movement. The road lives in a two-dimensional world: either this
  way or that way, The route and the destination are already determined. It's a road of death and conformity, a thick, black, deadly
  current.
- Remember to imagine yourself as each element and then link your
  experience to your waking life. For Kay, this brought the images
  into her waking life.
- Her dream's images became imaginal weapons and she could *feel*
  them in her life: that asphalt road would appear whenever she felt
  her creative resolve weakening, whenever she was tempted to get
  a *real* job, whenever she was tempted to "betray" her dreams and
  live only by "logic and reason."

Losing Myself

A young woman in her early twenties, whom I will call Melissa, had
just moved to Seattle to begin a new life. She recalled a mysterious recurring dream she had when she was thirteen years old:

I am in my childhood home but it looks different, bigger and
more square. I'm looking for our cat, Topper, who I love. I see

him through the window across the street on a bluff. When I call him to come home, he runs across the street in front and is run over, killed by a car. I'm horrified and very upset because it's my fault.

Melissa explained that Topper was independent, playful and stubborn—a totally unique, "really different" cat. For Melissa a cat also represented intuition, being natural, instinctive. Working on the dream, she realized that it had occurred precisely during the time in her life when she really began to feel social pressure to conform to outside standards and ideals. "I began losing myself, who I really was. I was more concerned with fitting in, with pleasing my parents." In her dream, it is that world of influences and pressures, the car on a *public* street, that runs over her natural, independent, unique individuality. Her psyche reached back into time, bringing her dream into her present life awareness and circumstances so that she would not step into the same trap, again trying to be someone or live an inauthentic, unnatural life under destructive societal and familial influences. Topper is hit when he tries to get across the pre-planned, paved road—a place where strict rules tell us what we should do and where we can and cannot go. And Melissa is also *in* her childhood home, *in* the structure containing and representing parental influences—good and bad.

This dream reconnected her to her own uniqueness and the deep significance of remaining true to herself, of not allowing family pressures and expectations to "run over" her "playful, stubborn, totally unique," authentic nature just when she had the opportunity to recreate her life. Melissa began identifying ideas and attitudes that belonged to her parents but were not a part of her real identity.

Down Under

Dreams frequently use the symbology of different countries to refer to unknown parts of ourselves. Someone once asked me at a conference about recurring dreams of Australia. I said, "Well, for most people living in our part of the world, Australia is a really big place they don't know much about, meaning a big chunk of unknown landscape in our own nature." That meaning immediately resonated. That's certainly not saying that all dreams of Australia have that meaning. We would have to place the image within the context of the dreamer's life, which would no doubt give us much more particular information.

When a country pops up in a dream, it is important to imagine that you *are* that particular place, feeling the geography, the cities, the people, and also asking yourself what it is like to be that country in *relation to* the other countries surrounding you. Often Westerners dream of being in a totalitarian state, or in a country ruled by a dictator. These dreams always refer to the fact that we are subjecting ourselves to some *outside* tyranny. A belief system has walled us in, each dogmatic idea another nail in the coffin of our creative life; we have erected our own prison, a barbed-wire-fenced border, our own iron curtain, which may be a particular religion, a political viewpoint, or any other cloned way of approaching life that blocks us from living out of the soul of our being.

And now we ready ourselves for some serious adventure, some dragon slaying. Time to gather our weapons, our "delicate magic," call upon our attendant spirits.

> *Where the spirit does not work with the hand,*
> *there is no art.*
> —Leonardo da Vinci

CHAPTER 10

☞

Slaying Dragons

Now she unweaves the web she hath wrought.
—William Shakespeare, *Venus and Adonis*

Staying in the Box: When Security Becomes a Trap

We should be about dismantling our social myths,
therefore, as pernicious things comparable to illusions
and neurotic distortions.

—Montague Ullman

The moment we get serious about changing our lives, new challenges and tests seem to appear out of nowhere, more determined than ever to steal our resolve. We meet dangerous enemies—some of our own making and others that are mental viruses: *dis-ease*, contamination, self-defeating ideas and rules spread by the masses that have cut deep grooves into our psyche. In the midst of this storm, our old life can feel compelling and seductive, like a safe harbor.

Insecurity, doubt, and fear march into our lives like invading armies. All the reasons we *should not* be on this quest swarm like hornets, sting-ing thoughts repeating themselves over and over in our heads. We have to fight our way out of the idea that security comes from conformity and adaptation to the expectations of others. Social pressure to make a good living, accumulate wealth and material possessions, impress others with our "success"—all combine to create an overwhelming barrier to living an authentic life. We need to think "outside the box," consider the im-possible, ignore well-intended "advice" from friends and family.

"Collective dragons" are the outer world's authority and influence preventing individuals from living their own lives; this is the dragon, Shakespeare's "many-headed beast," that one must slay. My dream research has convinced me that these influences and forces that have had us under their spell do not just let go; they attack in force to stop us from moving into our own lives.

During Hitler's reign in Germany, one woman dreamt that she tried to rip the swastika off the Nazi flag each night but it was always sewn on tightly again in the morning.[1] The swastika was the official emblem of Nazi Germany under Hitler. Her futile attempts to get it *off* the flag would be analogous to getting rid of a parasite that had not only attached itself to the German psyche but had also fastened its iron claws around her life. Her dream shows her how difficult it is to go against the current of any mass movement, even one that it is blatantly evil and destructive.

The Execution

During my voluntary incarceration in a New Age church, I had this dream:

> I was observing the cell floor of what had been a German concentration camp in World War II. As I looked at the old bloodstains on the floor, I could sense and feel the horror and suffering that had gone on in this place. Then, through a window, I saw a military firing squad in Nazi uniforms. They were executing a large group of seals. I was struck by the complete helplessness of the seals being slaughtered in an earthen pit. Then I was back in the cell area and walking down a hallway when suddenly one of the seals, who was furious with me, came after me trying to bite me.

The meaning of this dream remained a mystery to me for many years. Not until I ended my involvement in the church, which had become a horrendous dragon consuming all my time and energy, did I finally understand this dream. My unlived life was desperately trying to shock me into waking up from the group mind-set that had me completely under its control. For me the Nazis represented an extreme example of a political ideology run amuck. It also represented a totalitarian system with absolute authority invested in its leader, Hitler—a dynamic that felt just like my church and our very charismatic minister, who supposedly had an exclusive connection to God.

She, the minister, knew what we *should* be doing with *our* lives, and we were helpless, just like the seals in my dream, being led to the slaughter. Now this dream resonated deeply for me; I had put myself into an authoritarian religious group under a minister who, like the Third Reich, wielded ironclad authority over her subjects. And we, the dedicated disciples, spent our lives supporting and spreading the "word of God" for our teacher and minister, which translated into providing her with a very elegant lifestyle.

The seals in the dream are completely out of place, removed from the sea, their natural home, and their *authentic* existence. The dream presented me with a lethal obstacle, a collective circumstance that was killing my natural life. And it had created anger and fury—the seal that was "furious" with me—no doubt for removing him (myself) from his natural life.

The Kiss

Understanding this dream also solved another puzzling dream:

> I was sitting by the ocean on a rocky outcropping made of solid turquoise. It was a sunny, absolutely beautiful day. Suddenly a *seal* jumps up out of the sea and in midflight kisses me on my cheek, diving back into the ocean. I was not only surprised and shocked, I had the odd feeling that I knew that seal.

This once mysterious and even humorous dream became a rare diamond to me—a dream talisman, a symbol of an authentic part of myself, a natural part that is at home in the ocean, in the unconscious, but can also live on land. Maybe it is my "seal" nature that loves to dive into a dream and see what's there, bringing treasure up to the daylight world. Or perhaps each dream is a *kiss* from the unconscious.

So what about that outcropping of solid turquoise? With its brilliant blue and blue-green coloring, it represents the ocean for me. In the dream, I felt completely at home, right on the edge of the ocean, sitting on a piece of ocean, an outcropping of uncut dreams in the rough, wanting to become gemstones in the daylight world, soul currency for living an authentic life.

Following Whose Rules?

You recall Melissa, who moved to Seattle to begin a new life. Just as she was creating a plan to change her career and follow her passionate interest in social reform and liberal politics, she had a dream that exposed a rule she had internalized—a leash around her neck that severely limited her choices:

> I'm at some community college in a math or science class. I'm there to fulfill some requirement. But I'm not really part of the class and I feel completely lost in the class.

Melissa was also seriously considering returning to school full-time and getting a second degree in political science. She had already spent five years getting a teaching degree, only to discover she did not like teaching.

"I'm there because I have to be there," she said about the "requirement."

"If you're the college, what's your job in the dream?" I asked Melissa.

"My job is to make sure Melissa learns everything I think she should learn about political science before I give her a degree," she replied.

"When you think about your waking life, what comes up that feels like that 'requirement' and your job as the college?" I asked.

She explained. "I've been thinking about stepping outside the pattern of school-degree-job and getting myself more into a process mode, less drastic; I thought about approaching some individuals to check out work possibilities in the local government, maybe working for a senator—just bypass the whole school routine and go right where I can get the exact experience I need. It feels so freeing to think about that."

Melissa realized that the "requirement" that she follow the traditional route to qualify for a particular job did not originate with her at all. Instead *that requirement* was something she had accepted without ever questioning its logic or its consequences in her life. Getting rid of this one, internalized rule freed her to consider all sorts of creative ways to accomplish her dreams. She did not "have to" fulfill that requirement any longer. Her dream thoroughly demolished that cage.

Exploring the dream:

- Be alert for any dream reference to rules, laws, or requirements. Ask yourself:
  - Where does this particular idea come from?
  - Where did I learn this?
  - Who taught me this way of thinking?
  - If I followed this rule, what would the consequences be?

     – What would I do differently if this idea did not exist?
     – What do I think about the logic of this idea or rule?

Catching the Chameleon

    A bubbly, outgoing woman in her early twenties, Kelly could have been the weather forecaster on the evening news. But she complained of depression, and feeling directionless in her life. Armed with a teaching degree, she had plunged into teaching a class of second graders only to discover that teaching was definitely "not her thing." Discouraged and disappointed, Kelly was searching for herself, for her life, which remained a tantalizing but elusive mystery. At a particular low point she had a dream that became a treasure map for her:

> I couldn't talk. I wanted to be myself. I wanted to show my friend Judith that I could be myself. We were on Pelican Island, and I was wading through a stretch of water. Then the dream changed and I came to a warehouse and my sister was there and my boss from the department store where I work.

    Kelly described Judith as an old friend from childhood who was "very judgmental of me. She put up a front."

    "Pelican Island," according to Kelly, was "mysterious, wild, not populated, unique. It reminds me of Mexico: calm, nurturing, rich in nutrients," she said, describing the island and the water in her dream.

    Then I asked her about the warehouse. "It's my job. It's where I work and that's my actual boss—the jerk!" Kelly said, stiffening with a look that could kill. "He's demanding, all about work, work, work. He never lets up. He's impossible to please," she added.

    "It was my older sister in the dream. She's a parental figure for me, supportive as long as I do what she thinks I should do.

    "I was holding my tongue," Kelly said when I inquired about her inability to speak in the beginning of her dream. She explained that she always held herself back out of fear of making someone else feel bad. Kelly had assumed the role of making everyone around her feel good at the expense of *being herself*. The feeling in her dream was all too familiar. She often found herself unable to speak, as though her tongue had just turned to stone—trying desperately to understand how she *should* behave or what she *should* say in order to make others think well of her. Kelly had turned herself into a chameleon, a creature who survives by blending into the background, by disappearing, by changing color depending on the situation it finds itself in. Like Sisyphus's endless struggle to roll a massive stone up a hill in Hades only to have it roll down again on nearing the top, the impossible task of *always* pleasing others pushed Kelly's Authentic Self underground—the real Kelly had to remain invisible—trapped in a prison of her own making.

Kelly dreaded going to work. Teaching had not worked out for her and she found her current job at a large department store to be boring and depressing. She explained that her boss represented the many ways she tormented herself with unrealistic demands and obsessive self-talk from her "perfectionist" self who would not let her rest and reflect, just relax and think about her life.

Kelly's dream takes place on "Pelican Island," a mysterious, wild, . . . unique" place. For her, that wild and mysterious island represented the uncivilized, unexplored, untamed parts of her nature—a beautiful metaphor for her Authentic Self that would prove to be an oracle as well. And she described the water there as "calm, nurturing, rich in nutrients"; she had entered a rich, nourishing landscape.

Her dream shows her the immediate obstacles to freeing her Authentic Self: her friend Judith, who represented her own negative self-judgments and her ability to "put up a front," her perfectionist side, holding her tongue, and her *chameleon self*. Her dream had contained a mother lode of keys to her authentic life. Now she must use those keys in her waking life to unlock the prison built by an ego determined to survive at any cost.

A few months after her dream, Kelly decided to follow up on her life-long interest in the environment and nature. She found work as a guide for a group that organized nature expeditions. She was now creating her own path, a path taking her *into* her unlived life, into her essential nature.

Exploring the dream:

- Kelly's dream illustrates the significance of the *setting* of your dream: *Where* does your dream take place? Always explore places in your dream by imagining yourself *as* that place. Then ask yourself these questions:
  - What is it like to *be* this place?
  - What is different about me compared to other places around me?
  - What has happened to me?
  - What have I gone through in order to become what I now am?
  - What do I feel as the dreamer walks through/on/in me?
  - How do I survive as this place?

- When a setting in your dream resonates as an aspect of your Authentic Self, remember to create space in your waking life for what that place represents. Explore the image using art, collage, journaling.
- Find ways to allow that part of your authentic nature to express itself in your daily life.

Encountering Barriers and Beasts

Sometimes a dream animal becomes the canary in the mine shaft, showing us the consequences of some exterior influence or circumstance.

Following the Elephants

During the time I was in my spiritual group, I started having recurring dream encounters with elephants. It was not until I left the group that I began to understand the meaning and intent of these dreams. Over and over, the presence of these magnificent animals, their strength, their playfulness, their anger, and their magic, would leave deep tracks in the landscapes of my dreams. In retrospect, these dreams dramatically portrayed the effects of immersing myself in the group's belief system, which disconnected me from the qualities the elephant represents.

One of my first elephant dreams occurred about six months after I joined the group: In the dream I was riding a gray elephant when he suddenly collapsed and died. I felt a deep sadness. This dream, although I did not realize its significance at the time, was a clear warning shot fired over the road I had chosen. If I am that elephant, something is terribly wrong.

Another dream followed:

> I was traveling in a group and there were two small *white* elephants with us. We sat down to eat and one of the elephants was under the table and kept licking my face and bumping into my legs. It was very friendly but a nuisance.

For me, the "*white* elephants" were small but growing problems, soon to be big trouble, classic "white elephants," conspicuous endeavors that turn out to be burdensome failures. Another warning, perhaps, of something going on "under the table"? When I think of "white," I relate it to spirituality, purity, perfection, and a certain one-sided view of God—a God with no color or passion.

In another dream, I am in a boat with the minister and other members of our church going down a waterfall. A large elephant is in front of us and in the way. I'm afraid we're going to crash into it. Now the elephant presents itself as an obstacle in our path, that is, the spiritual path I was following, all of us in the same ideological boat.

In the next dream a chase unfolds:

> I'm in a multi-storied theater with a large group of people. I explain to someone how to get out without getting caught by the elephant. A large elephant is loose and coming after people. Some people were avoiding the elephant in a cowardly way and I knew this was wrong.

Now "we" are being chased by a "loose" elephant, implying that this elephant has escaped from somewhere. It's a common dream motif of an aspect of our essential nature after the dreamer. It would seem that my dreaming ego is becoming adept at avoiding elephants.

Five years after joining the group, my elephant dreams began to feel a lot more threatening. This next dream is an example:

> I saw a man in a rugged mountain area go into an animal pen for elephants. I watched in horror as he was dragged around the pen and slammed into the wall by an angry baby elephant.
>
> My elephants are evidently losing their patience and this one is angry and dangerous in spite of being a youngster—probably not happy at being penned up. Some other part of me is trying to keep my "elephant" nature locked up, walled off. In the next dream, I had somehow provoked several elephants, they were chasing me and they were angry! By now it's apparent that I'm not going to get rid of these elephants.

At a conclave, a weekend church gathering in Carmel, California, I had another encounter with an elephant:

> I encounter an elephant trapped in a large, red, iron-box-like container. Somehow I manage to set him free, but I know he's going to come after me. Then I set out to kill him with a knife. In the dream I am aware that this is a repeating dream.

As this elephant, I'm definitely removed from my natural environment; I'm *contained* inside an *iron* box, a *red* iron box. Red, for me, represents blood, vital life force, and passion in contrast to iron's cold, unyielding, unfeeling hardness—something once comprised of natural elements extracted from the earth, but refined, shaped, and manufactured. Maybe my "will of iron," my *absolute* adherence to the "teachings" and my 110 percent dedication to the "spiritual path" had manufactured my red iron tomb. Looking back on this dream, I was caught in between all that the elephants represented and what I was subjecting myself to by conforming to an exterior ideology. My "save the world" spiritual ego trip had to keep the elephants at bay, "in irons." No wonder I found myself, my dreaming ego, at times trying to kill the elephant. ·

More dreams followed of elephants dying. Then, nearing my tenth year of following my spiritual teacher and guru, I noticed some doubts creeping into my psyche. Some distant part of myself was beginning to question what I was doing with my life. Now, a different sort of elephant appeared:

> I saw one of the church leaders and [the leader's] family, all dressed in long mink coats. In the dream I knew they represented the money and luxury in which the ministers lived at the expense of the members. Then I was holding, very tenderly and affectionately, a baby elephant in my arms. This elephant then turned into a young boy about nine or ten years old. He had dark hair and an Asian or oriental complexion. Next we had come to a deep ravine in the earth, which I knew I had crossed before. I also knew that now I had to jump over it again, somehow get to the other side.

When I imagine being this boy's age, my father's death in an automobile accident when I was nine immediately comes to mind. We were very close and his death altered the course of my life. Overnight I changed from an extroverted, happy, confident child into an introverted, shy kid, profoundly grieving and furious with that Methodist God who let my father die. I retreated into myself and life was never the same for me. That "deep ravine" seems to me to represent that terrible wound, and I had to somehow "*get over it.*"

Thinking about this latest elephant dream, I resolved to begin taking care of that very hurt little boy, re-parenting him and giving him space in my adult world, letting him *out*, letting him play, dream, and have fun again. I also realized that this "baby elephant" was missing a parent! I could feel walls collapsing. I felt like a parent who had just found a lost child. And it dawned on me that the group had become a pseudo family for this hurt little guy, complete with a charming, charismatic, motherly woman/guru/teacher. No wonder *someone* in me felt warm all over every time she greeted me with, "Welcome home, John." I could hear the church walls crack, the earth starting to shift under my feet. My dreams were desperately trying to save my authentic life.

Then I had a dream in which I saw an elephant who was lying down as if dead. I knew he wasn't really dead, so I decided to get some water to revive him. Now I'm consistently connecting with the elephants and trying to help them. But just as I was reconnecting with my elephants, during the last two years of my involvement in the group, I regressed, meeting an elephant "trainer." Here's the dream:

> I'm watching a man who had once been with the elephants,
> training them. Now he had come back and they were unruly:
> One elephant chased him up a tree.

I can't help but identify with the elephant trainer, that part of my nature that can be so self-disciplined and strong-willed that I could force myself to do anything, just like I had been doing for years to keep myself in a religious cult. But the elephants, fortunately, are not putting up with this old "trainer," and instead chase him up a tree. The elephants are winning this epic battle. But my ego, intent on maintaining my spiritually superior status as a member of the church, had other ideas; it was not so willing to roll over and play dead. Hence a little setback for the wild side. I had this dream about a year before leaving the *mother ship*:

> I'm observing a huge rogue elephant, loose and knocking down
> buildings. I (guess who) get a high-powered rifle with one bullet:
> a ".235 Magnum," to kill the elephant. Someone tells me I can't
> kill that elephant with my size gun, but I reply that I can, by
> shooting him in the eye and hitting the brain.

Now there's big trouble afoot. Someone's survival is at stake. My dreaming ego is out to kill that "rogue" elephant, meaning a "vicious, solitary animal that has separated itself from its herd."[2] I had separated myself from who I was, from my writing, from my really understanding my dreams, from living my own life. There was a "rogue" in me that was pissed off, "knocking down buildings," collapsing the ideological, egocentric structures my ego had built in the group. In India, many rogue elephants are young ones who have lost their parents and become separated from other family members.

That dreaming/waking ego was messing with my mind, taking aim at the eye and hitting the brain, perhaps killing my ability to think for myself? Certainly exactly what had happened as a result of saturating myself in the murky waters of a religious system and brainwashing myself with *group-think*.

That ideologically bound, plastic visionary was done for—those *buildings* could no longer stand up against the emerging elephant, my emerging life. It now made sense to me that I had been feeling so angry and depressed and even occasionally thinking about suicide, which was a real shock. If I'm in such an enlightened spiritual group, then why do I feel suicidal?

Moving forward: About eighteen months before I left the church, I had another dream of an elephant in an unusual setting:

> I'm in a large room high in the mountains of what seems like Tibet. I could see tall mountains through the window and was thrilled with their beauty, struck by how exquisite they were! Then I'm with someone and we are sounding tones that could bring dead animals back to life, which we did. I remember specifically an elephant. Then I'm pulling his tail to get him moving forward through a mountain tunnel.

This dream gets straight to the point, awakening the dead—that being *me* of course; I had been efficiently executing my instinctual, authentic inner nature for years. In this dream, the "me" experiencing the dream feels very different, still the dreaming ego, but far removed from its familiar group terrain, high in an exotic, mysterious land. The dream says that we need to "get through" something, which it portrays as a "tunnel." I was finally moving towards the "light at the end of the tunnel," as I approached that immense door, the threshold *into* my own life at last.

Night-Blooming Jasmine

One year before finally leaving the church, I was walking a tightrope smack in the center of a furious storm of doubts about my life and the choices I had made. I was reading several books on philosophy by Eknath Easwaran that restored my spirit because, to my surprise and delight, they totally contradicted the teachings of my church. Here was another, entirely different approach to life. The spiritual life was not, after all, my group's exclusive property.

A retired English professor from the University of California at Berkeley, he spoke about world religions, meditation, and living a spiritual life. In 1960, he came to the U.S. from Kerala in South India on the Fulbright exchange program. A scholar of religions and the author of twenty-four books, including a biography of Gandhi, he believed a spiritual life meant living a life that somehow helped others in the world. When asked once what religion he followed, he replied, "I belong to all religions." It probably comes as no surprise that going to hear "another teacher" outside of our church would have been seen as a terrible betrayal of our teachers, the "ministry," and the "spiritual path."

Inspired by Easwaran's books, my wife and I began secret, weekly road trips from Los Angeles to Petaluma, a small coastal town about forty miles north of San Francisco. We went to hear Easwaran's evening lecture series. A slender, quiet man, then in his mid-seventies, dressed in an immaculate Indian suit and with his ever-present cup of herbal tea at his side, he would launch into commentary on Gandhi, the Upanishads, the Bhagavad-Gita, the environment, or how to protect the elephants in Africa from poachers, which was a special project of their group.

I know what you're thinking: Hey John, here's yet another "spiritual" group—and you are right. A large *group* of followers had sprouted up around Easwaran, one with many all too familiar group dynamics. But no matter, we were not about to "join" any other group. We wanted only to immerse ourselves in the clear, cool water of different ideas, other ways to look at life. And how curious: Here we were—my wife and I along with all my battle-weary dream elephants—listening to someone whose pet project was helping to save the elephants from extinction! That's when I had another elephant dream, but this one was a horse of a different color. Here's my dream:

> I was in the audience carefully listening to a very wise man, a philosopher, give a lecture. I knew he was Eknath Easwaran. I had followed him from city to city, extremely interested in what he had to say about life, its meaning and purpose. He was on his way back to his homeland. At the last city, I noticed *three elephants* had been quietly following him also. An exquisite fragrance from a bouquet of night-blooming jasmine he was carrying in his arms had attracted them. The elephants were homesick and the aroma from the jasmine reminded them of their home.

Easwaran represented an open, non-dogmatic spiritual perspective, a view suggesting that we fill our life with meaning and purpose by doing something meaningful with it. Very simple and straightforward. My wife and I loved the freedom and openness he expressed.

Looking back on this dream, I realized that at last my elephants were on their way *home*, back to where they belonged, drawn by the fragrance of a plant that blooms in the night, perhaps dreams blossoming in the night, in the unconscious,

We didn't realize it at the time but our adventures to hear those lectures about life and philosophy and elephants became our exit door, our way out of the prison compound, our *"setu,"** the bridge between this life and a new life.

Bitten by the Dream

The Spitting Black Cobra

Phillip, a thirty-five-year-old architect, had an unsettling dream that illustrates how repressive religious attitudes about sexuality can impact our adult life, pushing individuals into equally destructive opposite behavior. Phillip had to survive as a child with a mother who was a fundamentalist with a black and white, judgmental, religious world view, a concrete ideology that equated being "good" to *whiteness* and sinning to *blackness*. Getting caught in any extreme further separates us from the Authentic Self. Here's his dream:

> A black cobra was in my living room. It was spitting at me, peeing on the white carpet, and it bit my right thumb, which got infected. I was feeling afraid of it.

A native of Africa, the spitting cobra sprays deadly venom into the eyes of its victims. In this dream, we have opposite colors: the *black* cobra on the *white* carpet. The cobra—dark, animalistic, unconscious, deadly, primitive, and *natural*—not only bites the dreamer on his thumb, but pees—an expression of disdain, of being pissed off—on his *white* carpet. Whiteness, for Phillip, represented goodness, purity, perfection, and the Church, altogether a one-sided, *unnatural* state of existence that creates the *black* cobra: the vital, necessary "bite" from the

---

Setu is a Sanskrit word meaning a bridge between this life and what comes next.

unconscious—the psyche's attempt to restore itself to a more *natural* and genuine state.

"The most striking and psychologically painful event I can remember during this time [twelve to fourteen]," he told me, "was when my mother went snooping through my room and found some nude magazines that I had hidden. My mother's response was to make me go to the parish priest and talk to him. I can hardly recall any of our discussion, only huge amounts of shame and anger toward my mother. . . . There has been a recurring satisfaction from getting my way, getting away with things, and controlling events. Of course I feel the 'old shame' upon getting caught."

The drama occurs in his "living room," suggesting the *level* of his everyday, waking life where he attempted to maintain and present a "good image"—a completely white, level-with-puritanical-standards, moral *stance*, an *ideological-based*, puritanical carpet that covers the floor and the dark spaces beneath the floor. In such one-sided "whiteness," our dreams inevitably introduce powerful oppositeness, striving for a synergy, a yin and yang balance of forces. Indeed, the dreamer's "white carpet" stands as a form of threshold ogre preventing him from connecting with his own authenticity and depths. When the black cobra and the whiteness remained unacknowledged, he found himself irresistibly acting out, unconsciously, in the form of sexual promiscuity combined with putting women down.

After working on this dream, he underwent a transformation in his feelings and attitudes towards women, ironically feeling more of his own *conscience*. It did not surprise me when he told me about a disturbing dream in which he had killed his mother with poison and chopped up her body. His dream confirms that he is taking apart what Jungians would call a "mother complex," meaning that he has ended the negative influences of his mother.

What about the thumb? Von Franz explains that the thumb "is the dwarf of fingers and has mainly to do with creativity. . . . The dumbling or thumb is also the trickster. It is a spirit which enjoys its freedom and plays tricks on the dominating bourgeois world."[3] The dreamer had put his creativity on hold for his professional life. He had always wanted to write and travel. Thwarting his creative side was creating venomous moods, feelings of anger and irritability that were often projected on others. The thumb is also how we get a grip on things, the transmission of power through *oppositeness*. The dreamer's psyche wants to awaken this opposing power to get a grip on his creative side.

If we are to transform our life, then we must focus on what Jung calls the "creative center, the place of creative change. During this process people often dream of being 'bitten' by animals; in other words, we have to expose ourselves to the wild, animal impulses of the unconscious without identifying with them and without 'running away': ... we must hold our ground."[4] This means working with the dream's meaning in our waking lives and not unconsciously acting out on these powerful impulses. Of course, this creates a heightened tension between the unconscious and the conscious life, in particular such images confront the waking ego, who is always bent on maintaining the status quo even though the status quo has proven to be self-destructive; to the ego the status quo is known and hence deceptively comfortable.

To "spit" at or on someone evokes contempt and insult. In fact, the dreamer associated "spitting" with his attitudes towards women and holding them in contempt—an example of an unconscious dynamic projected onto the opposite sex. In reality, one is abusing one's own inner feminine nature. Shortly after bringing this drama to the surface in his dream, he noticed that his feelings about women were changing. He found himself looking at women with greater compassion and respect.

The Golden Leash

The Exiled Self

I met Alice and Ralph when they arrived at my office for couples counseling. In their mid-sixties, they had been together for over thirty years. Ralph could have passed for a scruffy ship's captain. Tall and powerfully built with a wild thicket of gray hair, he towered over Alice as he pushed her wheelchair through the door and into the office. Alice was a delicate orchid, her head bobbing like a thin rag doll struggling to keep herself sitting up straight. She was suffering from the advanced stages of multiple sclerosis.

"I want to be just like him," Alice explained, glancing lovingly at her husband, whom she clearly looked up to and admired. Ralph, on the other hand, complained, "She never tells me what she really thinks about things. I can't figure out what she's feeling." Their therapy sessions began to revolve around issues related to being authentic with each other, communicating their real feelings and opinions in the moment. As Alice tried to express more of her own feelings and desires, she realized she had lost a gigantic chunk of her own sense of self—she did not know *who* she really was. In the midst of this existential dilemma, she had a dream that worried her, a grisly drama she could not seem to get out of her head.

> I'm on a high desert, a desolate plateau with no vegetation. I'm traveling alone when I meet a solitary horse. The horse is just walking along. I know it needs care—water. A woman is suddenly there. I tell her the horse needs water and care. She sees maggots in the horse's shit and tells me, "That horse is really sick." I think to myself I should either get it water or shoot it.

Alice described the horse as gray-brown in color, friendly and gentle. When she imagined being the horse, she explained, "Something's really wrong. I need water. I need attention but I'm not getting it." She described the other woman in the dream as being unknown, maybe thirty years old and raggedly dressed. "She's lonely, she's been living by herself for a long time." Imagining herself as the "water" the horse needs, Alice said, "I'm a liquid that's absolutely necessary to stay alive—the source of life." As the desert, she felt "barren, like a wasteland with nothing living or growing anywhere."

"What about the maggots?" I asked.

Alice shivered. "As a maggot," she said, "I'm a parasite. I've been eating that horse from the inside—I'm killing it."

Alice realized the horse was her life and her illness, that she needed to "pay attention" to *her* life. She needed water, something essential "to stay alive." The unknown, lonely woman sees the maggots and knows the horse is gravely ill. It's as though an unknown part of herself knows what her life needs. Alice's dream presents her with a frightening ultimatum: "Either get it water or shoot it." Alice has reached a crossroads in her life and with her illness. Ironically, she and her husband were doing everything they could for her illness through traditional and alternative medicine, but they had not considered the effects of non-being, of living an inauthentic life. She must now save herself by reconnecting with her Authentic Self, her real nature—the lonely woman she had sent into exile in the desert—a consequence of wanting to make herself into someone else, "to be just like him," her husband. She needed to *be* herself. She needed to give up the tremendous effort to control who she is and simply relax into her essential nature.

Alice also realized she must rid herself of the maggots, which for her represented all the negative self-talk and pessimism about her illness that was *eating* away at her. She must get rid of her "shoot it" self. Her dream cut through the cords of conformity and impressed upon her the immediate necessity to begin living her own life. Alice began to feel back in control of her life and destiny for the first time in many years. Her illness no longer felt like a death sentence; it no longer loomed over her life like some devouring monster. When I last saw Alice, she still had MS but she was a changed person. "I don't want to be like him anymore," she said with a knowing smile and a wink as she was leaving our last session.

Exploring the dream:

- Once you separate what belongs to you in your dream from what does not belong to you, create a plan to eliminate those elements that are not a part of your Authentic Self in your waking life.
- When your dream pertains to any physical illness, it's extremely important to do your best to change your life based on the guidance in your dream. The immune system responds to our positive and negative attitudes and our will to live.
- Dreams inevitably zero in on aspects of our life that are adversely affecting our health.
- In a dream like Alice's, part of the interpretation will come from actually looking up "maggots" in an encyclopedia to understand what life is like as a maggot, how a maggot survives.
- Any dream image that represents an exterior, alien creature that has invaded your physical body needs to be objectively explored and understood in its natural state.

Snakes and Serpents: Protective Images in Dreams

> *We have scotch'd the snake, not kill'd it.*
> —Shakespeare, *Macbeth*

In mythology, various reptilian creatures such as snakes and dragons are often guardians of some sort of treasure. For example, a young man dreamed of a great snake guarding a golden bowl in an underground vault.[5] As the hero or heroine, we encounter such "threshold" presences when naturally in the process of connecting to the Authentic Self represented by the "golden bowl." The snake guards the treasure and in so doing protects the Self from the ego's outer world entanglements and conformity.

A snake in a dream gets our immediate attention. Whether symbolic or in a mythological context, a snake is "usually *down there*, on the ground—connected to the earth—moving in, around, over, through, under, slithering, gliding, sneaking—the "snake in the grass"—waiting silently, completely at home in its world. The Latin root of "serpent," *serpere*, means "to creep." Might not the psyche be drawing our attention down, grounding and terrifying the dreaming ego caught in flights of fancy—drawing our attention to a *deity* that wants to be integrated? The serpent's bite may be a god striking, awakening our sleeping, trapped-in-paradise, collectively drugged egos—*snaking* its way into our civilized, defended lives.

The *ego* often needs the serpent's bite, the transformative death experience. In such dreams, we are *both* the treasure *and* the guardian of our treasure. As Joseph Campbell wrote regarding fearsome encounters with snakes: "Such demons—at once dangers and bestowers of magic power—every hero must encounter who steps an inch outside the walls of his tradition."[6]

"Henry," a Sea Serpent

Not long after beginning my own inner exploration through dreams and meditation, I had a powerful dream that helped me to understand my own unique approach to the unconscious:

> I was standing at the edge of the ocean when suddenly a gigantic
> sea serpent, several stories tall, rose up vertically from the water.
> It had one enormous, dark eye and was looking straight at me
> with an enormous smile and said, "I'm Henry."

I awoke with a start and at first dismissed the importance of the dream—a smiling serpent named Henry? Give me a break! But after some reflection, I understood this dream was showing something important about my "Self," that the inner life I was intent upon opening was indeed gigantic, rising up from the depths of the unconscious—that perhaps my work would be to bring unconscious material into the daylight of my conscious awareness, and that humor would play an important role in my inner quest. And what about the curious name "Henry"? The origination of the name "Henry" completed the picture; it comes from the Teutonic meaning the "Ruler of the home: chief of the dwelling."[7] So I had just met the "Ruler" of my house!

Henry's appearance foretold a significant dream experience I had the very next morning:

> Again I found myself seated in a cross-legged meditation posture by the ocean when I suddenly felt a powerful sensation move up my spine, along the back of my neck, arch through the top of my brain and center itself in the center of my forehead. At this instant, "I" ceased to exist and what had been a sense of my waking ego-consciousness was utterly gone. I became "a center without any circumference," total awareness, seeing infinitely in all directions at once, as though I had become suddenly interconnected with everything that existed. I felt my consciousness instantaneously expand into spherical, timeless space all around me, and I knew that whatever I put my attention on would be known. A sparkling white cloud-like substance, difficult to describe in words, filled this space.

This dream experience was so startling and real that it awakened me in what seemed to be only a few seconds. After opening my eyes, I felt disoriented and had to struggle to reconnect to being in my physical body and its position on the bed; I had to reorient myself to physical space and time—a physical existence that now felt very limiting and confined. It left me with yet another profound understanding of how intimately we are interconnected with all life and how the human psyche is indeed a wondrous, remarkable, and mysterious creation. I had entered a realm where my physical-reality-ego-awareness could not go. The collectivized ego simply cannot contain an experience of the Self, of expanded consciousness and awareness. Such dreams are true gifts, milestones, markers on life's journey that we never forget. The Indian sage Ananda Coomaraswamy wrote, "No creature can attain a higher grade of nature without ceasing to exist."[7]

A world where we see and experience each other with dignity and respect cannot accommodate an ego saturated with mass-minded projections, group labels, and stereotypes. When we see others through the lens of dogma, we are unable to see the authentic individual. Ultimately, no ideology or tradition can contain the Self. Even if we meet the Buddha on the path, we must slay him. Thus the desire for God separates us from God.

My experience exemplified the erect serpent, which some traditions interpret as kundalini, "serpent power," spiritual awakening, wisdom. Snakes can also represent phallic symbolism, an *erection* of creative force—the Dionysian capacity for ecstasy, joy, and down-to-earth pleasures that are so lacking within most organized religious traditions. The Ophitic tradition viewed a serpent as a Redeemer and a Savior. However, all of the above are group labels and interpretations. I prefer to think of Henry as a creative life force emerging from the sea, from the source of life—a unique expression of who I am. And that snake in your dream is just that—your image and your "snake."

The White Cobra

Robert Johnson, in his book *Between Heaven and Earth*, described a dream he had that epitomizes this guardian aspect of snake imagery:

> I am out on a hill, dry like southern California. I am walking without shoes, and there are small cobras around me. I am very cautious, watching carefully where I step. They get more and more numerous, and I am having trouble finding space to put my feet down. I come to Dr. Jung's house; it's the only house in sight. It has a fence and a green yard with flowers. I pass through the front gate. There are no cobras in the yard. I ring the bell and Mrs. Jung is there. I explain my plight and ask if she has any shoes. "It is too dangerous to go on this journey without shoes," I say. She says she will see what might be done and invites me in.
>
> Mrs. Jung then goes to get Dr. Jung. I explain my predicament to him, and he tries to be helpful and looks all over the house but cannot find any shoes for me. He would do anything for me that he could, but he has no shoes that will fit me. I go out the back door, thanking him for being so kind to me, and I go out the gate to a dry, brown place again.
>
> Now the cobras get thicker and thicker as I get some distance from the house, until there is no place to put my foot down without stepping on a cobra. There is nothing to do but stand still. So I stop, and an extraordinary thing happens. The cobras make a circle in a curious way. Each one takes on an S shape. They lie close to one another, radiating out away from me, hundreds of cobras surrounding me. I am tired and sit down. I don't know what to do when a thought comes to me: are they facing me or facing out? When I look the tails are towards me and the heads are all facing out. Good God, I think, they are protecting me and I didn't know it. I talk to the cobras and say, Look, fellows, if I make an agreement not to move from here, if I promise

not to move, will you ease up on me? Instantly, all the cobras co-
alesce into one white cobra, three or four feet long.

Next the dream continues, with the white cobra coming to
me and winding up my body. I am frightened when he gets to my
shoulder and climbs to the top of my head. I am not repelled by
snakes, but this is a bit much. He climbs up and winds across the
top of my head with his head rising up from his coiled body
looking in the same direction that I am facing. The dream ends
with the two of us sitting there very still.[9]

Johnson's remarkable dream illustrates the protective aspect of the
human psyche, particularly when one's individuality and uniqueness is
at stake. He cannot fill Jung's shoes and must "leave" Jung's house. His
dream shows him that he must travel *his own path*, not someone else's
path. It is the "dream ego," not the Authentic Self, that believes it must
walk in someone else's shoes for the journey, and it is precisely the ego's
desire to follow another's path that the cobras defend against. There
were no cobras in Jung's idyllic setting: a "fence and a green yard with
flowers," meaning that Robert Johnson did not find his spiritual power,
the white cobra, by exactly following Jungian psychology. Instead, he
had to choose to enter the forest where there was no path, where no one
had gone before.

This is *the* crucial motif that we must follow in order to discover our
unique path in life. It does not mean that we do not encounter mentors,
guides, and many seemingly miraculous helps along the way. In fact, the
more we adhere to our unique track, the more we will meet, often at just
the right time, the precise help and circumstances we need.

The dream also points out the need for centering, to become immovable, to become the motionless center of one's existence—the "still
point" in the mandala of the Self. This stance transforms the cobras
from threatening to protective. Finally the cobra winds itself around the
dreamer like a *caduceus*, the dreamer becomes the *axis mundi*, a medi-
ating point between heaven and earth, the staff of life. As a result of
Robert Johnson's following his own path in spite of the difficulties this
presented for him, we now have the benefit of his unique insight and
wisdom. That kind of achievement can only come from one's innate authenticity and the struggle to discover and live one's own life.

Seeing Inside a Stone

Dreams of stones and other inorganic matter point to a relationship
between consciousness and matter that remains unresolved. Psycho-

somatic medicine struggles with this very issue. Throughout mythology we encounter references to God, spirit, or the transcendental being in everything. A passage in the Koran says, "withersoever ye turn, there is the Presence of Allah."[10] And Hindus say, "He is hidden in all things."[11] A Gnostic aphorism states, "Split the stick, and here is Jesus."[12] And physicists tell us that solid matter is essentially space between atomic nuclei. The "emptiness of all things," called "súnyatã," meaning "voidness" in Sanskrit, may in part refer to scientific reality about the real universe.

Some years ago, in the early morning hours, I had a powerful dream, more a vision, that to this day evokes in me an awe and reverence for the human spirit and for our natural world. I dreamt I was sitting on a rock at the edge of the ocean. Suddenly I became aware of a great background humming sound that permeated the atmosphere as well as the ocean depths; it seemed to be everywhere at once, but also moving toward me. Somewhat apprehensively, I felt this sound current reach the place where I was sitting, flow into my feet and throughout my body. This throbbing current then began reverberating up and down my spine and I experienced a complete and utter interconnectedness with everything. Suddenly the stone beside me I had been leaning on with my right hand drew my attention; the sound traveled down my arm into the stone, and to my amazement the stone transformed into uncountable, scintillating atoms—diamond-like points of brilliant light—and I knew that the stone had a form of consciousness. It was *alive*!

Looking at this experience, it's quite difficult to avoid a literal meaning. But in either case, or even from a *both-and* view, when I imagine being the stone or the sound current, my dream is telling me that we are all interconnected, that everything—dream, image, matter, space—has soul, consciousness. We are "alive" and so is our environment—inner and outer. The dream also points out the incredible vastness of the psyche, that we each are indeed a universe, as Origen, the Greek philosopher observed over two thousand years ago: "You yourself are even another little world and have within you the sun and the moon and also the stars."[13]

Dreams help us feel connected to life and to each other. As a result, people who pay attention to their dreams and work with applying their meaning (not literally) become instruments of peace and reconciliation in the world. The more we feel connected to ourselves, our innate being, the more we feel connected to others. When we do our best to live authentically, our life inevitably enriches society and our world. Perhaps the biggest dragon we must slay is our illusion of *separateness*.

CHAPTER 11

"Dying Inside the Dishes"

[W]e are bleeding at the roots, because we are cut off from the earth and sun and stars, and love is a grinning mockery, because, poor blossom, we plucked it from its stem on the tree of Life, and expected it to keep on blooming in our civilized vase on the table.

—D. H. Lawrence

Living Someone Else's Life

Sometimes a man stands up during supper
and walks outdoors, and keeps on walking,
because of a church that stands somewhere in the East.

And his children say blessings on him as if he were dead.

And another man, who remains inside his own house,
dies there, inside the dishes and in the glasses . . .
—Rainer Maria Rilke[1]

In a time of transition and change, people either disappear into an outer collective situation, the "church," or they stay inside the narrow cell of the ego's world, "dying inside the dishes and in the glasses." It is no easy task to loosen the waking ego's grasp of the familiar, the apparent safety and security of the known; it wants to keep us in its "own house," but that house is usually little more than a comfortable tomb.

Because of social pressure, media brainwashing, and family expectations, the vast majority of people end up living someone else's life, swallowed by manufactured lifestyles designed to make us into happy, consuming robots. Our dreams never give up trying to lift us from this deepest of pits. Even when people try to escape the living death "in the dishes and in the glasses," they are nearly always swept into the swift current of some group that promises wealth, salvation, or enlightenment, only to wake up years later still searching for that elusive missing piece, the elixir that will inject meaning and purpose into the corpse of a life consumed by the gangrene of conformity. Or people fill the emptiness with more stuff, becoming part of our "gross" national product.

Death and Dying in Dreams

Meeting the Creator

In his autobiography, Carl Jung described a dream that turned his traditional sense of reality upside down. His dream threatens death and his interpretation shows how easy it is to slip into being overly literal. Here's the dream:

> I was on a hiking trip. I was walking along a little road through a hilly landscape, the sun was shining and I had a wide view in all directions. Then I came to a small wayside chapel. The door was ajar, and I went in. To my surprise there was no image of the Virgin on the altar, and no crucifix either, but only a wonderful flower arrangement. But then I saw that on the floor in front of the altar, facing me, sat a yogi—in lotus posture, in deep meditation. When I looked at him more closely, I realized that he had my face. I started in profound fright, and awoke with the thought: "Aha, so he is the one who is meditating me. He has a dream and I am it." I knew that when he awakened, I would no longer be.[2]

It's as though Jung meets his "maker," an enigmatic aspect of his original Self, and this yogi has *his own face*. Most of us look at reality as anchored in the exterior world, in concrete forms, objects we can touch, see, hear, smell. The biggest part of life seems to be shaped and molded by exterior forces and experiences. The dream creates a "profound fright" for his *dreaming ego*, the assumed creator and master of reality, who runs smack into the *real* source of his "life."

In his dream, Jung is outside, in the natural world. He comes upon a "chapel," a place of worship where we go to find out about God, where we encounter earthly representations of God—a ritual space symbolizing a meeting of heaven and earth. But this dream chapel does not contain the usual religious icons. Instead it holds a "wonderful flower arrangement" and a yogi "in lotus posture, in deep meditation." The flower "arrangement"—a one-of-a-kind design, a choreographed dance between nature and the individual soul—becomes an exquisite metaphor for a unique life, a blossoming, the aesthetics of an authentic life.

Jung's dream tells him that it is his meditating, *self*-reflecting, inward-looking nature that has, in reality, created his life. And if he were to put an end to this inner exploration, he would no longer exist; his Authentic Self would be silenced—a silence that would effectively kill his life as a psychologist, writer, and philosopher. The beautiful flower arrangement would wither and die, no longer connected to its source of insight and creativity.

Exploring the dream:

- In dreams that threaten death or the possibility of life ending, remember to explore "death" as the ending of some aspect of your life that may well be the real reason why you are here. Ask yourself these questions:
  - Who or what is dying in my dream?
  - What are you thinking of ending in your life: a creative project, a relationship, a career? What would feel like a death if you stopped doing it?

Plunged into the Abyss

Most death imagery in dreams represents an ongoing, symbolic, transformative process of multiple deaths and rebirths. Dream images portray this drama with awesome accuracy because it is in this stage that the individual human psyche reacts to our inner resolve by alerting us to impending dangers, in particular those dynamics that keep us trapped in normality, locked up in some job that is really a hair shirt, or stuck inside rules and pressure to conform to the expectations of others.

But some dreams offer assurances that even physical death is not as final as we might imagine.* Consider this example from Inge Scholl's book, *The White Rose*:

> [It] was experienced by Sophie Scholl, the well-known student condemned to death for resistance. It occurred the night before

---

*See: Marie-Louise von Franz, *On Dreams and Death* (Boston: Shambhala Publications, 1987), for an excellent exploration of dreams recorded just prior to death.

her execution in 1943. Sitting on her cot, she gave her cellmate this account:

"It was a sunny day, and I was carrying a little child dressed in a long, white gown to be baptized. The path to the church led up a steep hill. But I was holding the child safely and securely in my arms. All of a sudden I found myself at the brink of a crevasse. I had just enough time to set the child down on the other side before I plunged into the abyss."

Attempting to explain the meaning of this simple dream, she told her cellmate, The child represents our idea, which will triumph in spite of all obstacles. We are allowed to be its trailblazers, but we must die before it is realized.[3]

Sophie's dream is fascinating in that it suggests that someone or something survives death on the "other side" of the "abyss"—perhaps her soul? Or possibly her *dream* survives—her example of courage and integrity in a society that has gone mad. Or are we moving on as physicist David Peat suggests, "the self lives on but as one aspect of the more subtle movement that involves the order of the whole of consciousness."[4] We can only speculate, but many dreams like Sophie's say over and over that *something* in the human spirit survives death.

"Walking at Dusk to My Funeral"

Rita, a woman in her mid-forties who had been suppressing an extremely creative side of her nature, had this profound dream which foreshadowed not a literal death but a significant transformation in her life:

I'm sitting in a paneled room. I have a list in symbolic form of all my possessions. An old girlfriend, Cindy, is sitting behind me. The Master of Ceremonies—debonair—comes in wearing a smoking jacket. He has a very old-world feeling. He talks to me, saying, "The bra I came in with looked very nice. What kind was it?" I was startled and pleasantly surprised. I had not been aware that I looked so good. I then looked at the list of symbolic possessions and decided to keep only the bra. I then gave the list to my friend, feeling very detached and knowing she would take care of it. This was the preparatory stage.

Next I was walking behind the Master of Ceremonies as he told me that his wife had been by him when he was dying, waiting to get his possessions. He laughed and said that he left her his clothes, since she was so interested . . . it was funny. Then he took me over to a kiln-like object and pulled out the bottom part which had oblong slots for tablets about three inches long and an inch-and-a-half wide. They were like pressed sage. I put two of them in. The second was for sulfur—the second stage of burning the body. The first was fire. I had to hurry so I wouldn't miss it—being cremated.

The third stage: I was out walking at dusk to my funeral, wearing a long, flowing dress, when I saw a car of teenagers dressed in suits going to my funeral. They recognized me and stopped. I recognized one of them, who I had known many years ago, just before I joined a religious group. I said, "Hi, and I had better hurry because I was coming back soon," as in reincarnation.

After the funeral, I was with a lot of people and a woman (unknown to me) gave me my house number: "6-C." I finally found the house on the left. They were duplexes with big porches. Suddenly a distraught woman called me for help. She was having a problem with this man who didn't know she was dead. But the first woman who gave me the house number (I knew she was an angel) said, "Tell her I can help her with the house number but about the other she's on her own." I relayed the message. Then I saw my husband and went to be with him. I told the woman with the problem that I couldn't help her, that I had to be with my husband. This was the last stage: bereavement, and it was to console him. I went to look for a place to sit with the sun coming in, not rain.

Her dream follows a ritual process of death and rebirth. There can be no doubt that her psyche has produced a drama about the death of something. The "Master of Ceremonies" (from the Latin, *caerimōnia*, a religious rite) fulfills a Hermes-like role, a messenger or a guide in her dream. In fact, when asked who she would cast in his part, she replied, "Vincent Price," describing him as "debonair—you know he has a dark integrity and *knows*." Her psyche produces this "dark and mysterious" figure as the "Master" of this ceremony.

Rita felt that the "bra" represented her femininity, which is the "only thing" she keeps, giving up all the rest of her possessions. In fact, the dream says that it is *the* part of her with all the possessions that is dying. She said that her friend Cindy represented qualities of creativity, discipline, and perfectionism; she is someone who can be trusted to get things organized and done. For Rita, the kiln was the container or place for her cremation, a type of funeral *pyre*.

Here it's worth looking at her dream's use of language. A "kiln" is an oven used for hardening, burning, or drying substances, especially a brick-lined oven used to bake or fire ceramics. The "burning and drying" are reminiscent of what the Alchemists referred to as a process of fire, or *calcinatio,* which meant a "purging, whitening fire" that "acts on the black stuff, the *nigredo,* and turns it white."[5] In actuality, calcination involves intense heat applied to some material in order to vaporize water and all other volatile ingredients. What remains is a dry, fine powder similar to ashes from a cremation. We could say that Rita's former world, her old life, ends in fire, a fire that burns away impurities— those attitudes, ideas, habits, and particularly all "her possessions, her stuff," that do not really belong to her essential nature.

The teenager she recognized in the dream was an actual friend she had known years ago just before joining a religious group. She remarked that he represented "complete freedom, lots of choices, doing whatever he wanted. And he was the only member of his family who did not get involved in a religious cult." The dreamer was nineteen years old when she joined a church that consumed the next twenty years of her life. When she finally left the church, she realized she had been in a cult, that she had not been able to live her own life. Here the dream shows her that part of this transformation involves the rebirth of creative freedom, self-determination instead of the totalitarian religious system she had subjected herself to.

And she says, "I'm coming right back soon as in reincarnation." If we take the dream literally, we might think, Well, she is going to die and reincarnate. But reincarnation as a metaphor yields a much more pertinent message that resonated for Rita: her youthful, free, *pre-church* Self will reincarnate in her present life. In this sense, her dream may actually be describing a rebirthing experience.

This transformative process intends to first separate Rita from all that would stand between her and her Authentic Self. Such dream symbolism connects one with powerful energies that are quite real, energies that intend to end the waking ego's grasp on collective values that block our authenticity. When one has dreams of this kind, sometimes referred to as "big" dreams, they often signify a life and death struggle on a soul level. The struggle is to save and bring into existence, incarnate our essential spirit.

Her dream alludes to two pellets "like pressed sage," one for fire and one "for sulfur." "Sage" comes from the Latin, *sapere,* meaning "to be wise." Rita described sage as "wild, hormonal, Native American, [its] scent mood altering." Dream references to "Native American" images, especially for people in the U.S., usually suggest a *native* or original state, the uncontaminated, natural, first inhabitants of the land and the psyche.

She felt that her dream portrayed the burning up of impulses and desires that would stand in the way of her own creativity and authenticity. To accomplish this, she needs fire, heat, and intense feelings. When Rita imagined *being* "sulfur," she said, "When I am smelled, everyone knows it's me—I'm unmistakably unique. I'm able to be beautiful colors like at Yellowstone."

New images appear at the end of her dream: "duplexes with big porches," which she described as "shared space yet separate—reminds me of my grandparents who loved my art and always encouraged my artistic side." The "distraught woman" who has a problem with a man, a part of Rita—". . . he did not know she had died." For Rita, this problematic male figure represented a logical, rational side that resists the ending of her old life. Then we have the house number, "6C." The letter "C" is difficult to interpret. But it may be as simple as "C" for creativity, which made sense for Rita. When she was six years old, she recalled loving art and always drawing, particularly at her grandparents' house.

Then she encounters a woman whom she knew was an "angel," which she described as "someone who knows." And she has to "console" her husband, who would represent once more the former way of relating to a masculine side of her nature. Rita described her husband as "sensitive, quiet, and disciplined; he does his passion."

Not long after this dream, Rita experienced not only the beginning of peri-menopause but also the sudden onset of a painful *inflammatory* malady in her joints. She felt "heat"—fire in her body, which had the effect of getting her instant attention. She also began to get serious about her creative life and to let go of former habits and ways of adaptation that were self-destructive. All that she needed to do to begin expressing her own creativity became clear to her.

The Trap of Synchronicity

What if we *attach* meaning to a dream, labeling it, for instance, a "precognitive dream," simply because a *synchronistic** event in our waking life occurs that *could* explain a dream's meaning? Might we be taking

---

*I use *synchronicity* to describe a coincidence of events that seem to be meaningfully related; a phenomenon where an event in the outside world coincides with a psychological state of mind, as conceived in the work of Carl Jung. Also "an essentially mysterious connection be-the easy way out, avoiding the real meaning of the dream? What if the dream is, as we have postulated, drawing its images out of the stream of time: past, present, and future? If this is indeed the case, then we must plunge back into the ocean depths, into the dream images, and once more allow them to speak to us. In this sense, synchronistic events that reconnect us to a particular dream may well be important road signs, bridges taking us back to our dream, another form of a recurring dream, not something that ought to be looked at as the ultimate meaning of the dream.

The End of Civilization

In 1913, Jung broke with Freud, who had been an important mentor for many years. It was a scary and traumatic experience for Jung. He was leaving the popular authority of his time; he was leaving a system of dream interpretation, a body of techniques, ideas, and theories of analysis. Shortly after disconnecting his life's work from Freudian psychology and setting out on his own, he had a dream-like vision while alone on a journey, a foreboding drama that seemed to predict a disaster.

> In October, while I was alone on a journey, I was suddenly seized by an overpowering vision: I saw a monstrous flood covering all the northern and low-lying lands between the North Sea and the Alps. When it came up to Switzerland I saw that the mountains grew higher and higher to protect our country. I realized that a frightful catastrophe was in progress. I saw mighty yellow waves, the floating rubble of civilization, and the drowned bodies of uncounted thousands. Then the whole sea turned to blood.
>
> Two weeks passed; then the vision recurred, under the same conditions, even more vividly than before, and the blood was more emphasized. An inner voice spoke. "Look at it well; it is wholly real and it will be so. You cannot doubt it."[6]

At first, Jung was concerned that his visions were predicting the onset of a psychosis. But on later reflection and world events, he believed they were warning him about the approaching world war, which began in August of 1914. Immediately after these disturbing images, Jung described going through a time of deep turmoil and self-reflection,

tween the personal psyche and the material world, based on the fact that at bottom they are only different forms of energy." See Daryl Sharp, *C.G. Jung Lexicon* (Toronto: Inner City Books, 1991), pp. 132–133.

attempting to find a way through the landscape of his own dreams, his fantasies, and their relationship to his life, to his work, and to political and social events unfolding throughout Europe. In his autobiography he wrote: "I was living in a constant state of tension; often I felt as if gigantic blocks of stone were tumbling down upon me. One thunderstorm followed another."[7]

First we need to place Jung's visions into the context of his life at the time. Jung was in a turbulent transition; he was leaving the "ordinary world" of Freud's psychology and striking out on his own, beginning to enter the forest where there was no path. He was stepping into the unknown and into his authentic life, and *then* he had the visions.

Next we need to imagine the images and the geography in his vision as the ground of his psyche, the landscape of his life at that time. If you imagine being the "monstrous flood," you are an elemental, powerful, unstoppable, natural force that some deep cataclysmic event has created, a shock wave, a spiritual tsunami moving up, out, and over the land. The ideological walls of convention cannot hold back or contain this aroused sea. For Jung, many of Freud's constructs about the unconscious and dreams, the *structures* that *contained* Freudian psychology, were collapsing. Now the flood begins to feel more like Jung's creative life and all that it contained being released, freed from the limitations of Freud's psychology—opening the floodgates of his potential. The waters cover all the "low-lying lands," which could mean all the common ground of popular psychology where nothing stands out; the areas of Jung's life in which he felt he had to lay low, conform, remain on a *level playing field* with Freud, were now in chaos.

Jung's home was in Switzerland, where, in his dream, the mountains "grew higher and higher to protect our country." The dream's *growing mountains* around Jung's *home-land* might well be saying that by his rising above the low-lying lands, by standing out with his own philosophy, that his "homeland," his life, his authenticity, and his creative potential will be protected. The flood is *after* the low-lying lands—conformity and the propensity in all of us to put down our creative ideas, telling ourselves, "That idea will never work. What makes you think you can make any difference anyway?" We are afraid to go against the world's accepted doctrines, to walk upstream against the current of popular ideas. So we "lay low," keeping our authentic life in exile in the "low-lying" land.

So what about the "floating rubble of civilization and the drowned bodies of uncounted thousands?" Here, we can see the dream referring to the collapsed structures of Freudian psychology that had contained

Jung and, until he broke with Freud, had prevented Jung from fully living his own life. The "drowned bodies" refer to the ideas, the *inhabitants* of Freud's world. The waters sweep away "civilization," everything that has been built on—*put upon*—the *low-lying* land. The dead bodies, a fairly common dream motif, would represent the death of old ideas that no longer fit into Jung's developing psychology—multiple deaths of ego-built structures based on Freud's theories. Of course, this would explain Jung's troubled state of mind just after his split with Freud and finally setting out on his own.

This brings us to the blood: "Then the whole sea turned to blood." If we imagined *being* a sea "turned to blood," we would probably feel disturbed, *bloodied*, changed from some traumatic event, a massive dying, an ending that has released its *lifeblood* into the sea. An *Alchemical* process is definitely underway, a mixture of blood and water. Blood released from the death of "uncounted thousands" of old ideas and theories that can no longer contain Jung's essential spirit. We could say that Jung's lifeblood—his essential nature—which had been circulating through the body of Freudian thought, is now useful, a necessary experience, a valuable ingredient in the new psychological being that would now rise from the *rubble of civilization*, the internal chaos created by leaving the house of Freud. As the sea, I've been changed—blood, the vital essence necessary for life, has moved into me (the sea). And for Jung, I am the *source* of his life, the unconscious, the "zone of magnified power," the mysterium, the *special world*. Jung's passion, his life's work that was "in his blood," has been freed, perhaps also telling him that his work would be to explore the "sea," the depths of the collective unconscious and its relationship to the individual psyche. Still glimmerings of a precognitive dream but with a very different slant: his dream provides a dramatic explanation of the sweeping consequences for Jung and his life when he pulled *Excalibur* from the monolith of Freudian psychology. By stepping wholly into *his* authentic life, Jung was free to create Jungian psychology, which has had a tremendous impact on the world.

Stone Soup

Fast-forward about ninety years and ten-thousand miles west of Zurich and meet Christine, an idealistic, forty-something founder of a home for abused young girls in the United States. She began having what she called a series of nightmares with a similar theme: losing everything, standing in rubble, in tattered clothing, the earth devastated in a disaster. Each time she would waken with a dreadful feeling that she described as "total nothing, nothing, nothing."[8]

Like Jung, Christine's dream was *not* a prophecy of some disaster in her waking world, although there have been plenty of candidates. Instead, her dreams were informing her that she was in the midst of a scary transition, a "black moment" that represented the total destruction of all the ideas and attitudes that were blocking the expansion of her work with children. Then she had what appeared to be another nightmare:

> I dream everything has finally been taken from me. I possess absolutely nothing—no clothing, no food, no love. I'm standing naked, though oddly I don't feel destitute. I'm really hungry, but all I have is a bowl filled with stones and water. I say in deep, final resignation, Well, I guess I'm just going to have to make some stone soup![9]

Christine felt that this last dream was not at all what she at first thought. In the dream, everything has been removed *except* "a bowl filled with stones and water," which she realized represented her center for at-risk children—each stone a child thrown out and rejected by society. The dream both inspired her and challenged her; she must create a new center, make "stone soup." Her dreams left her with her life and her work—nothing else. Now she began to experience a powerful sense of freedom to plan and create a unique center, an "earth-friendly facility, harmonious with the land,"[10] a magical soup that will nourish the souls of many children to come and enable Christine to life her own life, a life filled with purpose and meaning, a life that will be a creative *intervention* in society.

The Artist and the Tidal Wave

Terri, who had the dreams of her guru dying, had a frightening dream immediately after she joined her spiritual group and was in the process of moving in order to be near her spiritual teacher. Many years later, after she had left the group, we worked on that old dream that still puzzled her. Back then, her guru told her the dream was a reincarnation memory from Pompeii and that was the end of that. Here's her dream:

> I am on a beach at the ocean painting with an easel. There is a woman with me also painting. I then look out and see a gigantic tidal wave nearly on top us! Then I look back at my painting

and my friend and I realize everything has been swept away and I am under the water and will drown. I repeat a prayer but I feel the water filling my lungs and I am surprised there is no pain.

Terri's dream was to be an artist. Art was her passion in life. She told me, "I always dreamt I wanted to be a great painter." And her dream begins with her "painting" at the ocean. She described her friend as "someone I had known for a couple of years. She's an eccentric genius, a writer, but also somewhat self-destructive." Terri felt she accurately represented a part of herself—eccentric and talented as an artist but with a self-destructive side. I asked Terri to imagine being the tidal wave. "I'm going to overwhelm everything—wipe it out," she said, adding, "I was amazed I was dying and there was no burning, no pain."

"All the time I was in the group, my guru said art was not my right work. I accepted this without a fight, I just let go, exactly like dying in that tidal wave, without a struggle," she explained. Now Terri realized the tidal wave was the group's ideology that had killed her authentic life as an artist; it was the artist, her creativity that drowned under that wave so long ago. Now the dream made perfect sense. She told me, "Now after many years outside the group, I am struggling to find and uncover that artist, that painter that I let die."

Suicide and Dreams

Driven

Dreams about committing suicide are often interpreted literally because they seem to be literal warnings. But when we look at such dreams as symbolic warnings, they take on a very different significance, as in this example of an eighteen-year-old woman who deliberately drove her car over a cliff in an attempt to kill herself. She miraculously escaped with a broken shoulder and some minor bumps and bruises. The night before her suicide attempt, she had a dream: "I drove the car over that particular cliff and it killed me."[11]

In my experience and all my research on dreams, I have never found any evidence that our dreams intend our death. Only by taking a dream *literally* and then acting on the dream in a literal fashion do persons get into such dilemmas.

What if her dream really wanted her to look at her life, to see something she was doing to herself? Her dream is much more likely to be about a self-inflicted dynamic, how she is "driving herself to death," that she is "killing" herself by keeping herself in some restrictive life situation or circumstance that is soul-deadening, that prevents her from living her own authentic life. Perhaps some self-destructive pattern, or dynamic does needs to die. She might, for example, need to let go of a part of herself that always does what she believes *others* expect of her.

Exploring the dream:

- With any dream that includes suicidal feelings or actions, ask yourself:
  - *Who*, in me, wants to die?
  - *Who* or what *needs* to die?
  - *Where* have *I* come from (the part that wants to die)?
- Look at your waking life and determine *where* that part is active, where you see it impacting your life. If it's not a part of who you really are, your authentic nature, get rid of it! Replace it with thinking, attitudes, and values that come from the depths of *your* essential character.

David Raphling researched the dreams of individuals who had attempted suicide and found themes of "violence or destruction" and "explicit references to actual or threatened death, or dead persons."[12] One category of dreams that Raphling studied appears to actually idealize death. In such cases, physical death becomes a final solution, an ultimate transcending of what seems to be a life with no hope or meaning. But the great tragedy in looking at pre-suicidal dreams is that people have indeed acted on them in a literal sense and commited suicide, when in fact these dreams offer real healing help if looked at symbolically and as warnings from the psyche.

The Execution Chamber

Death in dreams sometimes can symbolize the end of a *structured* part of life, representing a collective experience that has blocked one's authenticity. Such dreams predict growing freedom and autonomy in the dreamer's life—more ability to think for ourselves and greater freedom to be authentic. Kate brought this disturbing dream to one of our group sessions, explaining that it left her feeling apprehensive and perplexed:

> I am climbing across the face and top of a brick wall with many other girls. We are all dressed in short red pleated skirts and

white tops. I am part of a girls' school. I next find myself going through an old building, with some colorful tiled waterways and pools. There are men cleaning and maintaining them. It seems like I am now in a boys' school.

The next scene is in the same building, but I am in what appears to be an execution chamber. There are men who are chained to regular chairs and my dream shows me a close-up of a blond girl, about ten, who smiles at me but who is going to be executed also. There is a big switch and the man pulls the switch and the people chained to the chairs are electrocuted.

Kate's dream takes place *in* and around a structure that is at first a "girls' school," and then becomes a "boys' school." When Kate imagined being this building, she described feeling "very solid, immovable, dark, wet—I'll be there forever." As a school, that structure's job description would include education and training for "girls" and for "boys," to prepare them to *fit into society*. Kate added that the girls' school felt to her "like the Catholic girls' school from her own childhood," a school "to keep those girls in line."

"I'm a cheerleader, exuberant, but I'm in a very repressive place," Kate said, as she imagined being dressed in a red pleated skirt with a white top. As for the ten-year-old blond girl, she recalled that when she was ten she was "boarded out" and lived with her aunt on a farm in Idaho, a very difficult time in her life. Kate realized that her dream was impressing upon her the gravity of what had happened to her back then, showing her that vital aspects of herself were executed, killed in a repressive school environment where she was "kept in line" and where the cheerleader, the exuberant part of herself, was "climbing the walls."

From her dream, Kate was able to look at her life and begin to rid herself of institutionalized stereotypes about men's and women's roles. She was also able to rid herself of repressive external ideas, rules, and attitudes that did not belong to her. Kate said the "regular chairs" were "utilitarian" ideas that tied her down, telling herself she had to do only things that were practical, pragmatic, logical, and useful. She began to create space for her natural exuberance and innate talent for encouraging herself and others. Kate's dream helped her get free of the internalized "girls' and boys' " school, accelerating the journey into her authentic life. She now must pull the "exuberant part of herself" from the red brick walls of that institution.

Exploring the dream:

- The "execution chamber" is inside the building, meaning that Kate's dream is referring to the collective influences the school represents, in particular those influences that "executed" the exuberant part of herself, the part that the institution would not accept.
- Her dream shows that the ten-year-old part of who she was wanted out of that structure. Her dream told her that she needs the qualities that little girl represents, and she needs them in her adult world.
- Kate's dream also implies that there are "men cleaning and maintaining" this institution, suggesting that certain masculine ideas are still working in her adult psyche for principles the school represented.
- Her dream is full of empowering solutions: Her dream puts the responsibility squarely on her shoulders to separate herself from those soul-killing, repressive brick walls.

Spiritual Death and Loss of Soul

The Mannequins

Sometimes our dreams use images of death to portray the consequences of events and circumstances in life that kill our ability to be ourselves, to be natural and authentic. Lynne, a twenty-nine-year-old art therapist, had just such a dream. It took her back to four deaths, parts of herself that survived in her family dynamic by becoming something else. Here is her dream:

> I am standing somewhere and I open a children's book. As I open it the story comes out of the book and becomes real. Some little girls have committed an offense of some sort and will be put to death. In this society or culture, this is not an unusual thing. It seems like there are four girls around the ages of eight, nine, or ten years old. One I remember is a beautiful, blond, curly-haired girl about eight years old. After they are killed, they are positioned like mannequins in a frozen style, like statues. The little blond girl has her hand raised, as if pointing upward, or motioning to something. A living little girl with short brown

hair is examining the bodies up close. She walks around and looks at them with a child's natural curiosity.

Lynne worked through this dream, exploring each of its images. A few days prior to having this dream she had been reading about the psychological death that many young girls experience just before or during puberty. "In addition," Lynne reflected, "I had been thinking about a relationship in which I feared losing the sense of self that I had worked hard to attain."

Her dream accurately portrayed the death of "a beautiful, blond, curly-haired girl"—the transformation of a living, vital creative life into a mannequin, a manufactured replica, a synthetic reproduction that fits society's idealized images.

Messenger, Guide, Trickster, Conductor of Souls

The Angel of Death

Marie-Louise von Franz published this initial dream of a fifty-two-year-old psychologist:

> He saw clouds grouping in the sky and a magically beautiful youth with winged shoes descending toward him. He awoke strangely shaken.[13]

She understood the magical youth to represent the Hellenistic Hermes as "the conductor of souls." In fact, the man's health was deteriorating and he was approaching death. Because his historical roots were in Italy, Hermes became his "angel of death," his guide into the death experience.

Hermes shows up often in dreams in assorted guises as a guide, teacher, a ferryman, or a trickster, as some figure helping us along the way, like Rita's "Master of Ceremonies." But Hermes also has a dark, *mercurial* side as the seducer of souls into dangerous trials.

To the ancient alchemists, Mercurius was quicksilver—mercury—on the surface, but inwardly, "the world-creating spirit concealed or imprisoned in matter."[14] During a time of recording a series of extremely helpful dreams, I dreamt that my father, who died many years ago, was showing me how to scoop up quicksilver with my right hand from inside the earth. I was "scooping up" valuable, transformative insight from "inside the earth"—the unconscious. For me, my father represented characteristics of daring, humor, and creativity. And he would always remind me, "There's no such word as 'can't,' " a comment that has stuck with me throughout my adult life.

Whenever I find myself limiting or restricting my life, I remember my dream; I imagine scooping up a handful of quicksilver from deep in the earth, and I say to myself, I "will" or I "won't," but never, I "can't."

> *Inside you there's an artist*
> *you don't know about.*
> —Rumi

CHAPTER 12

⎯⎯⎯
✑
⎯⎯⎯

"Circling Around the Ancient Tower"

Every spirit builds itself a house, and beyond its house a world, and beyond its world a heaven. Know then that world exists for you.

—Ralph Waldo Emerson

Dreams of Structures and Buildings

The building . . . stood narrow and glass-eyed.
—Doris Lessing, "Dialogue"

Dreams frequently use structures to represent snapshots of a work-in-process, a picture of where we are now in our inner journey and where we are in life. We encounter an enormous range of such images in dreams, portraying everything from low self-worth shacks to exquisite, unusual homes, and even cities that embody the Authentic Self. We may be trying to get out of our childhood home, running from a house on fire, *in* an "apartment" or a hotel—structures alluding to more of a collective containment, in contrast to an individual house.

The Narrow Cell

Or we confine our creative life to a narrow cell like Stefan, a talented writer who always found reasons why he could not pursue a writing career. He brought this dream to a group session:

> I was taking care of an old friend of mine. She was staying in a very narrow room like a cell. She couldn't walk. I said she needed a hospital bed. She says, "OK."

Stefan's old friend was actually a good friend he had known for years. She was now in her nineties and still quite active. "She's a maverick, a great artist," he explained. Stephan realized he was keeping his creative side trapped in that "narrow room like a cell." And his friend was deteriorating, now needing a hospital bed. His dream was warning him of the consequences of limiting his creativity.

The Voyager

Not all structures are land-locked. Many people dream of ships, from the *Titanic* to, in one example, a huge canoe stuck in a stairwell of an office building. At a time when I was beginning to feel deeply connected to my dreams and their intent in my life, I had a dream of a *tall ship,* a large, wooden, ocean-going sailing ship from a bygone era. I was observing this beautiful ship from above as it gracefully slipped through the water. Then I noticed a complex array of modern, high-tech satellite dishes and all sorts of antennas, some reaching high above the sails.

For me, this ship represented a vessel moving with the wind, a voyager at home on the sea, while all the high tech gear connected the ship to the heavens: listening devices, tuning in, intuition, receiving information, soul antennas. That dream of the *tall ship* encouraged me to continue working with dreams and the unconscious. It also impressed upon me that I was exploring the dream world in a unique craft: a ship that combined a classic, romantic windjammer with modern technology. The dream helped to explain my fascination with using aspects of the scientific method to explore dream images, and my intense curiosity about the intriguing connections between quantum physics, consciousness, and the world of dreams.

A Magical City

Our Authentic Self sometimes presents itself as a strange or unknown city in dreams. Lynne, our art therapist who dreamt about some little girls being put to death, told me about this dream journey to a wonderful stone city, but there was something not quite right about it:

> I'm sailing in a boat and we are approaching a large city. The buildings are white stone—all whitewashed—very elaborate and ornate. I tell my companion I don't recognize this city; it's like nothing I've ever seen. I feel as if we are in a strange and magical place. We are pulling in a bay or inlet so we are passing nearby

the buildings. There is a huge black metal sculpture like Mt. Rushmore sort of—four U.S. presidents. This seems like a clue to where we are.

Lynne's dream presents her with a dilemma: a "magical place" but with a glitch, the black metal sculpture and the "whitewashed" buildings. "I'm ancient, medieval, Greek maybe—European, magical," Lynne explained, imagining herself as the city. "But the four presidents are a collective thing." She added, "I want to think well of presidents but they often don't live up to expectations. It's all administrative, about rulers—comforting in a strange way. I do that to myself, follow the rules, do what I think others expect me to do," she said.

After exploring the images in her dream, Lynne felt the city did indeed represent her Authentic Self, a beautiful, ornate, ancient city. But she also knew something else was missing: The city had been covered up, whitewashed. No one could see its original, brilliant colors. Now, from her dream, she realized she needed color, passion, fire, brilliance, a full spectrum of feelings; she had "white-washed" her genuine nature, which was making it difficult for her to be genuine and direct in her waking life. She tended to be "nice," to clean up her emotions, even when that meant going against her real feelings. Suddenly Lynne began to feel much more authentic, free to be more herself. She felt the passion flowing back into her life, the true colors emerging through the *whiteness*.

Exploring the dream:

- In Lynne's dream the white paint is not a part of her authentic nature. Instead, it represents a behavior, a way of being in a world that had covered up her true colors, something inauthentic *put on* her original Self; it's like an artist's palette with only one color: white.
- The four black presidents also represent outside influences, social and governmental influences to conform. Powerful *shoulds* and *should nots* that Lynne had allowed to "rule" her life.
- In her dream these *"rule-ers"* are strangely "comforting." Her dream suggests that rules are indeed comforting to the *dreaming ego* who feels safe within known structures and within clearly defined *statutes*.
- The dream *does* show her "where" she is: She is approaching her Self, and now needs to remove the *whitewash* from her nature,

and escape the rules she has been imposing on her life that have prevented her from being herself and living authentically.

Our waking ego builds structures highly adapted to our collective world, and when we begin to reflect on the impact "fitting in" has had on our life, we often find that we have been living someone else's life, straying far off the path of our own authentic life. Hence dream after dream of structures, odd houses, and cities undergoing renovation, demolition, being consumed in fire—all showing the death of our old life and the transformative process of integrating the Authentic Self into our waking life and consciousness.

Under Construction

Construction debris, demolition, rubble, renovation—all are common indicators of change, particularly old ways of being and relating to our world and to others. Medard Boss, who looks at dreams through existential glasses, provides this example of a spiritual transition involving a religious structure:

> [This] dreamer saw himself standing on a rubbish heap near his church. The rubbish came from the ongoing total renovation and expansion of the church . . . [T]he previous day, the subject had realized the large extent to which the religious commands imposed on him . . . had given way . . . to a freer, and more loving relationship to the divine. While awake, then, he could recognize the crumbling of a narrow "intellectual" relationship to God, and its replacement by a novel relationship of freedom . . . [1]

This dream illustrates once more how dreams consistently use various structures to represent belief systems that tend to fall apart *if* they are preventing a person from living authentically. In the above dream, the expanding church structure would correspond to the dreamer allowing himself more intellectual freedom in his thinking and his views of religion. His dream is helping him out of a "narrow" relationship to his own spirituality. We can also look at a church as often representing a *ritual space* in between heaven and earth, a soul-making space *within* an individual, between our waking reality and our essential nature, or what we have been referring to as the Authentic Self.

Identifying Collective Structures in Dreams

Burning Down Dogma

Jeff, our aspiring actor, was struggling to extricate himself from certain religious training as a child when he had this dream:

> I dreamed that I'm in the neighborhood near my grandparents' old house. I see St. Joseph's Academy and it's on fire. I could hear the fire trucks on their way to put out a fire. I called my brother and told him that it was real smoky. It turned out that St. Joseph's dome was bombed and it no longer existed. I couldn't believe that I was nearby and didn't get hurt. There were a ton of fire fighters. The dome, looking down from above, was empty inside.

Jeff's dream is a great example of a building that for him represented "a Catholic institution where everything is structured, and I bought into it." He added, speaking for the academy, "My job is to educate people, keep people in line. I'm full of priests, full of rules." Regarding the bombed-out dome, he said, "My dome is what everyone sees, my identity, and it's gone." He explained that his grandparents represented "old world ideas—very strict religious people."

Jeff realized this dream marked an end to his self-critical thinking related to the church. He felt the dome symbolized his head, the religious structure and judgmental ideas that had gotten into his thinking. He did not have to be something shaped by institutional structure any longer; that academy was now "empty inside." He felt more himself and focused on separating his own thinking from negative religious influences from his grandparents and from the church.

Leaving the Mother's House

I first met Gretchen when she joined a dream therapy group. A soft-spoken woman in her late seventies with a youthful twinkle in her eyes, she was determined to make some real changes in her life. "I'm on a great adventure," she told me, commenting about her interest in dreams. She had recently moved across the continent, closing the door forever on her life as a nun. She brought this dream to one of our group sessions:

> I was at the university where I went to college, waiting for commencement exercises. There was some discussion with one of the

nuns regarding the delay and the next day was the last possible day for commencement.

The commencement was being held in a very large church. A priest sitting in the sanctuary in a large chair was distributing the diplomas. My name was called late in the program. When I received my diploma, it was a small greeting card that had frayed edges. I was furious about the quality of the diploma. This was garbage! I reflected that even the education had not been of good quality, especially the history courses.

Following the commencement dinner I returned to my room to get ready to return home. I was also concerned because when I went home I didn't have a job.

The university in her dream was the actual Catholic college she attended in her early twenties, which Gretchen described as "a very freeing time to be away from my parents and on my own—a very positive experience. I was an only child in a very strict Catholic family. You had to look good all the time. That's how I was brought up." She explained that seven years after graduating she joined a convent and became a nun. "I was back in the convent; my room and the halls were just like the convent," she said. Curiously, her dream connects three structures: the university, the church, and the convent. All three represent aspects of institutionalized education throughout her history, education that her dream debunks with the low quality diploma and her observation in the dream: "even the education had not been of good quality."

After working on this dream, Gretchen realized that although she had physically left her life as a nun, she was now crossing another threshold, leaving the *internalized* rules, the *habit*, and the training from her order and the male authority in the church: the "priest" or *priesthood* in the "very large church." And she was "furious" about the quality of the diploma, which she called "garbage." Gretchen, after imagining *being* the frayed diploma, said, "I'm supposed to be a vehicle for entrance into a lot of things, but I'm a joke, no good at all."

Finally, Gretchen doesn't have a job when she returns home, meaning that after leaving the church and the convent, her waking ego feels out of work; her career in organized religion has ended. Now she is freer to employ more of her authentic nature, and rid herself of the last internal remnants, the remaining implants from her experience—collective "garbage." Gretchen's dream portrays a death and a rebirth: leaving the structures of the Church and her convent, then going "home," probably meaning returning to her authentic life, where she really belongs.

A few weeks later, Gretchen told me, "You know, I've been looking back over my dreams for the last two or three years and I noticed I'm always inside different structures, some sort of institution, and I'm always angry. I'm getting rid of all this outside crap. I just want to find my own spiritual way without being told what I should do."

Exploring the dream:

- Here again is an important dream dynamic: When we are *in* a particular structure, it usually means that we are in or contained by what the structure represents. Leaving a structure then correlates to leaving a set of attitudes and ideas.
- Once we determine what a structure represents—self-destructive collective influences or aspects of the Authentic Self—we can sweep the negative influences out of our life, or, in the case of authentic characteristics, create room in our lives for those qualities.

Gretchen's dream also illustrates how difficult it is to get an ideology out of our psyches. Fortunately, dreams, like a spiritual immune system, seek out and attack alien ideas that have invaded the soul.

Through understanding our dreams we can "circle the ancient tower," explore the forgotten city; we can return to ourselves and help create a better world without subjecting our life to any tyranny over our creative spirit.

Self-Exploration: Origins

Get some colored markers and on a good size sheet of paper, draw the floor plan of your childhood home prior to age ten. Include all you can remember about each room. Include all the furnishings. When you have it as complete as possible, take yourself on an imaginal walk through the house. Make a note of smells, memories, colors, as much detail as you can recall. Notice if there are any rooms left blank, or areas you have no clear memories about. Be alert for any forgotten passions and interests you had as a child.

Then think about your current life and write about any connections you see: ideas, events, and experiences that still exert an influence in your adult world, good and bad. Where do you see childhood hope, spontaneity, and authenticity in your adult life? What has happened to your dreams?[2]

CHAPTER 13

✍

Going Home–Entering the City of God

I dreamed marvelously. I dreamed there was an enormous web of beautiful fabric stretched out. It was incredibly beautiful, covered all over with embroidered pictures. The pictures were illustrations of the myths of mankind but they were not just pictures, they were the myths themselves, so that the soft glittering web was alive. In my dream I handled and felt this material and wept with joy.
—Doris Lessing, *The Golden Notebook*

Return from Exile

As long as you do not know how to die and come to life again, you are a sorry traveler on this Dark earth.
—Goethe

Re-entry

In this stage of our journey into an authentic life, we are headed *home*. Our dreams have helped us change our lead into gold and now we are the architects of a new life. Our dreams say, "You've worked hard to understand us. Here's a surprise gift, another sacred stone for your journey."

We have "pulled the sword from the stone," extricated ourselves from the prison of following someone else's path. And we now have the *Elixir*, the lesson, the treasure, the sacred ring, the reason we are here. And we at least know what it is we must do. The challenge is twofold: how to place our treasure in the world and how to do so in a manner that benefits others and the world we live in. We need to *deliberately* engage the world with the Authentic Self.

It's not that we have "arrived," reached an ultimate goal, or an ending. But now life becomes a true creative adventure, as Nietzsche put it, "a wheel rolling of itself," a unique, invisible path where, as Joseph Campbell describes it, "difficulties melt and the unpredictable highway opens as [we go]."[1] The center of gravity of our existence has changed: we now live life from the *inside-out*.

A Curve Up Ahead

Once we have been through our initiatory trials; once we have our treasure in hand, we must find a place for it in the collective world. One of the more common dilemmas encountered by the returning hero can be found in the creative process. For example, an excellent artist had reached a impasse in his work which meant he would have to make a real effort to expand his art into the public realm. The prospect of having to promote his art felt intimidating to him and he found his day-to-day life more and more rushed, as he crowded all his spare time with trivial activities and classes that diverted him from his art. He then had this dream:

> I'm driving a sixties style convertible down the coast highway on a winding stretch of road that reminds me of the Monterey Peninsula area. It's absolutely beautiful—blue ocean, hills, trees, the air. I feel very free and alive. Suddenly I begin to worry that I'm going too fast for a curve up ahead. I try to apply the brakes but nothing happens. Instead, the car speeds up. I wake up feeling panicked.

For him, the convertible represented a carefree, fun, creative time in his life, and he said of the Monterey area, "It's the most beautiful spot in the world!" This "most beautiful spot in the world" relates to aspects of the dreamer's Self, that place where he feels utterly at home, where his creative spirit travels the border between the ocean depths and the land.

Of course, the *dream ego* drives and supposedly controls the car. But the ego wants to put the brakes on this journey—be in control, which it cannot do. He knew he was in his right place; he was immersed in doing his art yet he could sense a part of himself resisting leaving the status quo which was keeping his creativity walled-in, stopped just short of the recognition he deserves. Instead some saboteur in his nature devised all manner of diversions so that his creative side would have no time left for further development.

Going Too Fast

A week later he had a second dream very similar to the first one but with some significant changes:

> Albert and I are each driving separate cars down the same winding road. We're both going the same direction, but Albert starts laughing and going faster and faster. I realize there's a sharp turn up ahead and think that Albert is not going to make the turn. He is going so fast, he drives right off the road, through a fence, and comes to a stop in the middle of a lush green meadow. He's sitting in his car smiling at me. I pride myself in following the road and not going too fast. I feel righteous, doing things the right way, superior to Albert.

He described Albert as "an adventurous spirit, fun loving, fearless." When he imagined himself as the "winding road" he explained the road as "a safe place to be, guidelines, the rules, my risk level—my fear." Now the dreaming ego wants him to stay within the "guidelines, the rules," follow the "safe" path. When he role-played Albert, Albert's first comment, sitting in the "lush green meadow," was "See what you missed!" As Albert, he realized he did things "without fear of repercussions." Now his psyche clearly informs him that his life needs some of Albert's qualities, which will take his life where there is no predetermined route, off the beaten path—symbology that always alludes to the particular uniqueness and *un-common* characteristics of our essential spirit. Only when he stops following rules and guidelines does he end up "in green pastures."

From these dreams he realized that he needed to break some of the rules he had absorbed about his art, the collective authorities, the "shoulds" and expectations that were preventing his art from expressing his authentic, original nature.

Making a Difference

A Modern War Resister

Once in a while we have a dream that becomes the catalyst that propels us into our authentic life, gives us that last push, and then, off we go. Anthony Shafton, dream researcher and the author of *Dream Reader*, describes James Harrington's experience with just such a dream. Harrington's dream is fascinating because it so clearly illustrates the conflict between living his authentic life and the social pressures that often so easily overwhelm the best intentions. Here's Harrington's account:

I am a hospital corpsman in the United States Naval Reserve being readied for mobilization in the Persian Gulf conflict. What follows is an actual dream I had on July 3, 1990 . . . It has offered me spiritual and moral courage in speaking out for the necessity of finding alternatives to war. It has served as an initiation into social action against war in the Gulf. . . .

In the dream, *I know of no life outside the uniform I wear. I'm a gung-ho "Doc," and the Navy wants me to instruct the troops in the current strategy of how to "hold the enemy."* This is not actual Navy strategy but a dream phrase describing *a core military practice. Deep inside I know that if I teach or support the Navy's strategy on holding the enemy, I will betray the very core of my spiritual being.* So, at the start of the dream *I am plunged into a crisis between my identity and my spiritual self.*

My mind asks why I can't follow this order, and the answer comes in a vision of the mirage of personalities who make up the chain of command, from petty officers to Pentagon leaders to elected officials. They all wear outward clothes of warriorship, but none have inner qualities of warriorship to allow them to hold the enemy properly. They are all children with awesome outward power but no inner wisdom. None are worthy enough to be followed.

I refuse to present the Navy strategy on how to hold the enemy. This refusal is taken as an act of total insubordination. Even though I know of no life outside the uniform, I refuse to participate in the Navy. I am depressed for weeks as I wait for the court martial, and as I contemplate what has led me to this point, I realize the value of models in our lives. I see in the military a rich array of models for people to follow. I wonder what model it is I am now following.

In the certainty of dream knowing, *I know the answer to lie in a very sick dog. This is a faithful spiritual guide dog of my past that is now so sick that a sneeze alone may kill him.* This dog has been in my dreams in the past, ever since, as a boy, I nearly drowned . . . in a river. The dog and I have a deep psychic connection.

Military doctors and nurses are desperately trying to save the dog. They know full well it is only because the dog lives that they have power over me, and the dog remains alive, not because of their efforts, but because I won't let the dog go. But seeing him in such a desperate state breaks my heart, and I give the dog permission to die.

At once I am plummeted into a depth of depression previously unknown. I know that I will soon follow the dog into death.

Ten minutes before the court martial, I decide to get a haircut. I want to end things in a proper manner. I leave the base looking for a haircut and realize what I really want is initiation. I cross the country looking for a barbershop. . . . Places that look like barbershops end up turning out to be candy shops. Little time is left before the court martial, when I suddenly "know" the place to get a haircut is in Cambridge, Massachusetts, in an old Victorian house in the middle of the great universities there. I know of this house and know of some scissors in the bathroom there.

I begin to cut my own hair and have almost finished when I notice over my left shoulder, where the dog has always been, a strong fierce presence named Ali, a Muslim. His fierceness is surpassed only by his love and loyalty to God. I smile and he smiles. I know he is the sick dog reborn a man . . . This is the first time in the dream that I realize I have a life beyond the uniform I am forsaking.

Traveling back across the country, I look into the psyches of people. Each person is wearing a huge sombrero with a video monitor on the front. When the hats are flipped up, I can see the ideals of Star Trek *playing across each person's mind. Then, at a speed that astounds me, the hats flap down and the monitors show bombers and war films reminiscent of the Vietnam era. A voice within tells me the ideals of* Star Trek *are everlasting and are the ideals I need to support and not those of war.*

I wake up to my roommate throwing me some keys and telling me to get to work. I say, "This is my work," and get up. Soon after I realize I am still asleep and decide to get up "for real." The dream is over. (Iraq invaded Kuwait one month after Harrington's dream.)[2]

Harrington's remarkable dream reconnects him to his world in a way that requires him to first leave—the court martial—his ordinary world of the "uniformed" life. We can imagine how the "Navy" with all its collective power, authority, and "role models," gradually became implanted deep in the dreamer's psyche. He became the Naval establishment, but those implanted ideas and attitudes ran smack into his own innate being, who he really was, and that genuine person wanted *out* of *that uniform.*

We can also understand why the military doctors must save the sick dog in order to keep their "power" over the dreamer. In most dreams, dogs, "man's best friend," refer to highly *adapted* parts of our nature. A dog knows how to get along in our world. But Harrington knows he must let go of the ailing dog, give him "permission to die." In the dream, the dog reincarnates as a fierce warrior, clearly a transformation of adaptive, obedient characteristics into a "strong fierce presence," a powerful aspect of the dreamer's authentic nature. Now his life will indeed impact the world and society, not by "following" authoritarian, military leaders, but by removing his authentic life from those influences, getting them out of his psyche. He has pulled *Excalibur* from the iron hull of the military establishment.

His dream has given him a new model, *Star Trek,* which gives him an ideal, a vision of *peaceful* exploration of *other worlds*—to "*go where no man has gone before*"—into his unique life. He is now the captain of his own "*Star*" ship, the way of moving through a new life guided by the *stars*, by his destiny, living out of the center of his Authentic Self.

The City of God and Our Essential Nature

The Golden City

Dreams of an unusual, unknown home that has a tremendous nostalgic effect, a mysterious room or addition we have never seen before, ancient temple-like structures, and in some instances, a particular city can represent aspects of our real nature in a way that gives us an invaluable description of who we are and the nature of our relationship to the outside world. For example, many years ago, when activities and work for my church were consuming my life, I had this dream; about a year later I finally left the group:

> I was walking down a paved road that wound along the edge of
> a forest. Suddenly the light reflecting off something in the forest
> caught my eye. In the distance, up on the mountainside and
> through the trees to my right, I saw a city of gold glistening in

the sunlight. Amazed and excited, I stopped and tried to find a path to this golden city, but there was none. The dream ended. I felt deeply disappointed and frustrated.

I did not fully understand this dream until after I left the church. I then realized that the *golden city* was symbolic of my inner Self—my unlived, authentic life. But by walking on the group's known, *paved* road—a collective path designed for the masses—I could not get to this city, this unique part of myself that had no path leading to it. In the years that followed, I would have to create my own path through the forest, find my own way. I wasted a lot of precious time on that particular "paved road"!

This dream brought home the import of the Indian philosopher Krishnamurti's enigmatic comment, "Truth is a pathless land."[3] Radical Dreaming enables us to rediscover and unite with our own "City of Gold," to live in and through our unique, authentic nature.

Socrates was describing the ideal way of life to Glaucon, who complained, "Socrates, I do not believe that there is such a City of God anywhere on earth." Socrates replied, "Whether such a city exists in heaven or ever will on earth, the wise man will live his life after the manner of that city, having nothing to do with any other, and in so looking upon it, will set his own house in order." For me, Socrates's "City of God" and my inner "Golden City" are synonymous—representing an authentic life humanized with soulfulness, freedom, responsibility, and resurrected integrity.

Whether the City of God, the Tibetan mythical kingdom of Shambhala, the biblical "New Jerusalem," or the Renaissance city of Florence in a modern dream, our dreams give us remarkable glimpses of places that symbolize the Authentic Self—a state of being and living authentically in the world that turns life into a sacred garden for the human spirit.

The End Is the Beginning

Once you are real you can't become unreal again. It lasts for always.

—Margery Williams

We live in an exciting time and a critical time. As the planet strains under the pressures of population, consumerism, environmental decay, and increasing social and political fragmentation, we can but wonder if life as we know it will survive. How long can our earth sustain unlimited, *unconscious* growth? What role can you and I play in a world bombarded by seemingly insurmountable economic, social, cultural, and religious impulses? How do you and I make a meaningful connection and contribution in the midst of global chaos? How would we answer the question: "What does the earth need from us?"

Never have we had so much potential to rebuild our environment and our societies. Never in history have we had such a wealth of technology at our disposal. And yet, at the same time, extremist groups, political and economic factions threaten the very fabric of our common humanity.

How can one person make a difference in a world more and more saturated with media-driven images designed to turn human beings into robotic conformists, stereotypes, mechanical cogs in the vast, grinding machinery of conscienceless, mindless commerce?

How do we develop a sense of place, of history, of feeling at home in the midst of urban sprawl, tearing things down as fast as we build, felling forests and bulldozing farmland? How does living on a violated planet affect us psychologically, emotionally? How much of our epidemic depression, our existential emptiness, come from a vanishing natural world, from living and working in neon-lit, concrete, steel, and asphalt canyons? What happens spiritually when modern progress erases our environment?

Our dreams, inner and outer, hold creative solutions for what ails us, as a society and as individuals. Each day we each face a tremendous choice about how we live our lives, a choice between living an authentic, original life, or living a life of dreary conformity—living *someone else's life*. We each have the capacity to remake our lives and to change our world, but first we must redeem ourselves, resurrect our essential Spirit. It is, after all, up to each one of us to dream, to *create* a difference.

It ever was, and is, and shall be, ever-living Fire, in measures being kindled and in measures going out.
—Heraclitus

Tools: How to Improve Your Dream Recall

Recording and Remembering Your Dreams

Here are some practical techniques for recording your dreams that will also help you improve your dream recall:

- Find a journal that you like—something special just for your dreams. Keep it next to your bed. Before you sleep, open it to a blank page and leave a pen on it for the night's dreams. Think about getting a unique, unusual pen for your journal—for your dream journeying. Your preparation shows your psyche that you are serious, and inevitably you will begin to recall your dreams more clearly. Some people prefer to speak their dream into a tape recorder and then transcribe it into their journal later. Find the system that works best for you and then commit yourself to it. Don't give up!
- Use the back of your journal for a *symbol and image glossary* of your personal symbols, collective images, and recurring dream themes with dates that refer you back to particular dreams. Also consider keeping a blank page next to each page of dreams for future notes and interpretations. Over time, unique patterns unfold that are extremely helpful in understanding your own symbolic language and particular collective images that are impacting your Authentic Life.

- Write down your dreams immediately! Our connections to the unconscious are often fleeting and we tend to lose most dreams if they are not written down in the first few minutes after awakening. If you are unable to record your dreams right away, write down key words and images from them. This will usually bring the entire dream back. If you don't recall any dreams, use your journal to record how you felt when you awakened: relaxed, anxious, panicked, sad, depressed, etc. Your dreams play a major role in influencing how you feel, particularly when you first wake up. Writing about your feelings in your journal, even without remembering a particular dream, will help improve your dream recall.

- When you record your dreams or feelings from the night's sleep, don't *censor* any dream content. Record your experience no matter how strange or nonsensical it may appear to be. Also record the feelings from the dream. Trying to interpret your dreams when you first record them can be frustrating. We all have a tendency to immediately judge a dream through a left brain sort of logic—an intellectual approach that at first prompts us to think a dream is meaningless. Rest assured that your psyche does not waste any effort on meaningless dreams! You have to consciously override these first-impression judgments when you initially recall a dream.

- Consider including pertinent direct observations about dream figures and symbols in parentheses immediately after the motif/symbol to clarify known and unknown dream elements. For example, a dream might read: "I was in my grandparents' house (their actual house in Maryland)." As an alternative, connections to people and dream elements can be listed at the end of the dream.

- Keep your dream journal private! Well-intended judgments from friends and relatives can seriously hurt your dream work process. The only exceptions would be for legitimate dream groups, individual psychotherapy with someone experienced in dreamwork techniques, or a carefully selected "dreamwork partner," a close friend, partner, or spouse with whom you feel OK sharing and exploring each other's dreams. Finding a good dreamwork partner combined with ongoing practice in dream exploration and interpretive techniques is a tremendous aid to understanding your dreams and your life, especially if you prefer doing your own inner work instead of working with a psychotherapist. We are so close to our own dreams, it's often difficult to be objective, and hence working on our dreams alone is definitely more difficult.

However, do not tell your dreams to anyone who does not respect dreams or consider them important.

Improving Your Dream Recall

- Give yourself extra time to wake up gradually without using an alarm if possible. If you need an alarm, use the one that buzzes instead of a clock radio. Music or other programs tend to draw you into the waking world and make it more difficult to recall your dreams.
- Self-suggestion: As you go to sleep, speak to your psyche, repeating a brief sentence that clearly states your intent to remember your dreams, such as, "I will remember a dream when I awaken in the morning." Keep repeating your statement until you fall asleep. If you have difficulty focusing or find your mind wandering, number your statements in sequence: "One—In the morning I will remember a dream from this night. Two—In the morning I will remember a dream from this night," etc. Be patient and persistent with this process—no two people recall dreams alike. Don't feel anxious or pressured, but trust your own psyche.
- Avoid late meals, caffeine, alcohol, or other stimulants/depressants before sleep.
- "B" vitamins will often help dream recall, particularly B-6.
- Try to get enough sleep. Get enough rest to wake up naturally without an alarm. Exhaustion and stress can prevent or drastically reduce our dream recall.
- Give yourself time to unwind before sleep.
- If you notice that you are sleeping in a certain position when you recall most of your dreams, try to sleep in that position.
- If you rarely remember your dreams, try alternating your sleep patterns: Vary the times you go to sleep and the times you get up.
- Experiment with setting your alarm for ninety minutes, or two hours, or four and a half hours after you go to sleep in order to wake yourself during REM sleep. Or have your partner wake you when s/he detects your eyelids moving, indicating you are dreaming.[1]
- Try sleeping fully clothed on top of the bed covers. This may help you stay in a lighter sleep, which can help to improve your dream recall.
- Read or talk about your dreams just before you go to sleep.
- As you go to sleep, suggest to yourself that you will recall your

dreams upon the cue of some regularly occurring morning sound or event such as the alarms, birds, the sunrise, the smell of the coffee your partner is fixing, etc.[2]

- Try wearing clothing that is a color or design that reminds you of your dreams.
- Some people have had success taping a paperclip or similar object to their forehead to create a physical trigger to symbolize an antennae to receive and remember dreams.[3]
- Joining a dream group can stimulate and aid dream recall.
- The experience of interpreting and understanding your dreams aids recall, as does *acting* on your dreams' insight and guidance.
- Cultivate your imagination during your waking life, create daydreams and fantasies, read poetry you find inspiring.
- Use a timer that turns on a bedside lamp as an alternative to an alarm.
- When you wake up, give yourself a few minutes to lie very still and turn your attention inward. Sudden activity, like jumping out of bed, inhibits dream recall.
- Dream researcher and author Jeremy Taylor has found that "thinking backward," starting with the last dream image and using it to link your way back through the entire dream, helps dream recall. The regular practice of reviewing your entire day backwards at bedtime has been found to help dream recall, and in many instances, an entire night's dreams.[4]
- Simply retelling your dream to your partner or to someone during the day helps recall and can also bring out more details about the dream.

It helps to organize your dream journal with a dream index as well as a symbol and image glossary (with dates that refer you back to a particular dream). Early on, writing this book compelled me to go back and compile a dream log for my own dreams. I found myself recalling a particular dream and I had to look through five thick journals spanning the last twenty-four years and thousands of dreams to find it. Sometimes you will remember just a dream image and you can quickly locate it using your symbol glossary. Plus it's extremely informative to see what types of symbols and images repeat themselves in your dreams. Recurring themes in dreams, as well as recurring dreams, can indicate that you still have something important to work on that you have yet to understand.

Notes

Prologue: Modern Dreamwork—the Missing Piece

1. Stuart Holroyd, *The Supernatural Dream Worlds* (London: The Danbury Press, 1976), p. 72.

2. Rupert Sheldrake, *The Presence of the Past: Morphic Resonance and the Habits of Nature* (Rochester, Vermont: Park Street Press, 1988), pp. 248–49.

Introduction

1. Pindar, *Odes* (fifth century B.C.)

2. Marie-Louise von Franz, *Dreams: A Study of the Dreams of Jung, Descartes, Socrates, and Other Historical Figures* (Boston: Shambhala Publications, 1991), p. 112.

3. J. Sirven, *Les Années d'apprentissage de Descartes (1596–1628)* (Paris, 1925), pp. 50–51

4. *Writers Dreaming: Twenty-Six Writers Talk About Their Dreams and the Creative Process,* ed. Naomi Epel (New York: Vintage Books, 1993), pp. 234–235.

5. Cited in James Hillman, *The Dream and the Underworld* (New York: Harper & Row, 1979), p. 93.

6. Charlotte Beradt, *The Third Reich of Dreams,* trans. Adriane Gottwald (Chicago: Quadrangle Books, 1982).

7. David Bohm, *Wholeness and the Implicate Order* (New York: Routledge, 1983), p. 172. Bohm explains the *implicate order* as "the unbroken wholeness of the totality of existence as an undivided flowing movement without borders. . . . for in the implicate order the totality of existence is enfolded within each region of space and time. So, whatever part, element, or aspect we may abstract in thought, this still enfolds the whole and is therefore intrinsically related to the totality from which it has been abstracted."

8. Rupert Sheldrake, *The Presence of the Past: Morphic Resonance and the Habits of Nature* (Rochester, Vermont: Park Street Press, 1988), p. 371. Sheldrake describes *morphic resonance* as "The influence of previous structures of activity on subsequent similar structures of activity organized by morphic fields. Through morphic resonance, formative causal influences pass through or across space and time, and these influences are assumed not to fall off with distance in space or time, but they come only from the past."

9. Carl G. Jung, *The Structure and Dynamics of the Psyche* (New York: Pantheon Books, 1960) par. 342.

10. Cited in Marc Barasch, *Healing Dreams: Exploring the Dreams That Can Transform Your Life* (New York: Riverhead Books, 2000), p. 43.

11. Robert L. Van de Castle, *Our Dreaming Mind* (New York: Ballantine Books, 1994), p.11.

12. Doris Kearns, *Lyndon Johnson and the American Dream* (New York: Harper & Row, 1976).

13. Cited in Barasch, *Healing Dreams*, p. 137.

14. Ibid.

15. Stuart Holroyd, *The Supernatural Dream Worlds* (London: The Danbury Press, 1976), p. 74.

16. Ibid.

17. Ibid., p. 79.

18. Robert Johnson, *Inner Work: Using Dreams and Active Imagination for Personal Growth* (New York: Harper Collins Publishers, 1986), p. 98.

19. Ibid.

20. Wilhelm Stekel, *The Interpretation of Dreams: New Developments and Technique* (New York: Liverright, 1943), p. 152.

21. R. de Becker, *The Understanding of Dreams and Their Influence on the History of Man* (New York: Hawthorn Books, 1968), pp. 30–31.

22. Ibid., p. 69.

23. Ibid.

24. Cited in Barasch, *Healing Dreams,* p.161.

25. Ibid.

26. Ibid.

27. Ibid.

28. Gordon Globus, *Dream Life, Wake Life: The Human Condition through Dreams* (Albany: State University of New York, 1987), p. 151.

Chapter 1: Inner Revolution

1. Mary Oliver (Quoted in: *Utne Reader*, May-June, 2000), p. 13.

2. Joseph Campbell, *The Hero With a Thousand Faces*. (Princeton, NJ: Princeton University Press, 1968), p. 25.

3. From: Alfred W. Pollard, abridged from Malory, *The Romance of King Arthur and His Knights of the Round Table* (New York: Mayflower Books, 1979), p. 8.

4. Cited in Michael Talbot, *The Holographic Universe* (New York: Harper perennial, 1991), p. 63, private communication with author, October 31, 1988.

5. Kalle Lasn and Bruce Grierson, "Malignant Sadness," *Adbusters: Journal of the Mental Environment*, June/July, 2000, p. 37.

6. William Bridges, *The Way of Transition* (Cambridge, Massachusetts: Perseus Publishing, 2001), p. 155.

7. Cited in Bridges, *The Way of Transition*, p. 155.

8. T.S. Eliot, "The Hollow Men," p. 212., cited in: James Hollis, *The Archetypal Imagination* (College Station, Texas: Texas A&M University Press, 2000), p. 17.

9. Rollo May, *The Discovery of Being: Writings in Existential Psychology* (New York: W.W. Norton & Company, 1983), p. 107.

10. William Mattox Jr., *Journal of American Citizenship Policy Review* (Sept/Oct '98).

11. Roy F. Baumeister, *Escaping the Self*, cited in: "Malignant Sadness," *Adbusters Journal of the Mental Environment* (June/July 2000), p. 35.

12. Cited in "Malignant Sadness," *Adbusters Journal of the Mental Environment* (June/July 2000), p. 34.

13. Ibid., p. 3.

14. Mary Lutyens, *Krishnamurti: the Years of Fulfillment* (New York: Avon Books, 1983), jacket quote.

15. Ibid., p. 13.

16. Excerpted from *The American Heritage® Dictionary of the English Language,* Third Edition, Copyright © 1996 by Houghton Mifflin Company.

17. Cited in Robert L. Van de Castle, *Our Dreaming Mind* (New York: Ballantine Books, 1994), pp. 156-57.

18. Ibid., p. 157

19. Marc Barasch, "Night Eyes," *Utne Reader* (November/December, 2000), p. 71.

20. Edward L. Deci, *Why We Do What We Do* (New York: Grosset/ Putnam, 1995), p. 5.

21. Ibid., p. 4.

22. Marie-Louise von Franz, *The Psychological Meaning of Redemption Motifs in Fairy Tales* (Toronto: Inner City Books, 1980), p.78.

23. Montague Ullman, "Societal Factors in Dreaming," *Contemporary Psychoanalysis,* 1973, 9: 282–93, p. 284.

24. Marie-Louise von Franz, *Projection and Re-Collection in Jungian Psychology* (La Salle and London: Open Court Publishing, 1980), p. 189.

25. Ibid.

26. Ibid.

27. José Ortega y Gasset (1883–1955), Spanish essayist, philosopher. "In Search of Goethe from Within," in *Partisan Review* (New Brunswick, N.J., Dec. 1949; repr. in *The Dehumanization of Art and Other Essays, 1968*).

28. Excerpted from *The American Heritage ® Dictionary of the English Language,* Third Edition, Copyright 1996 by Houghton Mifflin Company.

29. Ibid.

30. Marcus Aurelius (121–180 A.D.), *Meditations,* bk. 3, sct. 5.

31. John Beebe, *Integrity in Depth* (College Station, Texas: Texas A & M University Press, 1992), p. 32.

32. The author uses the term "Dynamic Imagination" to describe his new approach to the imaginal world using the Radical Dreaming process.

33. Renee Weber, "The Enfolding-Unfolding Universe: A Conversation with David Bohm," in *The Holographic Paradigm,* ed. Ken Wilber (Boulder, Colo.: New Science Library, 1982), p. 72.

34. Michael Talbot, *The Holographic Universe* (New York: Harper Perennial, 1991), p. 48.

35. Cited in Joseph Campbell, *The Hero With a Thousand Faces* (Princeton, NJ: Princeton University Press, 1968), p. 18.

36. Jonathan Alter, "From the Prison of the 'Isms'," *Newsweek,* Jan. 1, 2000, p. 183.

37. Joseph Campbell, *The Hero With a Thousand Faces* (Princeton, NJ: Princeton University Press, 1968), p. 77.

38. Thomas Merton, "New Seeds of Contemplation," cited in: *Somewhere I Have Never Traveled,* Thomas Van Nortwick (New York: Oxford University Press, 1996), p. 183.

39. Rumi, "The Light You Give Off," trans. Coleman Barks and John Moyne. From *Unseen Rain,* translated by Coleman Barks and John Moyne (Putney, Vermont: Threshold Books, 1986).

Chapter 2: Approaching the World of Dreams

1. From the title page: "*A Portrait of the Artist as a Young Man,*" by James Joyce. The name of the hero is Stephen Dedalus, who created wings of art by which he flew.

2. Ralph Waldo Emerson, *Lectures and Biographical Sketches* (Cambridge: Riverside Press, 1883), pp. 7–8.

3. Wilhelm Stekel, *Fortschritte und Technik der Traumdeutung* (Wien—Leipzig—Bern: Verlag für Medizin, Weidmann und Cie., 1935), p. 37.

4. Joseph Campbell. Cited in: Sam Keen, *Your Mythic Journey* (Los Angeles: Jeremy P. Tarcher, 1989), p. 125.

5. See Bibliography for additional reference and resource materials.

6. See Patricia Garfield's book, *Creative Dreaming*, for further reading on this aspect of dreamwork.

7. Anthony Shafton, *Dream Reader: Contemporary Approaches to the Understanding of Dreams* (New York: State University of New York Press, 1995), p. 75.

8. Mary Watkins, *Waking Dreams* (Dallas: Spring Publications, 1984), p. 134.

9. William Wordsworth. Cited in: Mary Watkins, *Invisible Guests: the Development of Imaginal Dialogues* (Dallas: Spring Publications, 2000), p. 49.

10. *Hamlet*, I, ii, 137.

11. Cited in Ira Progoff, *At a Journal Workshop* (New York: Jeremy Tarcher/Putnam, 1992), p. 198.

12. Joseph Campbell, *The Hero With a Thousand Faces* (Princeton, NJ: Princeton University Press, 1968), p. 64–65.

Chapter 3: The Process—Breaking the Dream Code

1. William Burroughs, *Painting and Guns*, "The Creative Observer" (1992).

2. Rumi, "Four Quatrains by Rumi," trans. by Coleman Barks and John Moyne. From *Unseen Rain* (Putney, VT: Threshold Books, 1986).

3. Jung originated this method of inquiry: If a tiger appeared in a dream, Carl Jung's "I've just arrived here from another planet" perspective would pose this type of question: "Suppose I had no idea what the word tiger meant or what a tiger was, describe this object to me in such a way that I can not fail to understand what sort of thing it is." Cited in *Our Dreaming Mind*, by Robert L. Van de Castle (New York: Ballantine Books, 1994), p. 166.

4. Mary Oliver, from "Trilliums," *Dream Work* (New York: The Atlantic Monthly Press, 1986), p. 11. Used by permission of Grove/Atlantic, Inc., Copyright © by Mary Oliver.

5. William Morris, *For the Briar Rose*, BS XXXV.15, pl. 74, "The Rose Bower" and pl. 77, "The Briar Wood." P: Rodney Todd-White, London.

6. Ronan Coghlan, *The Illustrated Encyclopedia of Arthurian Legends* (New York: Barnes & Noble, 1993), p. 100.

7. Marie-Louise von Franz, *Shadow and Evil in Fairytales*. Cited in *The*

Ravaged Bridegroom by Marion Woodman (Toronto: Inner City Books, 1990), p. 130.

8. Charlotte Beradt, *The Third Reich of Dreams*, trans. Adriane Gottwald (Chicago: Quadrangle Books, 1982), p. 62.

9. Excerpted from: *The American Heritage Dictionary of the English Language*, Third Edition, Copyright © 1996 by Houghton Mifflin Company.

10. Heraclitus, fragment 46.

11. Galway Kinnell, *Flower Herding on Mount Monadnock* (New York: Houghton Mifflin Co., 1964).

Chapter 4: The Language of the Dream

1. Mary Oliver, from: "Dreams," *Dream Work* (New York: The Atlantic Monthly Press, 1986), p. 19. Used by permission of Grove/Atlantic, Inc., Copyright © 1986 by Mary Oliver.

2. Shakespeare, excerpted from *The American Heritage® Dictionary of the English Language, Third Edition* © 1996 by Houghton Mifflin Company.

3. Henry Corbin, *Creative Imagination in the Sufism of Ibn 'Arabi*, trans. Ralph Manheim (Princeton, NJ: Princeton University Press, Bollingen Series XCI, 1969), p. 4.

4. Daryl Sharp, *C. G. Jung Lexicon* (Toronto: Inner City Books, 1991), pp. 12-13.

5. Carl G. Jung, *The Structure of the Psyche*, CW 8, par. 342.

6. James Hillman, *Revisioning Psychology* (New York: Harper & Row, 1976), p. 12–13.

7. James Hillman, *The Force of Character and the Lasting Life* (New York: Random House, 1999), p. xxiv.

8. James Hillman, *The Dream and the Underworld* (New York: Harper & Row, 1979, p. 148.

9. Cited in: Robert L. Van de Castle, *Our Dreaming Mind* (New York: Ballantine Books, 1994), p. 170.

10. D. Sandler and N. Churchill, "Serpant as Healer," *Shaman's Drum* 10 (fall 1987): 32–34.

11. Ibid.

12. Ann Sayre Wiseman, *Dreams as Metaphor: The Power of the Image* (Cambridge, Massachusetts), p. 76.

13. Excerpted from *The American Heritage Dictionary of the English Language*, Third Edition, Copyright 1992 by Houghton Mifflin Company.

14. The Encarta® Desk Encyclopedia, 1998, Microsoft Corporation.

15. Ibid.

16. *Writers Dreaming: Twenty-Six Writers Talk About Their Dreams and the Creative Process*, ed. Naomi Epel (New York: Vintage Books, 1993), p. 80.

17. Excerpted from *The American Heritage Dictionary of the English Language,* Third Edition, Copyright © 1996 by Houghton Mifflin Company.

18. Ibid.

19. Cited in Marc Barasch, *Healing Dreams: Exploring the Dreams That Can Transform Your Life* (New York: Riverhead Books, 2000), p. 169.

Chapter 5: Who You Are Not

1. C. G. Jung, *The Archetypes and the Collective Unconscious*, trans. R.F.C. Hull (Princeton, NJ: Princeton University Press, 1969), par. 221.

2. Quoted in Ray Grasse, *The Waking Dream* (Wheaton, IL: Quest Books, 1996), p. 85.

3. Elias Canetti, *Crowds and Power* (New York: Farrar, Straus and Giroux, 1973), p. 203.

4. Amy Tan, Cited in: *Writers Dreaming: Twenty-Six Writers Talk About Their Dreams and the Creative Process*, ed. Naomi Epel (New York: Vintage Books, 1993), p. 286.

5. F. X. Newman, *Somnium: Medieval Theories of Dreaming and the Form of Vision Poetry* (Ann Arbor: University Microfilms International, 1983, p. 19).

6. Phyllis Koch-Sheras, Ann Hollier and Brook Jones, *Dream On: A Dream Interpretation and Exploration Guide for Women* (Englewood Cliffs, NJ: Prentice Hall, 1983, p. 100).

7. Robert Bly, *Eating the Honey of Words* (New York: HarperCollins, 1999), p. 236.

8. Excerpted from *The American Heritage Dictionary of the English Language*, Third Edition, Copyright © 1992 by Houghton Mifflin Company.

9. J. C. Cooper, *An Illustrated Encyclopedia of Traditional Symbols* (London: Thames & Hudson, 1978, p. 103).

10. Cited in: Anthony Shafton, *Dream Reader: Contemporary Approaches to the Understanding of Dreams* (New York: State University of New York Press, 1995), p. 278.

11. Ibid.

12. J. C. Cooper, *An Illustrated Encyclopedia of Traditional Symbols* (London: Thames & Hudson, 1978, p. 134).

13. *The Kabir Book: Forty-Four of the Ecstatic Poems of Kabir*, trans. Robert Bly (Boston: Beacon Press, 1977), p. 29.

Chapter 6: Someone Is Stealing Your Life

1. Marc Barasch, *Healing Dreams: Exploring the Dreams That Can Transform Your Life* (New York: Riverhead Books, 2000), pp. 273–74.

2. Marc Barasch, "Night Eyes," *Utne Reader,* November – December 2000, p. 68.

3. *The American Heritage Dictionary of the English Language,* Third Edition, Copyright © 1996 by Houghton Mifflin Company.

4. Michael Ventura *Letters at 3 AM: Reports on Endarkenment* (Dallas: Spring Publications, 1993), p. 48.

5. Edward C. Whitmont and Sylvia Brinton Perera, *Dreams, a Portal to the Source* (London: Routledge, 1989), p. 97.

6. Cited in Anthony Shafton, *Dream Reader: Contemporary Approaches to the Understanding of Dreams* (New York: State University of New York Press, 1995), p. 103.

7. Wilhelm Stekel, *Fortschritte und Technik der Traumdeutung* (Wien–Leipzig–Bern: Verlag für Medizin, Weidmann und Cie., 1935), p. 216.

8. Doris Lessing (b. 1919), British novelist. *The Grass Is Singing,* ch. 2 (1950).

9. Henry James, "The Jolly Corner." Cited in: *Somewhere I Have Never Traveled,* Thomas Van Nortwick (New York: Oxford University Press, 1996), p. x.

10. *The Encarta® 2000 New World Timeline* © Copyright 1998, Helicon Publishing Ltd. All rights reserved.

11. Henry James, "The Jolly Corner." Cited in: *Somewhere I Have Never Traveled,* Thomas Van Nortwick (New York: Oxford University Press, 1996), p. x.

12. Marie-Louise von Franz with Fraser Boa, *The Way of the Dream* (Boston & London: Shambhala, 1994), p. 80.

13. Edward Edinger. *Anatomy of the Psyche: Alchemical Symbolism in Psychotherapy* (La Salle, IL: Open Court, 1985), pp. 72–73.

Chapter 7: Turning Back—Refusing the Adventure

1. Campbell, Joseph. *The Hero With a Thousand Faces.* (Princeton, NJ: Princeton University Press, 1968), p. 60.

2. Robert Bly, "Snowbanks North of the House." From: *The Rag & Bone Shop of the Heart,* eds. Robert Bly, James Hillman, and Michael Meade (New York: Harper Collins Publishers, 1992), p. 112.

3. Emil A. Gutheil, *The Handbook of Dream Analysis* (New York: Washington Square, 1967), p. 159.

4. Proverbs, 1:24–27.

5. Joseph Campbell, *The Hero With a Thousand Faces.* (Princeton, NJ: Princeton University Press, 1968), p. 60.

6. Daryl Sharp, *C. G. Jung Lexicon* (Toronto: Inner City Books, 1991), p. 114.

7. Excerpted from *The American Heritage® Dictionary of the English Language,* Third Edition, Copyright © 1996 by Houghton Mifflin Company.

8. M. Sabini (1981a), p. 92, quoting J. Kirsch, "The role of instinct in psychosomatic medicine," *American Journal of Psychotherapy* 3, p. 257, 1949.

9. Ibid.

10. Cited in Marc Barasch, *Healing Dreams: Exploring the Dreams That Can Transform Your Life* (New York: Riverhead Books, 2000), p. 66.

11. Ibid., p. 66.

12. *Encarta® 98 Desk Encyclopedia* © & ℗ 1996-97 Microsoft Corporation.

13. Cited in Ernest Dimnet, *The Art of Thinking* (New York: Simon & Schuster, Inc., 1929), pp. 203–204.

14. *A Thousand and One Nights,* trans. Richard F. Burton (Bombay, 1885), vol. I, pp. 164-7.

15. Langston Hughes, *The Panther and the Lash* (New York: Alfred A. Knopf, 1951).

16. Charlotte Beradt, *The Third Reich of Dreams,* trans. Adriane Gottwald (Chicago: Quadrangle Books, 1968), pp. 5–6.

17. Ibid., p. 5.

18. Excerpted from *The American Heritage® Dictionary of the English Language,* Third Edition, Copyright © 1996 by Houghton Mifflin Company.

19. Beradt, p. 8.

20. Ibid., p. 9.

21. Ibid., p. 6.

22. Ibid., p. 13.

23. "Trapped by Nightmares," *ABC News,* 2002.

24. Ibid.

25. Frederick S. Perls, *Gestalt Therapy Verbatim* (Highland, New York: Gestalt Journal, 1992), pp. 190, 241.

Chapter 8: Invisible Guests

1. *The Kabir Book: Forty-Four of the Ecstatic Poems of Kabir,* trans. by Robert Bly (Boston: Beacon Press, 1977), p. 9.

2. Carl G. Jung. *Memories, Dreams, Reflections,* trans. Richard and Clara Winston (New York: Random House, 1973), pp. 103–104.

3. James Hillman, *Dream Animals* (San Francisco: Chronicle Books, 1997), pp. 4–5.

4. Cited in *Writers Dreaming: Twenty-Six Writers Talk About Their Dreams*

and the Creative Process, ed. Naomi Epel (New York: Vintage Books, 1993), p. 88.

5. Elias Canetti, *Crowds and Power* (New York: Farrar, Straus and Giroux, 1973), p. 84.

6. Excerpted from *The American Heritage® Dictionary of the English Language,* Third Edition, Copyright © 1996 by Houghton Mifflin Company.

7. Ibid.

8. Marc Barasch, *Healing Dreams: Exploring the Dreams That Can Transform Your Life* (New York: Riverhead Books, 2000), pp. 304–305.

9. Jane Lewis-White, "Beyond Freud and Jung: Seven Analysts Discuss the Impact of New Ideas About Dreamwork." A response by Jane Lewis-White. *Quadrant* (1992), 25(2): 98-99.

Chapter 9: Dreams at the Edge of the Forest

1. Robert Johnson, *Inner Work: Using Dreams and Active Imagination for Personal Growth* (New York: Harper Collins Publishers, 1986, p. 188).

2. Joseph Campbell, *Transformations of Myth Through Time* (New York: Harper & Row, 1990), pp. 210–11.

3. Cited in: Joseph Campbell, *The Hero's Journey* (New York: Harper Collins, 1990), p. 101.

4. Leonard S. Shultze, *Aus Namaland und Kalahari* (Jena, 1907, p. 392).

5. David Clement Scott, *A Cyclopaedic Dictionary of the Mang'anja Language spoken in British Central Africa* (Edinburgh, 1892), p. 97.

Chapter 10: Slaying Dragons

1. Charlotte Beradt, *The Third Reich of Dreams*, trans. Adriane Gottwald (Chicago: Quadrangle Books, 1982).

2. *The American Heritage Dictionary of the English Language,* Third Edition, Copyright © 1996 by Houghton Mifflin Company.

3. Marie-Louise von Franz, *The Way of the Dream* (Boston & London: Shambhala, 1994), p. 116.

4. Carl G. Jung, *Psychology and Alchemy*, trans. R.F.C. Hull (Princeton, NJ: Princeton University Press, 1969), par. 186.

5. Carl G. Jung, *Dreams*, trans. R.F.C. Hull (Princeton, NJ: Princeton University Press, 1974), pp. 77–78.

6. Joseph Campbell, *The Hero With a Thousand Faces.* (Princeton, NJ: Princeton University Press, 1968), p. 83.

7. Flora H. Loughead, *Dictionary of Given Names with Origins and Meanings* (Glendale, CA: The Arthur H. Clark Company, 1958), p. 60.

8. Ananda K. Coomaraswamy, "Akincanna: Self-Naughting" (*New Indian Antiquary,* Vol. III, Bombay, 1940), p. 6, note 14, citing and discussing Thomas Aquinas, *Summa Theologica,* I, 63, 3.

9. Johnson, Robert, *Balancing Heaven and Earth: A Memoir of Visions, Dreams, and Realizations* (New York: HarperCollins Publishers, 1998, pp. 183–84).

10. Koran, 2:115.

11. *Katha Upanishad,* 3:12.

12. Cited in Campbell, *The Hero With a Thousand Faces* (Princeton, NJ: Princeton University Press, 1968, p. 145).

13. Origen (A.D. 185?–254?), *Liviticum Homiliae.*

Chapter 11: "Dying Inside the Dishes"

1. Rainer Maria Rilke, "Sometimes a Man Stands Up During Supper." From *Selected Poems of Rainer Maria Rilke,* translated by Robert Bly (New York: Harper Collins Publishers, 1981).

2. Carl G. Jung, *Memories, Dreams, Reflections,* trans. Richard and Clara Winston (New York: Random House, 1973), p. 323.

3. Charlotte Beradt, *The Third Reich of Dreams,* trans. Adriane Gottwald (Chicago: Quadrangle Books, 1968), pp. 107–108, quoting I Scholl, *The White Rose.*

4. F. David Peat, *Synchronicity: The Bridge Between Mind and Matter* (New York: Bantam Books, 1987), p. 235.

5. Edinger, Edward. *Anatomy of the Psyche: Alchemical Symbolism in Psychotherapy.* (La Salle, Illinois: Open Court, 1985), p. 26.

6. Carl G. Jung, *Memories, Dreams, Reflections,* trans. Richard and Clara Winston (New York: Random House, 1973), p. 175.

7. Ibid., pp. 175–176.

8. Cited in: Marc Barasch, *Healing Dreams: Exploring the Dreams That Can Transform Your Life* (New York: Riverhead Books, 2000), pp. 30–32.

9. Ibid., p. 30.

10. Ibid., p. 33.

11. Robert E. Litman, "The Dream in the Suicidal Situation." In Natterson (1980a).

12. David L. Raphling, "Dreams and Suicide Attempts." *Journal of Nervous and Mental Disease* (1970), 151:404–10.

13. Marie-Louise von Franz. *Archetypal Dimensions of the Psyche.* (Boston: Shambhala, 1994), p. 3.

14. Carl G. Jung, *Psychology and Alchemy,* translated by R.F.C Hull (Princeton University Press, 1969), par. 404.

Chapter 12: "Circling Around the Ancient Tower"

1. Medard Boss, "*I Dreamt Last Night . . .*" (New York: Gardner, 1977), pp. 202–203.

2. Adapted from Sam Keen and Anne Valley-Fox, *Your Mythic Journey: Finding Meaning in Your Life Through Writing and Storytelling* (Los Angeles: Jeremy P. Tarcher, 1973), p. 37.

Chapter 13: Going Home—Entering the City of God

1. Joseph Campbell, *The Hero With a Thousand Faces* (Princeton, NJ: Princeton University Press, 1968), p. 345.

2. James Lawrence Harrington, "Dreams of War: the Unconscious Call to Initiation," *Men's Council Journal*, 1991, No. 8 (February):6–7.

3. J. Krishnamurti, from Mary Lutyens, *Krishnamurti: the Years of Fulfillment* (New York: Avon Books, 1983), jacket quote.

Tools: How to Improve Your Dream Recall

1. Anthony Shafton, *Dream Reader: Contemporary Approaches to the Understanding of Dreams* (New York: State University of New York Press, 1995), pp. 415–16.

2. Ibid., p. 416.

3. Janice Baylis, "Aids to Dream Recall," *Dream Network Journal* 10 (2&3): 49.

4. Jeremy Taylor, *Dream Work: Techniques for Discovering the Creative Power in Dreams* (New York: Paulist Press, 1983), p. 24.

Bibliography

Barasch, Marc. *Healing Dreams: Exploring the Dreams That Can Transform Your Life*. New York: Riverhead Books, 2000. This book explores the author's bout with a serious illness and how dreams aided his recovery.

Baumeister, Roy F. *Escaping the Self,* cited in: "Malignant Sadness," *Adbusters Journal of the Mental Environment* (June/July 2000).

Becker R. de. *The Understanding of Dreams and Their Influence on the History of Man*. New York: Hawthorn Books, 1968.

Beebe, John. *Integrity in Depth*. College Station, Texas, 1992.

Beradt, Charlotte. *The Third Reich of Dreams*, translated by Adriane Gottwald. Chicago: Quadrangle Books, 1968. An excellent book and a unique record of how the dreams of German citizens reacted to the social and political changes during Hitler's rise to power.

Bly, Robert. *Eating the Honey of Words*. New York: HarperCollins, 1999.

———, James Hillman, and Michael Meade, eds. *The Rag & Bone Shop of the Heart*. New York: HarperCollins Publishers, 1992.

Bohm, David. *Wholeness and the Implicate Order*. New York: Routledge, 1983. A physicist's perspective of how consciousness works.

Bosnak, Robert. *A Little Course in Dreams*. Boston: Shambhala, 1988.

Bridges, William. *The Way of Transition*. Cambridge, Massachusetts: Perseus Publishing, 2001.

Campbell, Joseph. *The Hero With a Thousand Faces*. Princeton, New Jersey: Princeton University Press, 1968. A beautifully written look at the "Hero's Journey" using myth and legend.

———. *The Hero's Journey*. New York: Harper Collins, 1990.

————. *Transformations of Myth Through Time*. New York: Harper & Row, 1990.

————. *The Inner Reaches of Outer Space: Metaphor as Myth and Religion*. New York: Harper & Row, 1989.

————. *An Open Life: Joseph Campbell in Conversation with Michael Toms*. New York: Harper & Row, 1989.

Canetti, Elias. *Crowds and Power*. New York: Farrar, Straus and Giroux, 1973. A unique perspective on group dynamics and human behavior in crowds.

Clift, Jean D., and Wallace B. Clift. *Symbols of Transformation in Dreams*. New York: Crossroad Publishing, 1986.

Cooper, J. C. *An Illustrated Encyclopedia of Traditional Symbols*. London: Thames & Hudson, 1978. This is a good reference book, not to interpret dream images, but to occasionally research the origins of a particular image or symbol and to get different cultural perspectives.

Corbin, Henry. *Creative Imagination in the Sufism of Ibn 'Arabi*, translated by Ralph Manheim. Princeton, New Jersey: Princeton University Press, Bollingen Series XCI, 1969.

Edinger, Edward. *Anatomy of the Psyche: Alchemical Symbolism in Psychotherapy*. La Salle, Illinois: Open Court, 1985. A very detailed and well-done exploration of the psychological symbolism of Alchemy.

Epel, Naomi. *Writers Dreaming: Twenty-Six Writers Talk About Their Dreams and the Creative Process*, edited by Naomi Epel. New York: Vintage Books, 1993. An excellent book showing how dreams work with the creative process.

Frankl, Viktor E. *Man's Search for Meaning: An Introduction to Logotherapy*. New York: Simon & Schuster, 1984.

Garfield, Patricia. *Creative Dreaming*. New York: Simon & Schuster, 1995.

Globus, Gordon. *Dream Life, Wake Life: The Human Condition through Dreams*. Albany: State University of New York, 1987.

Goldhammer, John D. *Under the Influence: the Destructive Effects of Group Dynamics*. New York: Prometheus Books, 1996. An exploration of the impact of group dynamics for the individual: social, political, religious, economic, and institutional. Compares healthy versus destructive group dynamics.

Hall, James A. *Jungian Dream Interpretation: A Handbook of Theory and Practice*. Toronto: Inner City Books, 1983. An excellent, concise book that explains the basic Jungian approach to dreamwork.

Harner, Michael. *The Way of Shaman*. New York: HarperCollins, 1980, 1990.

Hillman, James. *Dream Animals*. San Francisco: Chronicle Books, 1997.

————. *The Soul's Code: In Search of Character and Calling*. New York: Random House, 1996.

————. *The Dream and the Underworld*. New York: Harper & Row, 1979.

————. *Revisioning Psychology*. New York: Harper Collins, 1976.

Hollis, James. *The Archetypal Imagination.* College Station, Texas: Texas A & M University Press, 2000.

Inglis, B. *The Power of Dreams*, edited by T. Besterman. London: Paladin; Grafton, 1987.

Johnson, Robert. *Inner Work: Using Dreams and Active Imagination for Personal Growth.* New York: Harper Collins Publishers, 1986. One of the best books for a clear explanation of Jung's Active Imagination process.

———. *Balancing Heaven and Earth: A Memoir of Visions, Dreams, and Realizations.* New York: HarperCollins Publishers, 1998.

———. *Owning Your Own Shadow: Understanding the Dark Side of the Psyche.* San Francisco: HarperCollins Publishers, 1991.

———. *She: Understanding Feminine Psychology.* New York: Harper Collins Publishers, 1989.

Jung, Carl G. *Dreams*, translated by R.F.C. Hull. Princeton, New Jersey: Princeton University Press, 1974.

———. *Memories, Dreams, Reflections*, translated by Richard and Clara Winston. New York: Random House, 1973. Jung's autobiography and a good book to read as an introduction to the general concepts that characterize Jungian psychology.

———. *Psychology and Alchemy*, translated by R.F.C. Hull. Princeton, New Jersey: Princeton University Press.

———. *The Archetypes and the Collective Unconscious*, translated by R.F.C. Hull. Princeton, New Jersey: Princeton University Press, 1969.

———. *Symbols of Transformation*, translated by R.F.C. Hull. Princeton, New Jersey: Princeton University Press, 1967.

———. *The Undiscovered Self with Symbols and the Interpretation of Dreams*, translated by R.F.C. Hull. Princeton, New Jersey: Princeton University Press, 1990.

Kabir. *The Kabir Book: Forty-Four of the Ecstatic Poems of Kabir*, translated by Robert Bly. Boston: Beacon Press, 1977.

Kalweit, Holger. *Dreamtime and Inner Space: The World of the Shaman*, translated by Werner Wünsche. Boston: Shambhala Publications, 1984.

Kast, Verena. *Imagination as Space of Freedom: Dialogue Between the Ego and the Unconscious*, translated by Anselm Hollo. New York: Fromm International Publishing, 1993.

———. *The Dynamics of Symbols: Fundamentals of Jungian Psychother-apy*, translated by Susan Schwarz. New York: Fromm International Publishing, 1992.

Keen, Sam, and Anne Valley-Fox. *Your Mythic Journey: Finding Meaning in Your Life Through Writing and Storytelling.* Los Angeles: Jeremy P. Tarcher, 1973.

Koch-Sheras, Phyllis, Ann Hollier, and Brook Jones. *Dream On: A Dream*

Interpretation and Exploration Guide for Women. Englewood Cliffs, New Jersey: Prentice Hall, 1983.

Krippner, Stanley, and Joseph Dillard. *Dreamworking: How To Use Your Dreams for Creative Problem Solving*. Buffalo, New York: Bearly Limited, 1988.

Laberge, Stephen. *Exploring the World of Lucid Dreaming*. New York: Ballantine Books, 1990.

Lessing, Doris. *Prisons We Choose To Live Inside*. New York: Harper & Row, 1987. An excellent analysis of how we put ourselves in collective circumstances that are life-defeating.

Levoy, Gregg. *Callings: Funding and Following an Authentic Life*. New York: Harmony Books, 1997.

Lifton, Robert Jay. *The Protean Self: Human Resilience in an Age of Fragmentation,* New York: Basic Books, 1993.

Loughead, Flora H. *Dictionary of Given Names with Origins and Meanings*. Glendale, California. The Arthur H. Clark Company, 1958.

Lutyens, Mary. *Krishnamurti: the Years of Fulfillment*. New York: Avon Books, 1983.

Mahoney, Maria F. *The Meaning in Dreams and Dreaming*. Secaucus, New Jersey: The Citadel Press, 1966. A Jungian approach to dream interpretation.

May, Rollo. *The Discovery of Being: Writings in Existential Psychology*. New York: W.W. Norton & Company, 1983.

O'Connor, Peter. *Dreams and the Search for Meaning*. New York: Paulist Press, 1986.

Oliver, Mary. *Dream Work*. New York: The Atlantic Monthly Press, 1986. A great collection of poems that will inspire your dreaming and your imagination.

Paracelsus. *Paracelsus: Selected Writings*, edited by: Jolande Jacobi. Princeton, New Jersey, Princeton University Press, 1988.

Peat, F. David. *Synchronicity: The Bridge Between Mind and Matter.* New York: Bantam Books, 1987.

Ribi, Alfred. *Demons of the Inner World: Understanding Our Hidden Complexes*. Boston: Shambhala Publications, 1989.

Rilke, Rainer Maria. *Selected Poems of Rainer Maria Rilke,* translated by Robert Bly. New York: Harper & Row, 1981.

Samuels, Andrew. *The Political Psyche*. New York: Routledge, 1993. Samuels explores how the outer world's political convictions influence individual psychotherapy.

Shafton, Anthony. *Dream Reader: Contemporary Approaches to the Understanding of Dreams*. New York: State University of New York Press, 1995. Shafton's book gives an excellent overview of contemporary dream research and interpretive theories and techniques.

Sharp, Daryl. *C. G. Jung Lexicon*. Toronto: Inner City Books, 1991. A good resource for Jungian/depth psychology terminology.

Sheldrake, Rupert. *The Presence of the Past: Morphic Resonance and the Habits of Nature*. Rochester, Vermont: Park Street Press, 1988.

Siegel, Alan B. *Dreams That Can Change Your Life: Navigating Life's Passages through Turning Point Dreams*. Los Angeles: Jeremy P. Tarcher, 1990.

Stekel, Wilhelm. *The Interpretation of Dreams: New Developments and Technique*. New York: Liverright, 1943.

Talbot, Michael. *The Holographic Universe*. New York: Harper Perennial, 1991.

Taylor, Jeremy. *Where People Fly and Water Runs Uphill: Using Dreams to Tap the Wisdom of the Unconscious*. New York: Warner Books, 1992.

———. *Dream Work: Techniques for Discovering the Creative Power in Dreams*. New York: Paulist Press, 1983.

Van de Castle, Robert L. *Our Dreaming Mind*. New York: Ballantine Books, 1994. An outstanding, comprehensive review of dreaming and dream interpretation over the centuries; extremely well-researched.

Van der Post, Laurens. *Jung and the Story of Our Time*. New York: Vintage Books, 1975. A unique and interesting biography of Carl Jung.

von Franz, Marie-Louise. *Archetypal Dimensions of the Psyche*. Boston: Shambhala, 1994.

———. *On Dreams and Death*. Boston: Shambhala Publications, 1987. A fascinating exploration of dreams reported just before death.

———. *Dreams: A Study of the Dreams of Jung, Descartes, Socrates, and Other Historical Figures*. Boston: Shambhala Publications, 1991.

———. *Projection and Re-Collection in Jungian Psychology*. La Salle and London: Open Court Publishing, 1980.

———. *The Psychological Meaning of Redemption Motifs in Fairy Tales*. Toronto: Inner City Books, 1980.

———, with Fraser Boa, *The Way of the Dream*. Boston & London: Shambhala, 1994. An excellent Jungian-oriented book on dreams and dream interpretation.

Watkins, Mary. *Waking Dreams*. Dallas, Texas: Spring Publications, 1984.

Whitmont, Edward C., and Sylvia Brinton Perera. *Dreams, a Portal to the Source*. London: Routledge, 1989. Dreamwork from a Jungian perspective.

Wilhelm, Richard. *The I Ching or Book of Changes*, translated by Cary F. Baynes. New York: Bollingen Foundation, 1977.

Wiseman, Ann Sayre. *Dreams as Metaphor: The Power of the Image*. Cambridge, Massachusetts.

Wolf, Fred Alan. *The Dreaming Universe: A Mind-Expanding Journey Into the Realm Where Psyche and Physics Meet*. New York: Simon and Schuster, 1994.

Zeller, Max. *The Dream: The Vision of the Night*. Boston: Sigo Press, 1990.

Index of Dreams Described by Content

For more information about Radical Dreaming: workshops, classes and dream groups, visit us on the web at www.radicaldreaming.com.